T0280303

Lecture Notes in Artificial Intelligence   9791

Subseries of Lecture Notes in Computer Science

LNAI Series Editors

Randy Goebel
  University of Alberta, Edmonton, Canada
Yuzuru Tanaka
  Hokkaido University, Sapporo, Japan
Wolfgang Wahlster
  DFKI and Saarland University, Saarbrücken, Germany

LNAI Founding Series Editor

Joerg Siekmann
  DFKI and Saarland University, Saarbrücken, Germany

More information about this series at http://www.springer.com/series/1244

Michael Kohlhase · Moa Johansson
Bruce Miller · Leonardo de Moura
Frank Tompa (Eds.)

Intelligent Computer Mathematics

9th International Conference, CICM 2016
Bialystok, Poland, July 25–29, 2016
Proceedings

 Springer

Editors

Michael Kohlhase
Jacobs University Bremen
Bremen
Germany

Moa Johansson
Chalmers University
Göteborg
Sweden

Bruce Miller
National Institute of Standards
and Technology
Gaithersburg, MD
USA

Leonardo de Moura
Microsoft Research
Redmond, WA
USA

Frank Tompa
University of Waterloo
Waterloo, ON
Canada

ISSN 0302-9743   ISSN 1611-3349 (electronic)
Lecture Notes in Artificial Intelligence
ISBN 978-3-319-42546-7   ISBN 978-3-319-42547-4   (eBook)
DOI 10.1007/978-3-319-42547-4

Library of Congress Control Number: 2016944413

LNCS Sublibrary: SL7 – Artificial Intelligence

Printed on acid-free paper

This Springer imprint is published by Springer Nature
The registered company is Springer International Publishing AG Switzerland

Preface

Mathematics is "the queen of the sciences" (Friedrich Gauss), and "the language with which God has written the universe" (Galileo Galilei). This language is at the same time flexible enough to describe a wide variety of complex phenomena and rigorous enough to be verified in detail based on a small set of assumptions. But the collection of mathematical knowledge is exploding, and it can no longer be handled by the paradigmatic "pencil and paper" approach: Each year there are 120,000 new articles, and this week there was an announcement of a 200-terabyte "proof" of the Boolean Pythagorean triples conjecture.

The Conference on Intelligent Computer Mathematics (CICM) offers a venue for discussing and developing ways of involving computers in the process of "doing mathematics" in the broadest sense. The conference is the result of merging three independent meetings with considerable overlap: CALCULEMUS (integration of deduction and symbolic calculation), Mathematical Knowledge Management (MKM), and Digital Mathematical Libraries (DML). CICM has been held annually since 2008, with previous meetings in Birmingham (UK 2008), Grand Bend (Canada 2009), Paris (France 2010), Bertinoro (Italy 2011), Bremen (Germany 2012), Bath (UK 2013), Coimbra (Portugal 2014), and Washington, DC (USA 2015).

CICM 2016 was held in Białystok, Poland. As in previous years, we had several tracks: CALCULEMUS, Digital Mathematics Libraries (DML), and Mathematical Knowledge Management (MKM), which mirror the three main communities that form CICM, and a track each on "Systems and Data" and "Projects and Surveys." The papers accepted to these five tracks form the content of these proceedings. CICM 2016 had invited talks by John Harrison (Intel), Claudio Sacerdoti-Coen (University of Bologna), and Nicolas M. Thiéry (LRI University of Paris Sud). Additionally, the conference had seven workshops, two tutorials, a doctoral mentoring program, and an informal track for presenting work in progress; the proceedings of these events are published with CEUR-WS. The program of the meeting, as well as additional materials, is available at http://cicm-conference.org/2016/.

The track structure of CICM provides a framework for organizing the conference. The CALCULEMUS track examines the integration of symbolic computation and mechanized reasoning. The Digital Mathematics Libraries track deals with math-aware technologies, standards, algorithms, and processes. The Mathematical Knowledge Management track is concerned with all aspects of managing mathematical knowledge in informal, semi-formal, and formal settings. The Systems and Data track contains descriptions of systems and data collections, both of which are key to a research topic where theory and practice interact on explicitly represented knowledge. The Projects and Surveys track keeps the community informed of relevant projects and consolidates knowledge where the subject matter fits into one of the other four tracks.

This year, CICM had 41 submissions. Each submission received at least four reviews. The reviewing included a response period, in which authors could clarify points raised by the reviewers. This made for a highly productive round of deliberations before the final decisions were taken. In the end, the track Program Committees decided to accept 12 papers for these proceedings.

The Program Committee work for the tracks was managed using the EasyChair system. This year we modeled the multi-track Program Committee as a single committee and the track assignments as "keywords." This made track assignments and cross-track reviewing more flexible than in previous years. The fact that we had five chairs—the general chair and four track chairs—together with excellent conflict management made transparent and "safe" handling of submissions authored or co-authored by any of the chairs almost painless.

As in previous years, several workshops and informal programs were organized in conjunction with CICM 2015. This year these were:

- The CICM Doctoral Program, providing a dedicated forum for PhD students to present their on-going or planned research and receive feedback, advice, and suggestions from a dedicated research advisory board.
- The CICM Work-in-Progress Session, a forum for the presentation of original work not yet in a suitable form for communication as a formal paper.
- ThEdu 2016: Theorem Provers Components for Educational Software, with the goal of combining and focusing on systems from theorem proving, computer algebra, and dynamic geometry to enhance existing educational software and the design of the next generation of mechanized mathematics assistants. ThEdu was organized by Walther Neuper, Graz University of Technology, Austria, and Pedro Quaresma, University of Coimbra, Portugal.
- MathUI 2016: 11th Workshop on Mathematical User Interfaces, an international workshop to discuss how users can be best supported when doing/learning/searching for/interacting with mathematics using a computer. MathUI was organized by Andrea Kohlhase, University of Applied Sciences Neu-Ulm, and Paul Libbrecht, University of Education of Weingarten, Germany.
- Formal Mathematics for Mathematicians, a workshop dealing with developing large repositories of advanced mathematics. It was organized by Adam Naumowicz, University of Białystok, Poland.
- The 27th OpenMath Workshop. OpenMath is a language for exchanging mathematical formulae across applications (such as computer algebra systems and theorem provers). The workshop was organized by James Davenport, the University of Bath, Jan-Willem Knopper, Eindhoven University, and Michael Kohlhase, Jacobs University Bremen.
- The Proof Engineering Workshop, which brings together researchers interested in the new field of proof engineering, defined as the construction, maintenance, documentation, and presentation of large formal proof developments. This workshop was organized by David Aspinall (School of Informatics, University of Edinburgh, UK) and Christoph Lüth (DFKI Bremen and University of Bremen, Germany)

- The Tetrapod Workshop, which studies the deep interactions of (a) mathematical knowledge (formal and informal), (b) specification-based computation, (c) logic, and (d) algorithms and data structures. The workshop was organized by Jacques Carette, Bill Farmer (both McMaster University, Canada), Michael Kohlhase, and Florian Rabe (both Jacobs University Bremen, Germany)
- The Mizar Hands-On Tutorial by Adam Naumowicz et al.
- The MMT Tutorial by Florian Rabe et al.

We thank all those who contributed to this meeting. In particular we would like to thank the EasyChair team (Andrei Voronkov et al.) for the EasyChair system, which we found indispensable. We would like also to thank the invited speakers, the contributing authors, the reviewers, the members of the Program Committee, and the local organizers, all of whose efforts contributed to the practical and scientific success of the meeting.

June 2016

Michael Kohlhase
Moa Johansson
Bruce Miller
Leonardo de Moura
Frank Tompa

Organization

CICM Steering Committee

Volker Sorge (secretary)
Wolfgang Windsteiger (Calculemus representative)
Petr Sojka (DML representative)
Adam Naumowicz (MKM representative)
Bill Farmer (Treasurer)
Manfred Kerber (outgoing PC chair)
Michael Kohlhase (incoming PC chair)

CICM 2015 Organizing Committee

General Program Chair, Projects and Surveys Track Chair
Michael Kohlhase · · · · · · · · · Jacobs University Bremen, Germany

Conference Chair
Adam Naumowicz · · · · · · · · · University of Białystok, Poland

Calculemus Track Chair
Leonardo de Moura · · · · · · · · · Microsoft, USA

DML Track Chair
Frank Tompa · · · · · · · · · University of Waterloo, Canada

MKM Track Chair
Bruce Milller · · · · · · · · · NIST, USA

Systems and Data Chair
Moa Johansson · · · · · · · · · Chalmers University, Sweden

Doctoral Program Chair
Martin Suda · · · · · · · · · TU Wien, Austria

Publicity and Workshops Chair
Serge Autexier · · · · · · · · · DFKI Bremen, Germany

Program Committee

Akiko Aizawa (DML)	National Institute of Informatics, The University of Tokyo, Japan
Andrea Asperti (DML)	University of Bologna, Italy
David Aspinall (MKM)	University of Edinburgh, UK
Serge Autexier (Systems and Data)	DFKI Bremen, Germany
Thierry Bouche (DML)	Université Joseph Fourier (Grenoble), France
Christopher Brown (CALCULEMUS)	United States Naval Academy, USA
Jacques Carette (CALCULEMUS)	McMaster University, Canada
Joseph Corneli (DML)	Knowledge Media Institute, The Open University
James H. Davenport (CALCULEMUS)	University of Bath, UK
Leonardo de Moura (CALCULEMUS track chair)	Microsoft Research
Georges Gonthier (CALCULEMUS)	Microsoft Research
Gudmund Grov (MKM)	Heriot-Watt University, UK
Yannis Haralambous (DML)	Institut Mines-Télécom, Télécom Bretagne and UMR CNRS 6285 Lab-STICC, France
Mateja Jamnik (Systems and Data)	University of Cambridge, UK
Moa Johansson (Systems and Data track chair)	Chalmers Tekniska Högskola, Sweden
Cezary Kaliszyk (MKM)	University of Innsbruck, Austria
Andrea Kohlhase (Systems and Data)	University of Applied Sciences Neu-Ulm, Germany
Michael Kohlhase (Systems and Data)	Jacobs University Bremen, Germany
Laura Kovacs (Systems and Data)	Chalmers University of Technology, Sweden
Christoph Lange (MKM)	University of Bonn, Germany
Assia Mahboubi (CALCULEMUS)	Inria, France
Ursula Martin (CALCULEMUS)	University of Oxford, UK
Fiona McNeill (Systems and Data)	Heriot-Watt University, UK
Bruce Miller (MKM track chair)	NIST, Australia

Lawrence Paulson   University of Cambridge, UK
  (CALCULEMUS)
Jim Pitman (DML)   University of California at Berkeley, USA
Florian Rabe (MKM)   Jacobs University Bremen, Germany
Nicholas Smallbone   Chalmers University of Technology, Sweden
  (Systems and Data)
Elena Smirnova (MKM)   Texas Instruments, USA
Petr Sojka (DML)   Masaryk University, Czech Republic
Volker Sorge (DML)   University of Birmingham, UK
Adam Strzeboński   Wolfram Research Inc.
  (CALCULEMUS)
Geoff Sutcliffe   University of Miami, USA
  (Systems and Data)
Frank Tompa   University of Waterloo, Canada
  (DML track chair)
Josef Urban   Czech Technical University in Prague, Czech Republic
  (Systems and Data)
Abdou Youssef (DML)   George Washington University, USA
Richard Zanibbi (MKM)   Rochester Institute of Technology, USA

Additional Reviewers

Avigad, Jeremy   Krishnaswami, Neelakantan
Beeson, Michael   Megill, Norman
Brown, Chad   Müller, Dennis
Corzilius, Florian   Petersen, Niklas
Gauthier, Thibault   Reger, Giles
Iancu, Mihnea   Vahdati, Sahar
Kotelnikov, Evgenii   Yamada, Akihisa

Contents

Surveys and Projects

Systems and Data

CALCULEMUS

Mathematical Theory Exploration in Theorema: Reduction Rings

Alexander Maletzky$^{(\boxtimes)}$

Doctoral Program "Computational Mathematics" and
RISC, Johannes Kepler University, Linz, Austria
`alexander.maletzky@dk-compmath.jku.at`

Abstract. In this paper we present the first-ever computer formalization of the theory of Gröbner bases in reduction rings in Theorema. Not only the formalization, but also the formal verification of all key results has already been fully completed by now; this, in particular, includes the generic implementation and correctness proof of Buchberger's algorithm in reduction rings. Thanks to the seamless integration of proving and computing in Theorema, this implementation can now be used to compute Gröbner bases in various different domains directly within the system. Moreover, a substantial part of our formalization is made up solely by "elementary theories" such as sets, numbers and tuples that are themselves independent of reduction rings and may therefore be used as the foundations of future theory explorations in Theorema.

In addition, we also report on two general-purpose Theorema tools we developed for efficiently exploring mathematical theories: an interactive proving strategy and a "theory analyzer" that already proved extremely useful when creating large structured knowledge bases.

Keywords: Gröbner bases · Reduction rings · Computer-supported theory exploration · Automated reasoning · Theorema

1 Introduction

This paper reports on the formalization and formal verification of the theory of reduction rings in Theorema that has recently been completed. Reduction rings, introduced by Buchberger in [3], generalize the domains where Gröbner bases can be defined and algorithmically computed from polynomial rings over fields to arbitrary commutative rings with identity, and may thus become more and more an important tool in computational commutative algebra, just as Gröbner bases in the original setting already are. Since definitions, theorems and proofs tend to be technical and lengthy, we are convinced that our formalization in a mathematical assistant system has the potential to facilitate the further development of the theory in the future (e. g. to non-commutative reduction rings).

A. Maletzky—This research was funded by the Austrian Science Fund (FWF): grant no. W1214-N15, project DK1.

© Springer International Publishing Switzerland 2016
M. Kohlhase et al. (Eds.): CICM 2016, LNAI 9791, pp. 3–17, 2016.
DOI: 10.1007/978-3-319-42547-4_1

To the best of our knowledge, reduction rings have never been the subject of formal theory exploration[1] in *any* software system so far; Gröbner bases in polynomial rings over fields have already been formalized in ACL2 [9], Coq and OCaml [6,15] and Mizar [12], though. Moreover, a formalization in Isabelle by the author of this paper is currently in progress, and the purely algorithmic aspect (no theorems and proofs) of a variation of reduction rings has already been implemented in Theorema in [4]. Theorema is also the software system we chose for our formalization, or, more precisely, Theorema 2.0 (see [5,18] for an overview and [5] for a brief comparison to other systems). Note that Theorema 2.0 is quite new: it was released only two years ago, in summer 2014, meaning that it still lacks a couple of useful features that are available in many other proof assistants. This, however, was not a reason for not using the system for our work, but just the converse is true: on the one hand, we wanted to demonstrate what *can* be done with Theorema 2.0 already, and on the other hand we wanted to find out what exactly is still missing for effectively and efficiently formalizing mathematics in the system (some of these features have already been implemented in the meantime, see Sect. 5). Besides that, another motivation for using Theorema 2.0 was to formalize a handful of elementary mathematical theories (about sets, numbers, tuples, ...) as well, that may form the foundations of future theory explorations in the system.

The rest of this paper is organized as follows: Sect. 2 introduces the most important concepts of reduction rings and states the Main Theorem of the theory. Section 3 presents Buchberger's algorithm for computing Gröbner bases in reduction rings as well as its implementation in Theorema, and briefly gives an idea about its correctness proof. Section 4 describes the overall formalization of the theory and its individual components in a bit more detail, and Sect. 5 presents the interactive proving strategy and the TheoryAnalyzer tool that we developed and already heavily used in the course of the formalization and that will be useful also in future theory explorations. Section 6, finally, summarizes our findings and contains an outlook on future work.

2   Gröbner Bases and Reduction Rings

In this section we review the main concepts of the theory whose formal treatment in Theorema is the content of this paper. To this end, we first give a short motivation of Gröbner bases and reduction rings, and then present the most important definitions and results of the theory. A far more thorough introduction can be found in the literature, e. g. in [1].

Originally, the theory of Gröbner bases was invented for multivariate polynomial rings over fields. There, it can be employed to decide the ideal membership problem, to solve systems of algebraic equations, and many more, and hence is of great importance in computer algebra and many other areas of mathematics, computer science, engineering, etc.

---

[1] As one reviewer pointed out, *theory exploration* can be understood in several ways. In this paper, we use it as a mere synonym for *formalization of mathematical theories*.

Because of their ability to solve non-trivial, frequently occurring problems in mathematics, it is only natural to try to generalize Gröbner bases from polynomial rings over fields to other algebraic structures. And indeed, nowadays quite some generalizations exist: to non-commutative polynomial rings, to polynomial rings over the integers and other Euclidean- or integral domains, and many more. Reduction rings are a generalization as well, but in a slightly different spirit: in contrast to the other generalizations, reduction rings do not require the domain of discourse to have any polynomial structure. Instead, *arbitrary* commutative rings with identity element may in principle be turned into reduction rings, only by endowing them with some additional structure (see below). It must be noted, however, that not *every* commutative ring with identity can be made a reduction ring; known examples of reduction rings are all fields, the integers, quotient rings of integers modulo arbitrary $n \in \mathbb{N}$ (which may contain zero-divisors!), and polynomial rings over reduction rings.

2.1 Reduction Rings

Reduction rings were first introduced by Buchberger in 1984 [3] and later further generalized by Stifter in the late-1980s [13,14]; our formalization is mainly based on [14]. Here, we only recall the key ideas and main definitions and results of the theory. For this, let in the sequel $\mathcal{R}$ be a commutative ring with identity (possibly containing zero-divisors).

In order to turn $\mathcal{R}$ into a reduction ring, it first and foremost has to be endowed by two additional entities: a function $M : \mathcal{R} \to \mathcal{P}(\mathcal{R})$ that maps every ring element c to a set of ring elements (denoted by M_c) called the *set of multipliers* of c, and a partial Noetherian (i.e. well-founded) order relation $\preceq$. With these ingredients it is possible to introduce the crucial notion of reduction rings, namely that of *reduction*:

Definition 1 (Reduction). *Let* $C \subseteq \mathcal{R}$. *The reduction relation modulo* C, *denoted by* $\to_C$, *is a binary relation on* $\mathcal{R}$ *such that* $a \to_C b$ *iff* $b \prec a$ *and there exists some* $c \in C$ *and some* $m \in M_c$ *such that* $b = a - m\,c$.

As usual, $\to_C^*$ *and* $\leftrightarrow_C^*$ *denote the reflexive-transitive- and the symmetric-reflexive-transitive closure of* $\to_C$, *respectively. Moreover, for a given* $z \in \mathcal{R}$, a *and* b *are said to be* connectible below z, *denoted by* $a \leftrightarrow_C^{\prec z} b$, *iff* $a \leftrightarrow_C^* b$ *and all elements in the chain between* a *and* b *are strictly less than* z *(w.r.t.* $\preceq$*).*

Of course, the function M and the relation $\preceq$ cannot be chosen arbitrarily but, together with the usual ring operations, have to satisfy certain non-trivial constraints, the so-called *reduction ring axioms*. In total, there are 14 of them, with some being quite simple (0 must be the least element w.r.t. $\preceq$, for instance), others are extremely technical. The complete list underlying our formalization is omitted here because of space limitations but can be found in [7].

Example 1. In a field K, suitable definitions of M_c and $\preceq$ are $M_c := K \backslash \{0\}$ and $x \preceq y :\Leftrightarrow x = 0$. In $\mathbb{Z}_n = \mathbb{Z}/n\,\mathbb{Z}$, represented as $\{[0]_n, \ldots, [n-1]_n\}$, we have $M_{[c]_n} := \{[1]_n, \ldots, [k]_n, [n-k]_n, \ldots, [n-1]_n\}$, where k is the least positive integer such that $[c\,(k+1)]_n = [0]_n$; the ordering is simply defined as $[x]_n \preceq [y]_n :\Leftrightarrow x < y$.

In polynomial rings, finally, matters are a bit more complicated. There, the sets M_c and the ordering $\preceq$ not only depend on the respective objects in the coefficient ring, but also on an admissible *term order* [11] on the set of all power-products.

Note that in reduction rings $\leftrightarrow_C^*$ coincides with the congruence relation modulo the ideal generated by C. Hence, if it is possible to decide $\leftrightarrow_C^*$, then the ideal membership problem could effectively be solved—and this is where Gröbner bases come into play.

2.2 Gröbner Bases

We can start with the definition of Gröbner bases in reduction rings right away:

Definition 2 (Gröbner basis). *Let $G \subseteq \mathcal{R}$. Then G is called a Gröbner basis iff G is finite and $\to_G$ is Church-Rosser, i. e. whenever $a \leftrightarrow_G^* b$ there exists a common successor s with $a \to_G^* s$ and $b \to_G^* s$.*
For $C \subseteq \mathcal{R}$, G is called a Gröbner basis of C iff it is a Gröbner basis and $\langle G \rangle$ (i. e. the ideal generated by G over $\mathcal{R}$) is the same $\langle C \rangle$.

If reduction can effectively be carried out, i. e. whenever a is reducible modulo C then some b with $a \to_C b$ can be computed, and for any given $C \subseteq \mathcal{R}$ a Gröbner basis G of C exists and can be computed, then the problem of deciding membership in $\langle C \rangle$ can be solved: a given candidate a simply has to be totally reduced modulo G until an irreducible element h is obtained; then $a \in \langle C \rangle$ iff $h = 0$.

The axioms of reduction rings ensure that for every $C \subseteq \mathcal{R}$ a Gröbner basis does not only exist, but can even be effectively computed (see Sect. 3). This key result is based on the following

Theorem 1 (Buchberger's Criterion). *Let $G \subseteq \mathcal{R}$ finite. Then G is a Gröbner basis iff for all $g_1, g_2 \in G$ (not necessarily distinct) and all minimal non-trivial common reducibles z of g_1 and g_2, we have $a_1 \leftrightarrow_G^{\preceq z} a_2$, where $z \to_{\{g_i\}} a_i$ for $i = 1, 2$. (a_1, a_2) is called a* critical pair *of g_1 and g_2 w. r. t. z.*

The precise definition of *minimal non-trivial common reducible* (mntcr) is slightly technical and omitted here; the interested reader may find it in the referenced literature. Intuitively, a mntcr of g_1 and g_2 is an element that can be reduced both modulo $\{g_1\}$ and modulo $\{g_2\}$ in a *non-trivial* way.

Example 2. In a field K, the set of mntcrs of any two non-zero field elements is just $K \backslash \{0\}$. In $\mathbb{Z}_n$, the only mntcr of two non-zero elements $[c]_n$ and $[d]_n$ is $[\max\{\gcd(c,n), \gcd(d,n)\}]_n$. In $\mathcal{R}[X]$, the mntcrs of two non-zero polynomials p and q are all monomials of the form $c\tau$, where c is a mntcr of the leading coefficients of p and q in $\mathcal{R}$ and τ is the least common multiple of the leading power-products of p and q, w. r. t. the chosen term order.

Example 3. Let us consider $\mathbb{Z}_{24}[x, y]$ and the singleton $C := \{p := 16xy+2\}$ (we write 16 and 2 instead of $[16]_{24}$ and $[2]_{24}$, respectively, for the sake of brevity). No matter which term order we choose, the leading power-product of p is xy and its leading coefficient is 16, meaning that the only mntcr of p and p is $\gcd(16, 24)xy = 8xy$. Reducing $8xy$ modulo p once (in two different ways) yields the critical pair $(8xy - 2(16xy+2), 8xy - 17(16xy+2)) = ([20]_{24}, [14]_{24})$. Neither of the two constituents of the critical pair can be reduced further modulo C, meaning that the critical pair cannot be connected below $8xy$, and hence C is no Gröbner basis.

2.3 Contributions to the Theory

Before moving on to Buchberger's algorithm, we want to point out two contributions we managed to make to the theory of reduction rings itself. Namely, during the formalization, when turning to the computer-assisted verification of the results, we discovered two problems in the literature on reduction rings. The first of these problems is related to the notion of *irrelativity* as introduced in [14]: without going into details here, irrelativity basically is a binary relation on the set of all elements of a reduction ring, which clearly ought to be symmetric. Irrelativity according to [14], however, is *not* symmetric, and a close look at the proofs of the main results revealed that they contain a very subtle error mainly because of that reason. Therefore, the definition of irrelativity had to be adjusted in order to proceed with the formal verification, which we finally managed to do. More details can be found in [7].

The second problem concerns fields as reduction rings: in an infinite field, two elements have *infinitely many* mntcrs (see Example 2), although for an algorithmic treatment one axiom of reduction rings requires the number of mntcrs to be finite. Although this problem was already known in [3], no attempts have been made to fix it so far. We solved it by introducing an equivalence relation in reduction rings and weakening said axiom to require only the number of *equivalence classes* of mntcrs to be finite.

3 Buchberger's Algorithm

Theorem 1 not only yields a finite criterion for checking whether a given set G is a Gröbner basis or not, but it even gives rise to an algorithm for actually *computing* Gröbner bases. This algorithm, presented in Fig. 1, is a critical-pair/completion algorithm that, given an input set $C \subseteq \mathcal{R}$, basically checks the criterion of Theorem 1 for all pairs of elements of C, and if it fails for a pair (C_i, C_j), then C is *completed* by a new element h that makes the criterion hold for (C_i, C_j). Of course, afterward all pairs involving the new element h have to be considered as well.

Figure 1 presents the algorithm as implemented in a functional style in Theorema. Function GB is the main function that takes as input the tuple[2] C a

---

[2] GB is implemented for tuples rather than sets, for practical reasons.

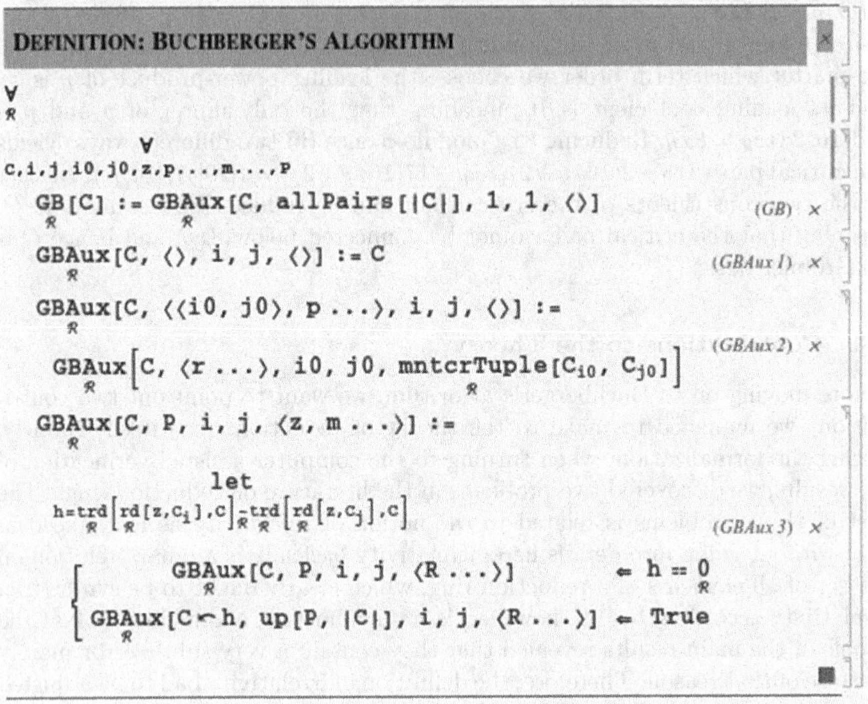

Fig. 1. Buchberger's algorithm in Theorema.

Gröbner basis shall be computed for. It then calls `GBAux` with suitable initial arguments, whose first argument serves as the accumulator of the tail-recursive function. Its second argument is the tuple of all pairs of indices of C that have not been dealt with yet, and its third and fourth arguments are the indices i and j of the elements currently under consideration. The last argument, finally, is the tuple of all mntcrs of C_i and C_j that still have to be checked. Formula (GBAux 3) is the crucial one: The constituents of the critical pair originating from C_i and C_j and mntcr z are totally reduced modulo the current basis C, and the difference is assigned to h. If $h = 0$, the critical pair can be connected below z according to the condition in Theorem 1, so nothing else has to be done in this case. Otherwise, h is added to C, ensuring connectibility below the new basis, and the index-pair-tuple is updated to include also the pairs involving the new element h.

Buchberger's algorithm, or, more precisely, function `GB`, can be proved to behave according to the following specification:

If $\mathcal{R}$ is a reduction ring and C is a tuple of elements of $\mathcal{R}$, `GB` terminates and returns again a tuple G of elements of $\mathcal{R}$. G is a Gröbner basis of C.

The proof of this claim was carried out formally in Theorema. It heavily depends on Theorem 1, of course, but also quite some other technicalities (concerning the

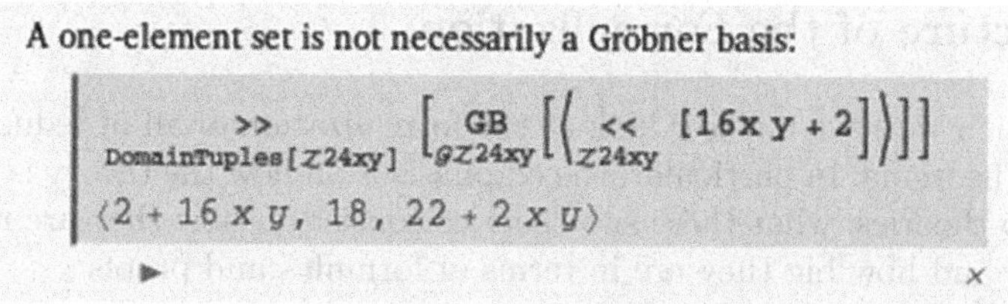

A one-element set is not necessarily a Gröbner basis:

$$\left|\ _{\text{DomainTuples}[Z24xy]}^{>>} \ \left[\ _{gZ24xy}^{GB}\ \left[\left\langle\ _{Z24xy}^{<<}\ [16x\,y+2]\right]\right)\right]\right]$$

⟨2 + 16 x y, 18, 22 + 2 x y⟩

▶   ✕

Fig. 2. A sample computation in Theorema. The "<<" and ">>" are only responsible for the in- and output of polynomials and do not affect the actual computation.

indices, for instance) have to be taken into account. Furthermore, termination of GBAux is by no means obvious: its second argument, which must eventually become empty, is enlarged in the second case of (GBAux 3), meaning that this case must be shown to occur only finitely often. A separate reduction ring axiom is needed to ensure this.

Function GB is not only of theoretical interest for our formalization, but can also be executed on concrete input to actually compute Gröbner bases, provided that the underlying domain $\mathcal{R}$ is a reduction ring and implements a couple of auxiliary functions GB depends upon (most importantly, the usual ring operations). At the moment, the following domains included in the formalization meet these requirements; the proofs thereof are part of the formalization, of course (see also Sect. 4.2):

– all fields, in particular the Theorema built-in fields $\mathbb{Q}$, $\mathbb{R}$ and $\mathbb{C}$,
– $\mathbb{Z}$,
– $\mathbb{Z}_n$ for arbitrary $n \in \mathbb{N}$,
– multivariate polynomial rings over the aforementioned domains.

Function GB always returns provenly correct results when used in these domains. Figure 2 shows a sample computation in $\mathbb{Z}_{24}[x, y]$, carried out directly within Theorema 2.0: as discussed in Example 3, $\{16xy+2\}$ is no Gröbner basis, because the constituents of the critical pair $([20]_{24}, [14]_{24})$ cannot be connected. Therefore, their difference $[14]_{24} = [15]_{24}$ must be added to the basis in a first step. Figure 2 reveals that this is still not sufficient, since one further element must be added afterward.

For the sake of completeness we have to point out that Buchberger's algorithm and Theorem 1 as presented here were simplified a bit compared to our actual formalization. For one thing, the sets of multipliers M_c have to be split into several (finitely many) indexed subsets M_c^i, and the notion of mntcr depends on these indices; mntcrs for *all* pairs of indices have to be considered separately, both in the theorem and in the algorithm. Also, the actual implementation of GB employs the so-called *chain criterion* for avoiding useless reductions; this criterion, hence, increases efficiency and works in reduction rings in pretty much the same way as in the original setting of polynomials over fields, see [2]. The interested reader is referred to [7] for an unsimplified statement of Theorem 1, and to [8] for a more detailed discussion of Buchberger's algorithm in our formalization.

4   Structure of the Formalization

In this section we have a closer look at the formalization of all of reduction ring theory in Theorema. In particular, the emphasis is on how the theory is split into smaller sub-theories, what these sub-theories consist of, how they are related to each other, and how big they are in terms of formulas and proofs.

Before, however, some remarks on theory exploration in Theorema 2.0 *in general* are in place. Theorema theories are essentially *Mathematica* notebooks consisting of both formal (mathematical formulas) and informal (explanatory text, diagrams, tables, etc.) content. Users are free to compose such notebooks in whatever way they want, making use of *Mathematica*'s rich typesetting capabilities, yielding nicely-formatted documents. Proving proceeds by first setting up *proof tasks* and then either calling an automatic prover or an interactive proof strategy (see Sect. 5). In any case, the resulting proofs are stored as abstract *proof objects* in external files; they can be inspected in automatically generated *proof documents* displaying the proofs in a human-readable form that closely resembles the way how proofs are usually presented in mathematical text-books (again, heavily relying on *Mathematica*'s typesetting capabilities). Since this paper does not aim at presenting Theorema 2.0, and in particular how theory exploration in the system proceeds, in detail, the interested reader is referred to our recent article [5] instead.

Although the paper has only been about reduction rings so far, it must be noted that a substantial part of our formalization is actually concerned with rather basic concepts, such as sets, algebraic structures, numbers, tuples (or lists) and sequences that are themselves independent of reduction ring theory and merely serve as its logical backbone. In this respect, our formalization can also be regarded a major contribution to a structured knowledge base of elementary mathematical theories in Theorema 2.0 that can be reused in future theory explorations. Such a knowledge base did not exist in Theorema 2.0 before, which justifies, in our opinion, presenting it just alongside the formal treatment of reduction rings in this section (only superficially, though).

Figure 3 shows the dependencies of the individual sub-theories on each other. Each node represents a sub-theory, contained in a separate Theorema notebook, and a directed edge from theory A to theory B means that B logically depends on A in the sense that formulas (i. e. definitions or theorems) contained in A were used in the proof of a theorem in B. Theories corresponding to framed nodes are directly related to reduction rings (see Sect. 4.2), whereas all other theories belong to the knowledge base of elementary theories (see Sect. 4.1). Note also that transitive edges are omitted for better readability, e. g. theory Numbers.nb not only depends *indirectly* on theory LogicSets.nb (via AlgebraicStructures.nb), but also *directly*; this fact is not reflected in Fig. 3.

The total number of proved theorems in the whole formalization in 2464, the total number of unproved definitions and axioms is 484. Hence, the total number of formulas is **2948**. The complete formalization is available online from http://www.risc.jku.at/people/amaletzk/Formalizations.html.

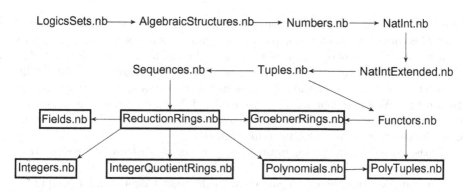

Fig. 3. The theory dependency graph.

4.1 Elementary Theories

Most of the sub-theories in this category have rather self-explanatory names, and we will not go into details regarding their contents. Some remarks are still in place, though.

Theories Numbers.nb, NatInt.nb and NatIntExtended.nb are all about natural numbers and integers: the very definition of natural numbers by purely set-theoretic means, as well as the definition of integers as some quotient domain of pairs of natural numbers are contained in Numbers.nb, and the other two theories basically consist of hundreds of results about linear and non-linear arithmetic, division with quotient and remainder, the greatest common divisor, finite sums and mappings from $\mathbb{N}$ to $\mathbb{N}$ (needed for infinite sequences).

Theory Functors.nb contains a couple of general Theorema functors, mainly for constructing product domains from given ones.[3] The most important functor in this theory, LexOrder, maps two ordered domains to their lexicographic product; this functor was needed for proving termination of function GB (see Sect. 3). Functors.nb also proves that the order in the new domain is still partial/total/Noetherian if the orders in the original domains are.

4.2 Reduction Ring Theory

ReductionRings.nb contains the definitions of several auxiliary notions in reduction rings, like reducibility, the reduction relation (and its various closures) and properties of binary relations (confluence, local confluence, Church-Rosser), as well as the definitions of reduction rings and Gröbner bases. Reduction rings are defined through a unary predicate, isReductionRing, that is simply the conjunction of all reduction ring axioms together with the axioms of commutative rings with identity.

Besides these definitions, the main contents of ReductionRings.nb are the Main Theorem of reduction ring theory, Theorem 1, and the theorem that states

---

[3] For information on functors and domains in Theorema, see [4,17].

that the symmetric-reflexive-transitive closure of the reduction relation modulo a set C coincides with ideal congruence modulo the same set C, together with their proofs. The proof of Theorem 1 is non-trivial and lengthy, which is reflected by the fact that many auxiliary lemmas were needed before it could finally be completed, and one of these lemmas in fact deserves special attention: the *Generalized Newman Lemma*. The Generalized Newman Lemma is a general result about sufficient conditions for binary relations to be confluent (and thus Church-Rosser) that was first introduced in [19].

Please note that everything in this theory is *non-algorithmic* in the sense that no single algorithm is implemented or specified. All algorithmic aspects of our formal reduction ring theory, in particular Buchberger's algorithm for computing Gröbner bases, are part of GroebnerRings.nb.

GroebnerRings.nb contains all the algorithmic aspects of the formalization, like the implementation and specification of Buchberger's algorithm. More precisely, the theory contains a functor called GroebnerRing that extends a given input domain D by the function GB that implements Buchberger's algorithm and can thus be used for computing Gröbner bases. GB is defined in terms of auxiliary functions provided by the underlying domain D, such as the basic ring operations and the partial Noetherian ordering in reduction rings. However, following a general principle of functors and domains in Theorema, D can be completely arbitrary: it does not need to be a reduction ring, nor even a ring, meaning that some operations used in function GB are possibly undefined – and this is perfectly fine, except that one cannot expect to obtain a Gröbner basis when calling the function. But if D *is* a reduction ring, i.e. isReductionRing[D] holds, then the function really behaves according to its specification. The proof of this claim is non-trivial, even if Theorem 1 is already known, and also contained in GroebnerRings.nb.

In addition to the implementation, specification and correctness proof of Buchberger's algorithm, various sample computations of Gröbner bases in different domains ($\mathbb{Z}_{24}, \mathbb{Z}_{24}[x,y], \mathbb{Q}[x,y,z]$, for instance) are included in GroebnerRings.nb as well.

Fields.nb contains a Theorema functor, ReductionField, that takes an input domain K and extends it by those objects (function M and relation $\preceq$) that turn K into a reduction ring. These new objects are defined in such a way that if K is a field, then the extension really *is* a reduction ring – otherwise nothing can be said about it. The proof of this claim is of course also contained in Fields.nb, and actually it is quite straight-forward.

Integers.nb contains a Theorema functor, ReductionIntegers, that does not take any input domains but simply constructs a new domain whose carrier is $\mathbb{Z}$ and that provides the additional objects for turning $\mathbb{Z}$ into a reduction ring, following [3]. The proof of this claim is included in the theory as well.

IntegerQuotientRings.nb contains a Theorema functor, ReductionIQR, that takes a positive integer n and constructs a new domain whose carrier is the set $\{0,\ldots,n-1\}$ and that provides the additional objects for turning $\mathbb{Z}_n$, represented by $\{0,\ldots,n-1\}$, into a reduction ring, following [13]. The proof of this claim is of course included in the theory as well. Surprisingly, although turning $\mathbb{Z}_n$ into a reduction ring is more involved than $\mathbb{Z}^4$, fewer auxiliary results were needed in IntegerQuotientRings.nb than in Integers.nb. This is due to the fact that the reduction ring ordering $\preceq$ in $\mathbb{Z}_n$ is much simpler than in $\mathbb{Z}$.

Polynomials.nb contains the general result that the n-variate polynomial ring over a reduction ring is again a reduction ring, if the sets of multipliers and the order relation are defined appropriately. This is accomplished by first introducing the class of *reduction polynomial domains* over a coefficient domain $\mathcal{R}$ and a power-product domain $\mathcal{T}$. A domain $\mathcal{P}$ belongs to this class iff it provides the usual ring operations, a coefficient function that maps each power-product from $\mathcal{T}$ to a coefficient in $\mathcal{R}$, a set of multipliers for each element in $\mathcal{P}$ (i. e. the function M), and an order relation $\preceq$, and all these objects satisfy certain constraints (e. g. the coefficient function must have finite support and must interact with $+$ and $\cdot$ in the usual way, the sets of multipliers must be of a particular form, and the ordering must be defined in a certain way). These constraints, whose precise formulations can be found in [3], ensure that if $\mathcal{R}$ is a reduction ring and $\mathcal{T}$ is a domain of commutative power-products, then $\mathcal{P}$ is a reduction ring as well. This is one of the fundamental results of reduction ring theory, and its proof is very complicated and tedious (even more complicated than the proof of Theorem 1). Nevertheless, it has been entirely completed already and is also part of Polynomials.nb.

Note that all definitions and results in this theory are on a very abstract level: no concrete representation of multivariate polynomials, be it as tuples of monomials, as iterated univariate polynomials, or whatsoever, is ever mentioned in the whole theory, but instead polynomials are essentially viewed as functions from $\mathcal{T}$ to $\mathcal{R}$ with finite support. This approach has the advantage that the results can easily be specialized to many *different* representations of polynomials, if necessary, and this is just what is made use of in theory PolyTuples.nb.

PolyTuples.nb contains a functor, `PolyTuples`, that takes two domains $\mathcal{R}$ and $\mathcal{T}$ as input and constructs the domain $\mathcal{P}$ of reduction-polynomials over coefficient domain $\mathcal{R}$ and power-product domain $\mathcal{T}$ represented as ordered (w. r. t. the ordering on $\mathcal{T}$) tuples of monomials. Monomials, in turn, are represented as pairs of coefficients and power-products. $\mathcal{P}$ provides the additional functions and relations needed to prove that it belongs to the class of reduction polynomial domains, and thus is a reduction ring thanks to the key result in Polynomials.nb.[5] The proof of this claim is part of the theory, of course.

Besides functor `PolyTuples`, three additional functors for constructing domains of commutative power-products are also contained in PolyTuples.nb: one for a purely lexicographic term order, one for a degree-lexicographic term order, and one for a degree-reverse-lexicographic term order. In either case, power-products are represented as tuples of natural numbers.

---

[4] The first attempt in [3] was erroneous.

[5] Once again, this is only true if $\mathcal{R}$ is a reduction ring and $\mathcal{T}$ is a domain of commutative power-products.

5   New Tools

In this section we present two useful tools that we developed in the course of the formalization of reduction rings: an interactive proof strategy and a mechanism for analyzing the logical structure of Theorema theories. As will be seen in the following two subsections, the tools are general-purpose tools and thus completely independent of our concrete formalization, and hence may be used in any other theory exploration in Theorema as well. For that reason, they are planned to be integrated into the official version of the system in the near future.

5.1   Interactive Proof Strategy

In contrast to most other proof assistants, the interactive proof strategy in Theorema 2.0 described below is not text-based, but *dialog-oriented* (similar to the one in Theorema 1 [10]): whenever a new proof situation that cannot be handled automatically[6] arises during the proof search, a dialog window pops up. This window displays the current proof situation, characterized by the current proof goal and the current set of assumptions, and asks the user how to proceed. He may now either

- choose an inference rule to apply,
- choose a different pending proof situation where to continue with the proof search,
- inspect the proof *so far*, in a nicely-formatted proof document,
- inspect the internal representation of the proof object for debugging,
- save the current status of the proof in an external file,
- adjust the configuration of the prover (maybe even switching from the interactive mode to a fully automatic one), or
- abort the proof attempt.

When choosing an inference rule that shall be applied (or, more precisely, *tried*), the user even has the possibility to indicate the formula(s) to be considered by the rule (for instance, if one of several universally quantified assumptions is to be instantiated). Furthermore, he may then be asked to provide further information about the concrete application of the rule (like specifying the concrete term a formula shall be instantiated with); this, however, solely depends on the implementation of the inference rule and is thus not affected by our interactive proof strategy.

Figure 4 shows a screen-shot of the interactive dialog window. In the middle, the current goal (top) and the current assumptions (bottom) are displayed. Above, the inference rule to be applied next, as chosen by the user, is indicated, and the menu bar is located at the very top.

---

[6] So, there is still *some* automation of very trivial tasks.

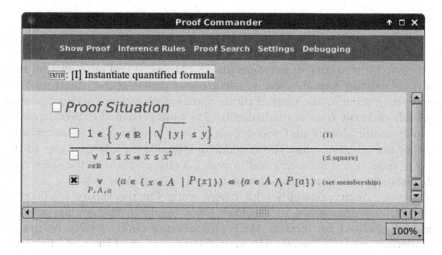

Fig. 4. A "Proof Commander" dialog window for interactive proving.

5.2   TheoryAnalyzer

The TheoryAnalyzer is a *Mathematica* package that provides a collection of functions for analyzing the logical structure of Theorema theories and the logical dependencies of formulas on each other. If theories grow big, as in our case, it becomes more and more difficult to keep track of which formulas were used in the proofs of which other formulas, which formulas are affected when another formula is modified, and whether the order of formulas in a notebook agrees with their logical order. It is clear, however, that these questions are of utmost importance for a consistent, coherent and systematic development of a mathematical theory; after all, if a formula φ is modified, then all of its consequences (that is, the theorems that use φ as an assumption in their proofs) *must* be re-proved, and so one needs to know what these consequences are in the first place—and this was the main motivation for the development of the TheoryAnalyzer.

Summarizing, the TheoryAnalyzer allows to automatically

- inspect all direct or indirect assumptions of a given theorem,
- inspect all direct or indirect consequences of a given formula,
- ensure that theories do not contain circular arguments,
- check whether the order of formulas in a notebook agrees with their logical order, and
- draw nicely-formatted theory-dependency-graphs (as the one in Fig. 3) and formula-statistics-diagrams.

6 Conclusion

The work described in this paper is expected to have, and already had, various positive effects on theory explorations in Theorema 2.0 and on reduction ring theory: the existing formalization, in particular of the elementary mathematical theories, may serve as the basis of future theory explorations, perhaps even in completely different areas of mathematics. The tools presented in Sect. 5 proved extremely useful already and will definitely be of use for other users as well, once they are integrated into the system. And, finally, the contributions to the theory of reduction rings mentioned in Sect. 2.3 give evidence to the claim that mathematics profits from being treated formally in computer systems.

There are many possibilities for future work. On the theory level, other aspects of, and approaches to, Gröbner bases (again in the original setting) could be formalized, for instance the computation of Gröbner bases by matrix triangularizations [16]. For this, the further improvement of the tools described in Sect. 5 and the development of new tools might be necessary (more flexible interactive proving strategy, proof checker, . . .).

Acknowledgments. I thank the anonymous referees for their valuable remarks and suggestions.

This research was funded by the Austrian Science Fund (FWF): grant no. W1214-N15, project DK1.

References

1. Adams, W.W., Loustaunau, P.: An Introduction to Gröbner Bases. Graduate Studies in Mathematics, vol. 3. American Mathematical Society, Providence (1994). doi:10.1090/gsm/003. ISSN: 1065-7339, ISBN: 0-8218-3804-0
2. Buchberger, B.: A criterion for detecting unnecessary reductions in the construction of Gröbner bases. In: Ng, E.W. (ed.) EUROSAM 1979. LNCS, vol. 72, pp. 3–21. Springer, Heidelberg (1979)
3. Buchberger, B.: A critical-pair/completion algorithm for finitely generated ideals in rings. In: Börger, E., Hasenjaeger, G., Rödding, D. (eds.) Logic and Machines: Decision Problems and Complexity. LNCS, vol. 171, pp. 137–161. Springer, Heidelberg (1984)
4. Buchberger, B.: Gröbner Rings in Theorema: A Case Study in Functors and Categories. Technical report 2003-49, Johannes Kepler University Linz, Spezialforschungsbereich F013, November 2003
5. Buchberger, B., Jebelean, T., Kutsia, T., Maletzky, A., Windsteiger, W.: Theorema 2.0 computer-assisted natural-style mathematics. J. Formalized Reasoning **9**(1), 149–185 (2016)
6. Jorge, J.S., Guilas, V.M., Freire, J.L.: Certifying properties of an efficient functional program for computing Gröbner bases. J. Symbolic Comput. **44**(5), 571–582 (2009)
7. Maletzky, A.: Exploring reduction ring theory in theorema. Technical report 2016-06, Doctoral Program "Computational Mathematics", Johannes Kepler University Linz, Austria, July 2015

8. Maletzky, A.: Verifying Buchberger's algorithm in reduction rings. In: Jebelean, T., Wang, D. (eds.) Proceedings of PAS 2015 (Program Verification, Automated Debugging and Symbolic Computation, Beijing, China, 21–23 October 2015. arXiv:1604.08736
9. Medina-Bulo, I., Palomo-Lozano, F., Ruiz-Reina, J.L.: A verified common lisp implementation of Buchberger's algorithm in ACL2. J. Symbolic Comput. **45**(1), 96–123 (2010)
10. Piroi, F., Kutsia, T.: The *Theorema* environment for interactive proof development. In: Sutcliffe, G., Voronkov, A. (eds.) Logic for Programming, Artificial Intelligence, and Reasoning. LNCS, vol. 3835, pp. 261–275. Springer, Heidelberg (2005)
11. Robbiano, L.: Term orderings on the polynomial ring. In: Caviness, B.F. (ed.) EUROCAL 1985. LNCS, vol. 204, pp. 513–517. Springer, Heidelberg (1985)
12. Schwarzweller, C.: Gröbner bases — theory refinement in the mizar system. In: Kohlhase, M. (ed.) MKM 2005. LNCS (LNAI), vol. 3863, pp. 299–314. Springer, Heidelberg (2006)
13. Stifter, S.: A generalization of reduction rings. J. Symbolic Comput. **4**(3), 351–364 (1988)
14. Stifter, S.: The reduction ring property is hereditary. J. algebra **140**(89–18), 399–414 (1991)
15. Thery, L.: A machine-checked implementation of Buchberger's algorithm. J. Autom. Reasoning **26**, 107–137 (2001)
16. Wiesinger-Widi, M.: Gröbner Bases and Generalized Sylvester Matrices. Ph.D. Thesis, Johannes Kepler University Linz (2015). http://epub.jku.at/obvulihs/content/titleinfo/776913
17. Windsteiger, W.: Building up hierarchical mathematical domains using functors in theorema. In: Armando, A., Jebelean, T. (eds.) Proceedings of Calculemus 1999, Trento, Italy. ENTCS, vol. 23, pp. 401–419. Elsevier, Amsterdam (1999)
18. Windsteiger, W.: Theorema 2.0: a system for mathematical theory exploration. In: Hong, H., Yap, C. (eds.) ICMS 2014. LNCS, vol. 8592, pp. 49–52. Springer, Heidelberg (2014)
19. Winkler, F., Buchberger, B.: A criterion for eliminating unnecessary reductions in the Knuth-Bendix algorithm. In: Colloqium on Algebra, Combinatorics and Logic in Computer Science, pp. 849–869 (1983)

Formalization of Bing's Shrinking Method in Geometric Topology

Ken'ichi Kuga$^{(\boxtimes)}$, Manabu Hagiwara, and Mitsuharu Yamamoto

Department of Mathematics and Informatics, Faculty of Science, Chiba University,
Yayoi 1-33, Inage-ku, Chiba City 263-0022, Japan
{kuga,hagiwara,mituharu}@math.s.chiba-u.ac.jp

Abstract. Bing's shrinking method is a key technique for constructing homeomorphisms between topological manifolds in geometric topology. Applications of this method include the generalized Schoenflies theorem, the double suspension theorem for homology spheres, and the 4-dimensional Poincaré conjecture. Homeomorphisms obtained in this method are sometimes counter-intuitive and may even be pathological. This makes Bing's shrinking method a good target of formalization by proof assistants. We report our formalization of this method in Coq/Ssreflect.

Keywords: Formalization · Geometric topology · Bing's shrinking method · Coq · Ssreflect

1 Introduction

The Jordan curve theorem is one of the classical theorems in topology that has been successfully formalized using proof systems (in HOL Light [10], and in Mizar [9]). These formalizations in topology show significant differences between traditional proofs based on geometric/topological intuition and computer checking of those traditional proofs. In fact, trained geometers and topologists can reproduce mathematically rigorous proof steps by reading traditional arguments appealing to geometric intuition, but this reproduction process can frequently be nontrivial to formalize. When it comes to the Schoenflies problem, which is an essential refinement to the Jordan curve theorem, formalization becomes even less trivial.

The Schoenflies problem asks whether the region bounded by a Jordan curve is topologically equal to the disk. In the category of topological spaces, we say two objects are "equal" when there exists a homeomorphism between them. However, finding a homeomorphism is a fairly non-trivial issue even when the two spaces appear similar. In fact, while the original 2 dimensional Schoenflies problem can be affirmatively answered using a fairly nontrivial topological argument or applying Carathéodory's theorem in complex analysis ([1]), the 3 dimensional analogue fails to hold due to the existence of counter-intuitive examples such as Alexander's horned sphere ([2] Fig. 1). This pathological phenomenon is a

M. Kohlhase et al. (Eds.): CICM 2016, LNAI 9791, pp. 18–27, 2016.
DOI: 10.1007/978-3-319-42547-4_2

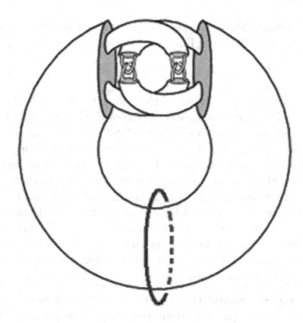

Fig. 1. Alexander's horned sphere [16] The complement of this wild sphere in the 3-dimensional sphere S^3 is not homeomorphic to the standard 3-dimensional ball. This follows from the observation that the linking circle depicted in the picture is not contractible in the complement. However, gluing two copies of the complement along the horned sphere yields the standard 3-dimensional sphere S^3. Bing constructed this counter-intuitive homeomorphism using his shrinking method in 1952 [3].

characteristic aspect of geometric topology in the topological category, and this counter-intuitive aspect makes geometric topology a good target of computer formalization.

To avoid the pathology of Alexander's horned sphere and recover the Scheon-flies problem in arbitrary dimensions, a correct assumption to impose on the topological embeddings of the $n - 1$ sphere in the n sphere turned out to be "local flatness": An embedding of the $n - 1$ dimensional sphere S^{n-1} into the n dimensional sphere S^n, $\phi : S^{n-1} \rightarrow S^n$, is *locally flat* when there exists a topological embedding $\overline{\phi} : S^{n-1} \times \mathbb{R} \rightarrow S^n$ such that $\overline{\phi}(x, 0) = \phi(x)$ for all $x \in S^{n-1}$.

Thus in 1960 Morton Brown succeeded in proving the following theorem [4]:

Generalized Schoenflies Theorem (GST). Let $\phi : S^{n-1} \rightarrow S^n$ be a locally flat topological embedding. Then the closure of each connected component of the complement of $\phi(S^{n-1})$ is homeomorphic to the n dimensional disk D^n.

Here, the n dimensional sphere S^n is most often concretely defined as the unit sphere in the Euclidean $n + 1$ space:

$$S^n := \{(x_1, x_2, \cdots, x_{n+1}) \in \mathbb{R}^{n+1} \mid x_1^2 + x_2^2 + \cdots + x_{n+1}^2 = 1\}$$

with subspace topology. Similarly, the n dimensional disk D^n is usually defined concretely as the unit disk in the Euclidean n space:

$$D^n := \{(x_1, x_2, \cdots, x_n) \in \mathbb{R}^n \mid x_1^2 + x_2^2 + \cdots + x_n^2 \leq 1\}$$

However, we may also define D^n to be the cube $D^n := [0,1]^n$, the standard n simplex, or some appropriate compactification of Euclidean n space.

The choice of these concrete definitions of S^n or D^n or any space in topology is mathematically immaterial, but it does change the resulting formalization significantly and makes it less portable. Hence it is a better idea to abstract the essential property of disks and spheres required in the proof of the **GST** to a greater extent in formalization than in traditional mathematics. The essential property of these spaces needed for constructing required homeomorphisms is certain self-shrinkability of disks and spheres. We will briefly explain some abstraction of this self-shrinkability later, but the point here is this property ensures that any surjection $f : D^n \to D^n$ with finitely many nontrivial inverses is "shrinkable" in the following sense.

Definition (Bing Shrinkability). Let $f : X \to Y$ be a continuous mapping between compact metric spaces with metrics d and d' respectively. We say f is called *Bing shrinkable* if for each positive $\epsilon > 0$ there exists a homeomorphism $h_\epsilon : X \to X$ such that for all $y \in Y$, $\mathrm{diam}_d h_\epsilon(f^{-1}(y)) < \epsilon$ and for all $x \in X$, $d'(f(x), f(h_\epsilon(x))) < \epsilon$.

This property is the key property when we wish to show two topological spaces are "equal" because of the following theorem.

Bing Shrinking Theorem (BST). Suppose $f : X \to Y$ is a continuous surjection between compact metric spaces and f is Bing shrinkable. Then f can be approximated by homeomorphisms, that is, for each positive δ there exists a homeomorphism $k_\delta : X \to Y$ such that for all $x \in X$, $d'(f(x), k_\delta(x)) < \delta$. In particular X and Y are homeomorphic.

This shrinking method was first invented and used by R. H. Bing in 1952 when he produced an exotic involutive self-homeomorphism of the three sphere S^3 whose fixed point set is the Alexander horned sphere [3]. In his construction, a certain map $f : S^3 \to Y$ from the three sphere to a potentially non-manifold space Y was approximated by homeomorphisms. Hence it follows that the target space is actually a three sphere.

Other applications of this shrinking construction of non-trivial homeomorphisms include the celebrated double suspension theorem of J. Cannon and R. Edwards, and M. Freedman's proof of the 4-dimensional Poincaré conjecture. Homeomorphisms obtained in this theorem are relatively general and beyond what can be easily understood concerning equality of topological spaces, which makes this theorem an attractive target of formalization.

The purpose of this paper is to report our formalization of this method in Coq/Ssreflect. We note that our formalization is essentially non-constructive. In fact, a characteristic feature of the shrinking construction is the appearance of infinite iterations producing possibly conter-intuitive homeomorphisms.

Thus Bing's Shrinking criterion in its generality requires the Axiom of Choice in the form of the Baire Category Theorem. Our formalization also uses a topology library by Schepler [13] which assumes the classical propositional logic in the standard library of Coq.

2 Formalization

In this section we explain our formalization of the previously stated Bing Shrinking Theorem in Coq/Ssreflect. Our formalization uses the current version of Coq(Coq-8.5) with the Standard Library and its Ssreflect extension contained in Mathcomp-1.6. Our formalization also uses the Topology library in Coq by Daniel Schepler in [12] as our starting point. We also made a small library of topological lemmas, LemmasForBSC.v, and a formalization of the Baire Category Theorem, BaireSpaces.v, needed in our main formalization BingShrinkingCriterion.v. These files with complete code are in [11].

In [12] (or more or less in any topology library in Coq, e.g. [13–15]) topological spaces are formalized according to the axiom for the system of open subsets:

```
Record TopologicalSpace : Type := {
  point_set : Type;
  open : Ensemble point_set → Prop;
  open_family_union : ∀ F : Family point_set,
    (∀ S : Ensemble point_set, In F S → open S) →
    open (FamilyUnion F);
  open_intersection\,2: ∀ U V:Ensemble point_set,
    open U → open V → open (Intersection U V);
  open_full : open Full_set
}.
```

Here we remark on one aspect where our formalization might look different from informal arguments. That is about subspaces of Xt (we reserve X for the underlying type point_set Xt of the topological space Xt). A subset A of Xt: TopologicalSpace is of type

```
Ensemble (point_set Xt) := (point_set Xt) → Prop.
```

There is a natural topology, say At, on A induced from Xt called a relative topology or a subspace topology. Informally, a subset U of A is open in At if and only if $U = A \cap V$ for some open set V of Xt. Formally, however, U is an element of the type

```
Ensemble {x : point_set Xt | A x}
```

Especially when subsets are nested, $X \supset A \supset B$, identifications of various induced topologies become non-trivial.

Another factor which complicates this situation is that we begin with metric spaces $(X, d), (Y, d')$ where d and d' are distance functions $(d : X \to X \to R)$ $(d' : Y \to Y \to R)$ and R is the set of real numbers. These metrics are subject to the standard metric space axioms such as the triangle inequality. These metrics induce a metric topology on X and Y yielding topological spaces Xt and Yt. If A is a subset of X, then d restricts to a metric dA on A. Then the metric space (A, dA) induces a topology on A which is equivalent to the subspace topology from Xt. Again this identification is non-trivial.

2.1 Bing Shrinking Criterion

Let's begin with X Y: Type as underlying point sets and (d: X → X → R) (d': Y → Y→ R) as metrics on them. These metrics define topological spaces Xt and Yt. Then the Bing Shrinkability for compact spaces is formalized as

```
Hypothesis X_compact: compact Xt.
Hypothesis Y_compact: compact Yt.
Definition Bing_shrinkable (f:X→Y): Prop:=
  ∀ eps:R, eps>0 →
    ∃ h : point_set Xt → point_set Xt,
     homeomorphism h ∧
     (∀ x:X, d' (f x) (f (h x)) < eps) ∧
     (∀ x1 x2:X, (f x1) = (f x2) → d (h x1) (h x2) < eps).
```

Defining the conclusion as approximability by homeomorphisms, the **BST** is formalized as follows.

```
Definition approximable_by_homeos (f:X→Y): Prop:=
  ∀ eps:R, eps>0 →
    ∃ h:point_set Xt → point_set Yt,
     homeomorphism h ∧
     (∀ x:X, d' (f x) (h x) < eps).


Theorem Bing_Shrinking_Theorem:
  ∀ f: point_set Xt → point_set Yt,
  continuous f → surjective f →
  (Bing_shrinkable f → approximable_by_homeos f).
```

We formalized the proof of the Bing Shrinking Theorem following the line of argument of R.D.Edwards' ICM talk in 1978 [5]. Edward's argument is different from Bing's original proof and quite succinctly outlined. This is made possible by going to the function space of continuous functions. This function space becomes a metric space with uniform topology. This formalization is a good example where formal proof becomes considerably longer than the intuitively outlined proof because of various non-trivial identifications of topologies on subspaces of function spaces with metrics, etc., which are usually unnoticed by experts in topology.

We thus consider the function space

```
Let CMap :=
  {f:X→Y | bound (Im Full_set
            (fun x:X⇒ d' (y0 x) (f x)))∧
          @continuous Xt Yt f}.
```

This CMap becomes a complete metric space with a uniform metric. Mathematically the boundedness condition is redundant as it follows immediately when the spaces are compact. However, it is added to make the definability of a uniform metric on CMap obvious.

We then suppose f : CMap satisfies the Bing shrinking criterion: Bing_shrinkable f.

```
set fH : Ensemble (point_set CMapt) :=
   fun gP : CMap ⇒ ∃ hx : point_set Xt → point_set Xt,
          homeomorphism hx ∧
          ∀ x : point_set Xt, (proj1_sig gP) x = f (hx x).
```

```
set CfH := closure fH.
set CfHt := SubspaceTopology CfH.
```

Then we can check that CfHt becomes a complete metric space and hence by applying the Baire Category Theorem this space is a Baire space:

```
have CfHt_baire : baire_space CfHt.
apply BaireCategoryTheorem
          with um_restriction um_restriction_metric.
```

We construct a sequence of open dense subsets of CfHt by setting:

```
Let W (eps:R):
 Ensemble (point_set CMapt) :=
 fun g : CMap ⇒  ∀ (x1 x2:X),
  (proj1_sig g x1) = (proj1_sig g x2) → d x1 x2 < eps.
```

From the reasons mentioned above the openness of W is not as straightforward as it might look:

```
Lemma W_is_open : ∀ (eps:R),
                    eps > 0 → open (W eps).
```

The point of the Bing shrinkability is that this property amounts to saying each such W is dense.

Then

```
set Wn : IndexedFamily nat (point_set CfHt) := fun n:nat ⇒
   inverse_image (subspace_inc CfH)  (W (/ INR (S n))).
have WnOD : ∀ n : nat, open (Wn n) ∧ dense (Wn n).
```

Then applying the Baire property, the intersection of W_n's is dense.

```
have IWn_dense : dense (IndexedIntersection Wn).
apply CfHt_baire.
by apply WnOD.
```

This intersection consists of the desired homeomorphisms, which completes the formalization.

2.2 Baire Category Theorem

As we needed the Baire Category Theorem (**BCT**) in our formalization of the **BST**, we formalized the **BCT** for compact metric spaces.

```
Variable T: Topological_space.
Definition baire_space : Prop :=
 ∀ V : IndexedFamily nat (point_set T),
   (∀ n: nat, (open (V n)) ∧ (dense (V n))) →
   dense (IndexedIntersection V).
```

Let X be a point set (Type) and d a metric $(X \to X \to R)$ defining a metric topology on X. Then

```
Theorem BaireCategoryTheorem :
             complete d d_metric → baire_space.
```

Our formalization follows a more or less straightforward argument of choosing an appropriate convergent sequence. One point we need to mention here is that to choose this sequence it is inevitable to assume the Axiom of Choice. In this sense, our formalization is essentially non-constructive. Explicitly we used the following form of the Axiom of Choice:

```
Axiom FDC : FunctionalDependentChoice_on
             (point_set X * {r:R | r > 0} * nat).
```

(In our code in BaireCategory.v [11], it is a lemma derived from the Coq standard library.)

3 Relation to Some Theorems in Geometric Topology

In this section, to give an idea how Bing's shrinking method is used in more concrete geometric situations, we first sketch a traditional proof of the Generalized Schoenflies Theorem using this method (Details can be found in [4,7]).

3.1 Proof Sketch of the GST Using Bing's Shrinking Method

Consider a map $f : S^n \to \Sigma S^{n-1}$, where ΣS^{n-1} is the suspension of S^{n-1}, i.e., the compact space obtained from the infinite cylinder $S^{n-1} \times \mathbb{R}$ by adding two ideal points $+\infty$ and $-\infty$. Define f to be the map collapsing two bounded regions of $S^n - \overline{\phi}(S^{n-1} \times \mathbb{R})$ and mapping them to the corresponding ideal points $\pm\infty$. By drilling a small ball from the image of $\overline{\phi}$, the **GST** becomes the $k = 2$ case of the following 'Disk to Disk Theorem'.

Theorem (Disk to Disk Theorem). Suppose $f : D^n \to D^n$ is a map such that there are only finitely many points (say k points) p_i with the property $\mathrm{Card}(f^{-1}(p_i)) > 1$. If all p_i are in the interior of $\mathrm{Im}(f)$ then f is Bing shrinkable.

For the sake of simplicity we assume there is only one such point $p_i = p$. To shrink the point inverse $f^{-1}(p)$, consider the homeomorphism $h : D^n \to D^n$ obtained by applying the Relative Annulus Property of (D^n, N, B) where N is a standard thin collar neighborhood of ∂D^n and B is a small ball around p.

Then the map $\sigma : D^n \to D^n$ defined by $\sigma(x) = x$ for $x \in f^{-1}(p)$ and $\sigma(x) = f^{-1}(h(f(x)))$ for $x \in D^n - f^{-1}(p)$ turns out to be a homeomorphism. This σ is used to produce nested neighborhoods of $f^{-1}(p)$, which then shows the Bing Shrinkability of f.

3.2   Abstract Property of Disks Necessary for Shrinking Arguments

A problem which arises as soon as we try to formalize concrete theorems in Geometry/Topology is that geometric objects are usually given concretely in terms of some specific representation using coordinates. However, formalizations based on these specific representations make them less portable. Thus we state our example using an abstraction of disks from our on-going formalization of a key property of subsets called cellularity.

Suppose D is the standard disk D^n in the Euclidean space formalized using coordinates in some specific way. Given a point x in the interior of D, an open neighborhood U of x, and a closed subset K in the interior of D, we can construct a concrete homeomorphism h of the Euclidean space which moves interior points of D towards x until K is contained in U while at the same time fixing exterior points of D. This is the property abstracted in the following definition. (Here, a coercion from TopologicalSpace to Sortclass is defined).

```
(* Definition of abstract cell *)
Definition abstract_cell (D : Ensemble X) : Prop :=
  Inhabited (interior D) ∧ closed D ∧
  ∀ (x : X) (U K : Ensemble X),  open U → In U x
     → Included U D → closed K → Included K (interior D) →
  ∃ h : X → X, homeomorphism h ∧ h x = x ∧
        Included (Im K h) U ∧
        (∀ y : X, In (Complement D) y → h y = y).
```

This abstract property of disks is sufficient for us to formulate a property of subsets called cellularity, and it makes formalizations of the main body of the proofs using cellularity independent of concrete coordinate representations of disks.

Also, in this definition, abstract_cell is defined not as a property of topological spaces but of subsets of a fixed ambient type X, and each homeomorphism h is defined all over X. This kind of flattening is important in practice, especially for dealing with infinitely nested structures. Cellularity, abstractly defined below, is a typical example of such an infinite nesting. Concretely, a subset of a manifold (such as the n-disk or the n-sphere) is cellular if it is the intersection of some decreasing sequence of disks in the manifold. When a subset is cellular, we can shrink it explicitly without using the Baire Category Theorem. Our abstract cellularity is:

```
(* Definition of abstract cellularity *)
Definition abstract_cellular (K : Ensemble X) : Prop :=
  ∃ D : IndexedFamily nat X,
    (∀ n : nat, abstract_cell (D n) ∧
     Included (D (S n)) (interior (D n)) ) ∧
    IndexedIntersection D = K.
```

If a surjective map between spheres (of the same dimension) has only finitely many non-trivial point-inverses, then these point-inverses are inevitably cellular and that map can be approximated arbitrarily closely by homeomorphisms. The Generalized Schoenflies Theorem corresponds to the case of two non-trivial point-inverses. The Sphere to Sphere theorem in the next section corresponds to the case of countablely many nontrivial point-inverses:

3.3 Future Plan

M. Freedman's proof of the 4-dimensional Poincaré Conjecture is a triumph of geometric topology. The Bing shrinking construction of homeomorphisms we have discussed in this article plays an essential role in this proof. In fact the core theorem in [6] asserts certain topological objects, called the Casson handles, are homeomorphic to $D^2 \times \mathbb{R}^2$. This result is obtained by placing a Casson handle CH in the 4 dimensional sphere S^4 and applying the following theorem to construct a homeomorphism $CH \approx S^2 \times \mathbb{R}^2$.

Theorem (Sphere to Sphere Theorem)) [6,8]. Suppose $f : S^n \to S^n$ is a surjective map such that there are only countably many points p_i, $(i \in \mathbb{N})$ with the property $\mathrm{Card}(f^{-1}(p_i)) > 1$. We assume $\lim_{i \to \infty} \mathrm{diam}(f^{-1}(p_i)) = 0$ and the subset $\{p_i \mid i \in \mathbb{N}\} \subset S^n$ is nowhere dense. Then f is Bing shrinkable.

This theorem is the Disk to Disk Theorem for $k = \infty$ and its proof can be restated in terms of abstract_cells defined in Sect. 3. Thus formalization of this theorem may not be far from our formalization of the Bing Shrinking method.

4 Conclusion

We formalized the Bing shrinking theorem, a basic method of constructing possibly wild and even pathological homeomorphisms in geometric topology. We also extracted an abstract property of the disk to further facilitate formalization of arguments using the shrinking method.

References

1. Carathéodory, C.: Mathematische Annalen (Springer, Berlin / Heidelberg) 73(2), 305–320 (1913)
2. Alexander, J.W.: An example of a simply connected surface bounding a region which is not simply connected. Proc. Nat. Acad. Sci. U.S.A. 10(1), 8–10 (1924)
3. Bing, R.H.: A homeomorphism between the 3-sphere and the sum of two solid horned spheres. Ann. Math. 56, 354–362 (1952)
4. Brown, M.: A proof of the generalized Schoenflies theorem. Bull. Amer. Math. Soc. 66, 74–76 (1960)
5. Edwards, R.D.: The topology of manifolds and cell-like maps. In: Proceedings of the ICM, Helsinki, pp. 111–127 (1978)
6. Freedman, M.H.: The topology of four-dimensional manifolds. J. Differ. Geom. 17(3), 357–453 (1982)
7. Freedman, M.H.: Bing topology and Casson handles, notes by S. Behrens, Santa Barbara Lectures (2013)
8. Freedman, M.H., Quinn, F.: Topology of 4-Manifolds. PMS, vol. 39. Princeton University Press, Princeton (1990)
9. Mizar formalization of the Jordan curve theorem. http://mizar.uwb.edu.pl/jordan/
10. Hales, T.: The Jordan curve theorem, formally and informally. Am. Math. Mon. 114(10), 882–894 (2007)
11. BingShrinkingCriterion. https://github.com/CuMathInfo/Topology/tree/master/BingShrinkingCriterion
12. Schepler, D.: Topology/v8.5 in coq-contribs. https://scm.gforge.inria.fr/anonscm/git/coq-contribs/coq-contribs.git
13. https://github.com/c-corn/corn/tree/master/metric2
14. http://www-sop.inria.fr/marelle/Guillaume.Cano/
15. http://coquelicot.saclay.inria.fr/html/Coquelicot.Coquelicot.html
16. "Alexander Horned Sphere" From MathWorld–A Wolfram Web Resource. http://mathworld.wolfram.com/AlexandersHornedSphere.html

SC²: Satisfiability Checking Meets Symbolic Computation
(Project Paper)

Erika Ábrahám[1], John Abbott[12], Bernd Becker[2], Anna M. Bigatti[3],
Martin Brain[11], Bruno Buchberger[4], Alessandro Cimatti[5],
James H. Davenport[6(✉)], Matthew England[7], Pascal Fontaine[9],
Stephen Forrest[10], Alberto Griggio[5], Daniel Kroening[11],
Werner M. Seiler[12], and Thomas Sturm[8,13]

[1] RWTH Aachen University, Aachen, Germany
abraham@cs.rwth-aachen.de
[2] Albert-Ludwigs-Universität, Freiburg, Germany
[3] Università Degli Studi di Genova, Genova, Italy
[4] Johannes Kepler Universität, Linz, Austria
[5] Fondazione Bruno Kessler, Trento, Italy
[6] University of Bath, Bath, UK
[7] Coventry University, Coventry, UK
[8] CNRS, LORIA, Inria, Nancy, France
[9] LORIA, Inria, Université de Lorraine, Nancy, France
[10] Maplesoft Europe Ltd., Aachen, Germany
[11] University of Oxford, Oxford, UK
[12] Universität Kassel, Kassel, Germany
[13] Max-Planck-Institut für Informatik, Saarbrücken, Germany

Abstract. *Symbolic Computation* and *Satisfiability Checking* are two research areas, both having their individual scientific focus but sharing also common interests in the development, implementation and application of decision procedures for arithmetic theories. Despite their commonalities, the two communities are rather weakly connected. The aim of our newly accepted SC² project (H2020-FETOPEN-CSA) is to strengthen the connection between these communities by creating common platforms, initiating interaction and exchange, identifying common challenges, and developing a common roadmap from theory along the way to tools and (industrial) applications. In this paper we report on the aims and on the first activities of this project, and formalise some relevant challenges for the unified SC² community.

Keywords: Logical problems · Symbolic computation · Computer algebra systems · Satisfiability checking · Satisfiability modulo theories

© Springer International Publishing Switzerland 2016
M. Kohlhase et al. (Eds.): CICM 2016, LNAI 9791, pp. 28–43, 2016.
DOI: 10.1007/978-3-319-42547-4_3

1   Introduction

The use of advanced methods to solve practical and industrially relevant problems by computers has a long history. While it is customary to think that "computers are getting faster" (and indeed, they were, and are still getting more powerful in terms of multicores etc.), the progress in algorithms and software has been even greater. One of the leaders in the field of linear and mixed integer programming points out [9, slide 37] that you would be over 400 times better off running today's algorithms and software on a 1991 computer than you would running 1991 software on today's computer. The practice is heavily inspired by the theory: [9, slide 31] shows that the biggest version-on-version performance advance in software was caused by "mining the theory". *But* this progress has been in what is, mathematically, quite a limited domain: that of linear programming, possibly where some of the variables are integer-valued.

There has been also much progress in the use of computers to solve hard non-linear algebraic[1] problems. This is the area generally called *Symbolic Computation* (or *Computer Algebra*). It includes solving non-linear problems over both the real and complex numbers, though generally with very different techniques. This has produced many new applications and surprising developments: in an area everyone believed was solved, non-linear solving over the reals (using cylindrical algebraic decomposition — CAD) has recently found a new algorithm for computing square roots [35]. CAD is another area where practice is (sometimes) well ahead of theory: the theory [18,29] states that the complexity is doubly exponential in the number of variables, but useful problems can still be solved in practice ([3] points out that CAD is the most significant engine in the "Todai robot" project).

Independently and contemporaneously, there has been a lot of practical progress in solving the SAT problem, i.e., checking the satisfiability of logical problems over the Boolean domain. The SAT problem is known to be NP-complete [27]. Nevertheless, the *Satisfiability Checking* [8] community has developed SAT solvers which can successfully handle inputs with millions of Boolean variables. Among other industrial applications, these tools are now at the heart of many techniques for verification and security of computer systems.

Driven by this success, big efforts were made to enrich propositional SAT-solving with solver modules for different theories. Highly interesting techniques were implemented in *SAT-modulo-theories (SMT) solvers* [6,42] for checking easier theories, but the development for quantifier-free non-linear real and integer arithmetic (see Footnote 1) is still in its infancy.

Figure 1 shows a non-exhaustive history of tool developments in these two areas. It illustrates nicely the historically deeper roots of computer algebra systems, but also the high intensity of research in both areas. The resulting tools

---

[1] It is usual in the SMT community to refer to these constraints as *arithmetic*. But, as they involve quantities as yet unknown, manipulating them is *algebra*. Hence both words occur, with essentially the same meaning, throughout this document.

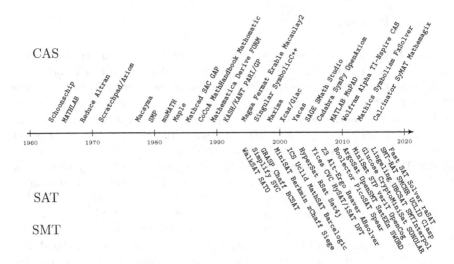

Fig. 1. History of some computer algebra systems and SAT/SMT solvers (not exhaustive; years approximate first release as far as known and as positioning allowed) [2]

are successfully applied in several academic and industrial areas, however, the current state is still not satisfactory, as described in [51]:

> *"Despite substantial advances in verification technology, complexity issues with classical decision procedures are still a major obstacle for formal verification of real-world applications, e.g., in automotive and avionic industries."*

Both communities address similar problems and share the challenge to improve their solutions to achieve applicability on complex large-scale applications. However, the Symbolic Computation community and the Satisfiability Checking community are largely in their own silos and traditionally do not interact much with each other.

To connect these communities, we successfully applied for a European Horizon 2020 *Coordination and Support Action*, with an envisaged project start in July 2016. The overall aim of this project is to create a new research community bridging the gap between Satisfiability Checking and Symbolic Computation, whose members will ultimately be well informed about both fields, and thus able to combine the knowledge and techniques of both fields to develop new research and to resolve problems (both academic and industrial) currently beyond the scope of either individual field. We call the new community SC^2, as it will join the communities of **S**atisfiability **C**hecking and **S**ymbolic **C**omputation.

The contributions of this paper are twofold: Firstly, we discuss the potentials of closer connection and more intensive exchange between the two communities, and list a number of challenges that are currently out of reach but could be tackled by a unified SC^2 community (Sect. 3). Secondly, we discuss what is needed to trigger and support these developments, and describe the actions of our project to satisfy these needs (Sect. 4).

2 Background

Before describing our project, we give a short description of the state-of-the-art in Satisfiability Checking and Symbolic Computation. Parts of this section are taken from [2].

2.1 Symbolic Computation and Computer Algebra Systems

Computer Algebra, the use of computers to do algebra rather than simply arithmetic, is almost as old as computing itself, with the first PhD theses [41,50] dating back to 1953. This initial work consisted of programs to do one thing, but the focus soon moved on to 'systems', capable of doing a variety of tasks. One early such system was Collins' SAC [24], written in Fortran. Many of the early systems were written in LISP, largely because of its support for recursion, garbage collection and large integers. The group at M.I.T. developed Macsyma [45] in the 1960s. about the same time, Hearn developed Reduce [38], and shortly after a group at IBM Yorktown Heights produced SCRATCHPAD, then AXIOM [39], a system that attempted to match the generality of Mathematics with some kind of generic programming, to allow algorithms to be programmed in the generality in which they are conventionally stated, e.g., polynomials over a ring.

Symbolic Computation was initially seen as part of Artificial Intelligence, with major triumphs such as [54] being "A Heuristic Program that Solves Symbolic Integration Problems in Freshman Calculus", firmly in the AI camp. By the end of the 1960s, this approach to integration had been replaced by an algorithm [46], which had the great advantage that, when backed up with a suitable completeness theorem [52] it could *prove* unintegrability: "there is no formula made up of exponentials, logarithms and algebraic functions which differentiates to e^{-x^2}", in other words "e^{-x^2} is unintegrable".

The 1960s and 70s also saw great advances in other areas. We had much more efficient algorithms to replace naive use of Euclid's algorithm for greatest common divisor computation (and hence the simplification of fractions), far better algorithms than the search-based methods for polynomial factorisation, and so on. All this meant that Symbolic Computation firmly moved into the camps of algorithmics and complexity theory, and the dominant question became "what is the worst-case complexity of this algorithm".

Gröbner bases. One great success of this period was the method of *Gröbner bases* [20]. This allows effective, and in many cases efficient, solution of many problems of polynomials over algebraically-closed fields (typically the complex numbers, though applications over finite fields and in cryptography abound). This notion paved the way for the discovery of numerous effective methods for polynomial ideals; many applications in other areas of Mathematics quickly followed. Buchberger's algorithm for computing a Gröbner basis is a prime example of the huge gulf that can separate an abstract algorithm from a usably efficient implementation. Over the fifty years since its initial publication, research into the algorithm's behaviour has produced several significant improvements: the modern refined version is typically thousands of times faster than the original. The search for further improvements continues today.

The remarkable computational utility of Gröbner bases prompted the development of a number of distinct, independent implementations of refined versions of Buchberger's algorithm. The main commercial general-purpose computer algebra systems (including MAGMA [12], Maple [43], Mathematica [58]) can all compute Gröbner bases; researchers needing the flexibility and ability to experiment with new algorithms also use computer algebra systems such as CoCoA/CoCoALib [1], Macaulay/Macaulay2 [37] and Singular [32] and Reduce [38] which are freely downloadable from their respective websites.

Cylindrical algebraic decomposition. Another great success of the 1970s was the development of *cylindrical algebraic decomposition* (*CAD*) in [25]. This replaced the non-elementary complexity (no finite tower of exponentials bounds the complexity) of Tarski's method for real algebraic geometry, by a doubly exponential method. A CAD is a decomposition of $\mathbb{R}^n$ into cells arranged cylindrically (meaning their projections are equal or disjoint) and described by semi-algebraic sets. For a detailed description of modern CAD, see [15].

Hong created a C version of both the SAC library and the comprehensive CAD code, which is now open-source and freely available as SACLIB and QEPCAD-B [17]. Another example is the Redlog package [33] of the computer algebra system Reduce, which offers an optimised combination of the cylindrical algebraic decomposition with virtual substitution (see below) and Gröbner basis methods.

Virtual substitution. To mention a last algorithm, *virtual substitution* [57] focuses on non-linear real arithmetic formulas where the degree of the quantified variables is not too large. Although the method can be generalised to arbitrary degrees, current implementations are typically limited to input, where the total degree of the quantified variables does not exceed 2. In practice, this limitation is somewhat softened by employing powerful heuristics like systematic *degree shifts* or polynomial factorisation. One key idea is to eliminate existential quantifiers in favour of *finite* disjunctions plugging in test terms that are derived from the considered formula.

These methods and their numerous refinements belong to the usual tool box of state-of-the-art computer algebra systems, and enable them to tackle hard arithmetic problems.

2.2   Satisfiability Checking

In the 1960s, another line of research on *Satisfiability Checking* [8] for *propositional logic* started its career. The first idea used *resolution* for quantifier elimination [31], and had serious problems with the steeply increasing requirements on computational and memory resources with the increase of the problem size. Another research line [30] suggested a combination of *enumeration* and *Boolean*

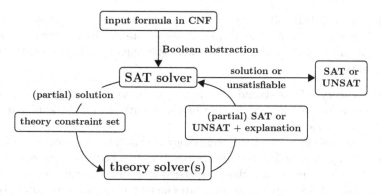

Fig. 2. The functioning of SMT solvers

constraint propagation (BCP). A major improvement was achieved in the 1990s by *combining* the two approaches, leading to *conflict-driven clause-learning* and *non-chronological backtracking* [44]. Later on, this impressive progress was continued by novel efficient implementation techniques (e.g., sophisticated decision heuristics, two-watched-literal scheme, restarts, cache performance, etc.), resulting in numerous powerful *SAT solvers*.

Driven by this success, big efforts were made to enrich propositional SAT-solving with solver modules for different existentially quantified theories. Highly interesting techniques were implemented in *SAT-modulo-theories (SMT) solvers* for checking, e.g., equality logic with uninterpreted functions, array theory, bit-vector arithmetic and quantifier-free linear real and integer arithmetic, but the development for quantifier-free non-linear real and integer arithmetic is still in its infancy. For further reading, see, e.g., [6,42].

Modern *SMT solvers* typically combine a *SAT solver* with one or more *theory solvers* as illustrated in Fig. 2. First the input formula is transformed into conjunctive normal form (CNF), a conjunction of disjunctions (clauses); this transformation can be done in linear time and space using Tseitin's transformation on the cost of additional variables. Next, the resulting CNF is abstracted to a pure Boolean propositional logic formula by replacing each theory constraint by a fresh Boolean proposition. Intuitively, the truth value of each fresh proposition defines whether the theory constraint, which it substitutes, holds. The SAT solver tries to find solutions for this propositional abstraction and during solving it consults the theory solver(s) to check the consistency of the theory constraints that should hold according to the current values of the abstraction variables.

On the one hand, theory solvers only need to check *conjunctions (sets)* of theory constraints, instead of arbitrary Boolean combinations. On the other hand, theory solvers should have the following properties for being *SMT-compliant*:

– They should work *incrementally*, i.e., after they determine the consistency of a constraint set, they should be able to take delivery of some additional constraints and re-check the extended set, thereby making use of results from the previous check.

– In case of unsatisfiability, they should be able to return an *explanation* for inconsistency, e.g., by a preferably small inconsistent subset of the constraints.
– They should support *backtracking*, i.e., the removal of previously added constraints.

Optimally, theory solvers should also be able to provide a *satisfying solution*, if the problem is satisfiable, and a *proof of unsatisfiability* for the explanation, if the problem is unsatisfiable.

A great advantage of the SMT technology is that it can employ decision procedures not only in isolation, but also *in combination*. For example, solving non-linear arithmetic formulas can often be speeded up by first checking linear abstractions or linear problem parts using more efficient decision procedures, before applying heavier procedures. Additionally, theories can also be combined already in the input language of SMT solvers. For example, deductive program verification techniques generate verification conditions, which might refer to arrays, bit-vectors as well as integers; in such cases, dedicated SMT solvers can apply several decision procedures for different theories in combination.

When combining decision procedures, *incomplete* but *efficient* procedures are also valuable, if they guarantee termination but not necessarily return a conclusive answer. Such incomplete methods are frequently applied in SMT solving, a typical example being interval constraint propagation, based on interval arithmetic. Some solvers combine such incomplete methods with complete decision procedures, in order to guarantee the solution of the problem, while increasing efficiency. Other solvers even sacrifice completeness and might return a "don't know" answer, but still they are able to solve certain extremely large problems, which are out of reach for complete methods, very fast. Furthermore, incomplete procedures are the only way to support problems from undecidable theories, like formulas containing exponential or trigonometric functions.

SAT and SMT solvers are tuned for efficiency. Combining complete and incomplete decision procedures, making use of efficient heuristics, learning not only propositional facts but also (Boolean abstractions of) theory lemmas at the SAT level allow modern SMT solvers to solve relevant large-size problems with tens of thousands of variables, which could not be solved before by single decision procedures in isolation. For some example applications see, e.g., [5].

Examples for solvers that are able to cope with linear arithmetic problems (either in a complete or in an incomplete manner) are Alt-Ergo [26], CVC4 [4], iSAT3 [36,53], MathSAT [22], OpenSMT2 [19], SMT-RAT [28], veriT [13], Yices2 [34], and Z3 [48]. A further interesting SMT-approach for linear integer arithmetic is proposed in [16].

Much less activity can be observed for SMT solvers for non-linear arithmetic. A few SMT tools embedded some (complete as well as incomplete) decision procedures. Such a solver is iSAT3, which uses interval constraint propagation. The SMT solver MiniSmt [59] tries to reduce non-linear real arithmetic problems to linear real arithmetic and can solve only satisfiable instances this way. We are aware of only two SMT solvers that are complete for non-linear real arithmetic: Firstly, the prominent Z3 solver developed at Microsoft Research, which uses an elegant SMT-adaptation of the cylindrical algebraic decomposition method [40]. Secondly, SMT-RAT [28], using solver modules for simplex, the cylindrical algebraic decomposition, the virtual substitution method, Gröbner bases, interval constraint propagation, branch and bound, and their strategic combination [47].

Even fewer SMT solvers are available for non-linear integer arithmetic, which is undecidable in general. A linearisation approach was proposed in [11]. The SMT solving spin-off of AProVE [23] uses bit-blasting. To our knowledge, Z3 implements a combination of linearisation and bit-blasting. iSAT3 uses interval constraint propagation, whereas Alt-Ergo combines the idea of [10] with an axiom-based version of interval constraint propagation. SMT-RAT can tackle this theory using a generalised branch-and-bound technique.

The increasing variety of the theories considered by SMT solvers created an urgent need for a common input language. The *SMT-LIB* initiative [7] defined a *standard input language* for SMT solvers with a first release in 2004, and provides a large and still increasing number of *benchmarks*, systematically collected for all supported theories. *SMT-LIB* also enabled the start of *SMT competitions*; the first one took place in 2005 with 12 participating solvers in 7 divisions (theories, theory combinations, or fragments thereof) on 1360 benchmarks, which increased in 2014 to 20 solvers competing in 32 divisions on 67426 benchmarks. The *SMT-LIB* standard and the competitions not only intensified the SMT research activities, but also gave visibility and acceptance for SMT solving in computer science and beyond. Once a problem is formulated in the *SMT-LIB* language, the user can employ *any* SMT solver to solve the problem.

3   Some Scientific Challenges and Opportunities

On the one hand, SMT solving has its strength in efficient techniques for exploring Boolean structures, learning, combining solving techniques, and developing dedicated heuristics, but its current focus lies on easier theories and it makes use of Symbolic Computation results only in a rather naive way. There are fast SMT solvers available for the satisfiability checking of linear real and integer arithmetic problems, but just a few can handle non-linear arithmetic. On the other hand, Symbolic Computation is strong in providing powerful procedures for sets (conjunctions) of arithmetic constraints, but it does not exploit the achievements in SMT solving for efficiently handling logical fragments, using heuristics and learning to speed-up the search for satisfying solutions.

The Satisfiability Checking community would definitely profit from further exploiting Symbolic Computation achievements and adapting and extending them to comply with the requirements on embedding in the SMT context. However, it is a highly challenging task, as it requires a deep understanding of complex mathematical problems, whose embedding in SMT solving is not trivial.

Symmetrically, Symbolic Computation could profit from exploiting successful SMT ideas, but it requires expertise in efficient solver technologies and their implementation, like dedicated data structures, sophisticated heuristics, effective learning techniques, and approaches for incrementality and explanation generation in theory solving modules.

In this section we describe some ideas of how algorithms and tools from both communities could be made more powerful by exploiting scientific exchange and technology transfer.

3.1 Symbolic Computation Techniques for Satisfiability Checking

Many practical decision procedures, designed by the Symbolic Computation community, are implemented in computer algebra systems (e.g., linear real and integer arithmetic, non-linear real arithmetic, linear programming, quantified formulas, Gröbner and involutive bases). To use them in a Satisfiability Checking context, some scientific and engineering issues need solutions, notably to find new ways of *incremental* solving, *explaining* unsatisfiability and generating *lemmas*.

Whereas for linear real arithmetic useful procedures have been adapted to satisfy the requirements for SMT embedding, many opportunities remain to be explored for non-linear arithmetic. For example, there are (to the best of our knowledge) just two SMT solvers, Z3 and SMT-RAT, which make use of the CAD method, but in a different way: Z3 uses a very elegant solution to explore the state space by a close integration of theory decisions and theory propagation in the Boolean SAT search, and constructs CAD only partially to explain conflicts in the above search (more precisely, to compute a semi-algebraic description of CAD cells that do not satisfy a given sign condition). In contrast, SMT-RAT implements an incremental version of the CAD method, which works hand-in-hand with the search at the logical level. For this latter approach, the power of heuristics (variable and polynomial ordering for incremental projection, choice and order of sample points for lifting) and the generation of lemmas (most importantly the computation of explanations for unsatisfiability) is still far from being fully exploited.

There is still great potential for improvements not only for the SMT embedding of the CAD method, but also other non-linear arithmetic decision procedures like virtual substitution or Gröbner bases, and their strategic combination with each other and further light-weight methods such as interval constraint propagation.

Another important aspect is the Symbolic Computation community's expertise in simplification and preprocessing. The complexity of the problems this community handles is often extremely high, and no practical procedure would exist without significant techniques to prepare the input problems. Such techniques do exist for Satisfiability Checking, but they rather focus on easier theories. A transfer of the savoir-faire in simplification and preprocessing for non-linear real and integer arithmetic would certainly be highly profitable.

3.2 Satisfiability Checking Techniques for Symbolic Computation

A key ingredient in the success of the Satisfiability Checking tools is the use of *learning* and *non-chronological backtracking* techniques to speed up the search through tree-shaped search structures. Traditionally (and in the majority of cases) CAD proceeds through a two stage process: first, projecting the problem through lower dimensions; then lifting: incrementally building a solution in increasing dimensions. An alternative approach using triangular decomposition was introduced in [21] where first the complex domain is cylindrically decomposed and then refined to a CAD of the real domain, where all data is in a tree-shaped structure.

Other techniques are certainly amenable for learning with the non-chronological backtracking approach. For instance, first prototypes integrating CDCL-style learning techniques with virtual substitution for linear quantifier elimination have been successfully created and studied. Integration of learning techniques with the computation of comprehensive Gröbner bases [56] should also be investigated.

Incrementality, which played an important role in the success of Satisfiability Checking, may also be used to make Symbolic Computation techniques more efficient. The alternative CAD construction method described above is also incremental in nature [14] and so may offer one option here. An incremental CAD-based decision procedure for solving polymial constraint systems was proposed in [55]. There exist algorithms for computing Gröbner bases which exploit known mathematical facts about the ideal generated by the basis like its Hilbert function or some syzygies. Traditionally, this has been seen as a way to speed up computations. However, these approaches can naturally be adapted into incremental algorithms.

A central aspect of Satisfiability Modulo Theories is the combination frameworks for theories and decision procedures. Combining theories in Symbolic Computation (combined real/floating point theories, interval constraint propagation with other arithmetic theories) might also bring a number of advantages and possibilities, for instance, more expressive languages, or efficiency due to hierarchical reasoning. While combination of theories in Symbolic Computation are typically very specific and ad hoc, the SMT community systematically uses the generic Nelson–Oppen framework [49] for disjoint theories. Such a framework can of course not be used as it is, but it might be an inspiration for a modular approach in Symbolic Computation.

3.3 Standard Languages and Benchmarks

The initiation and maintenance of a common problem specification language standard *SMT-LIB* [7] and of competitions form an important part of the Satisfiability Checking community effort. Besides providing a stimulating event for tool developers to exhibit their systems, the competitions are also a vehicle for publishing practical progress. Competition results are advertised, and consulted by users to pick the best tools and techniques to solve problems.

The Symbolic Computation community does not have a similar tradition, and indeed, to quote one major system developer: "it is very hard to get any practical improvements published — the reviewers will often say this is not hard science". Although it is not good to only focus on a small library of benchmarks and have the competition as sole goal, competitions do have a tremendously positive effect on tools and techniques, as witnessed in the Satisfiability Checking community, especially if the competition challenges are concrete industrial challenges. Such driving forces could be also established in Symbolic Computation.

Though in Satisfiability Checking the standard input language allowed to provide large benchmark sets to the community, benchmarks for non-linear arithmetic theories are still rare, and harder to describe without ambiguity. Therefore, also the Satisfiability Checking community would profit from a common standard with an increased number of non-linear arithmetic benchmarks.

4 Project Actions

The solution of challenging problems, as mentioned in the previous section, could be within reach, when supported by a stronger collaboration between both SC^2 research areas, creating an infrastructure for dialogue and knowledge transfer. However, the research areas of Satisfiability Checking and Symbolic Computation are still quite disconnected, as reflected in their communication platforms and support structures. Symbolic Computation has its own conferences (ACA, CASC, ISSAC, etc.), several dedicated journals (e.g., AAECC, JSC, MSC), and the SIGSAM forum. Similarly, Satisfiability Checking is supported by its own conferences (CADE, IJCAR, SMT, etc.) and journals (e.g., JAR), the SatLive forum to keep up-to-date with research, SMT standards, and SAT- and SMT-solver competitions.

The main aims of our project are to create *communication platforms* and propose *standards* to enable the interaction between the two communities, and to use these platforms to *initiate discussions and cooperation* and to *identify potentials, challenges and obstacles* for future research and practical applications. In the following we shortly describe planned actions of our SC^2 project to achieve these goals.

Communication Platforms. To bridge the SC^2 communities, we will initiate platforms to support the interaction of the currently disjoint groups. We organised a Dagstuhl Seminar *Symbolic Computation and Satisfiability Checking*[2] 15–20th November, 2015, which already led to numerous interesting discussions and interactions. At CASC 2016, we will organise a *topical session* devoted to topics from the cross-community SC^2 area. Furthermore, we will establish a workshop series in the area of SC^2, covering the interests of both communities, and having its first edition affiliated with SYNASC 2016. These workshops will serve as platforms for scientific exchange, discussion and cooperation within and between the currently disjoint communities. To support and attract young new community

---

[2] http://www.dagstuhl.de/en/program/calendar/semhp/?semnr=15471.

members, we will organise a dedicated summer school aimed at interested young researchers from SC^2 areas, with courses specifically tailored to their needs.

Research Roadmap. The above platforms will initiate cross-community interactions, and help to clearly identify unused potentials. We aim at initiating discussions on what the communities can learn from each other, what are the common challenges which they can solve together, what Satisfiability Checking could learn from Symbolic Computation achievements, and which Satisfiability Checking results could be adapted to improve Symbolic Computation solutions.

Our long-term objective is to create a research roadmap of potentials and challenges, both to the two traditional subject silos, but also challenges that only the new joined SC^2 community can address. This roadmap should identify, within the problems currently faced in the industry, the particular points that can be expected to be solved by the SC^2 community in the short and middle term, and will provide recommendations for spin-off projects.

Standards, Benchmarks, Competitions. We aim to create a standard problem specification language capable of representing common problems of the SC^2 community. We plan on extending the *SMT-LIB* language, which is already mature and fully accepted among the SMT (Satisfiability Checking) community, to handle features needed for the Symbolic Computation community. This will be done in a modular way, with a particular focus on extensibility for new features.

Agreeing on a common language, and being able to share challenging problems is an essential aspect for building a dynamic community. This will foster further discussions and uncover problems that can be solved by the SC^2 community altogether, set clear challenges on which various approaches can be evaluated, classify the approaches according to their strength and weaknesses on the various kinds of problems. Mixed approaches will naturally emerge, to tackle problems exhibiting several orthogonal difficulties. The standard could also serve as a communication protocol for platforms mixing tools, to build meta-tools to solve large and difficult problems out of reach of current techniques often specialised to just one kind of job.

How to Become an Associate? This project cannot reach its aims by involving just a small number of core project members. To be able to cover sufficiently wide research and application areas and to take into account their needs and interests, there are currently 37 SC^2 *associates* from both research communities as well as from industry. Our associates will be regularly informed about the project activities and they will be invited to take part in the corresponding events.

The SC^2 Coordination and Support Action will be an optimal platform for industrial and academic partners and associates to form smaller working groups and initiate specific projects. If you would like to participate in the project as an associate, please contact the Project Coordinator James Davenport[3].

---

[3] Email contact: J.H.Davenport@bath.ac.uk.

5   Conclusions and Future Work

In this paper we gave a short description of the aims and actions of our upcoming
EU Coordination and Support Action SC^2.
   The SC^2 project will maintain a website (http://www.sc-square.org) making
readily accessible all the public information of the project (e.g., contact information, details of past and forthcoming SC^2 workshops and other similar events).

Acknowledgements. We thank the anonymous reviewers for their comments. We
are grateful for support by the H2020-FETOPEN-2016-2017-CSA project SC^2 (712689)
and the ANR project ANR-13-IS02-0001-01 SMArT. Earlier work in this area was also
supported by the EPSRC grant EP/J003247/1.

References

1. Abbott, J., Bigatti, A.M., Lagorio, G.: CoCoA-5: a system for doing computations
   in commutative algebra. http://cocoa.dima.unige.it
2. Ábrahám, E.: Building bridges between symbolic computation and satisfiability
   checking. In: Proceedings ISSAC 2015, pp. 1–6. ACM (2015)
3. Arai, N.H., Matsuzaki, T., Iwane, H., Anai, H.: Mathematics by machine. In: Proceedings ISSAC 2014, pp. 1–8. ACM (2014)
4. Barrett, C., Conway, C.L., Deters, M., Hadarean, L., Jovanović, D., King, T.,
   Reynolds, A., Tinelli, C.: CVC4. In: Gopalakrishnan, G., Qadeer, S. (eds.) CAV
   2011. LNCS, vol. 6806, pp. 171–177. Springer, Heidelberg (2011)
5. Barrett, C., Kroening, D., Melham, T.: Problem solving for the 21st century: efficient solvers for satisfiability modulo theories. Technical report 3, London Mathematical Society and Smith Institute for Industrial Mathematics and System Engineering, Knowledge Transfer Report (2014). http://www.cs.nyu.edu/~barrett/
   pubs/BKM14.pdf
6. Barrett, C., Sebastiani, R., Seshia, S.A., Tinelli, C.: Satisfiability modulo theories.
   In: Biere, A., Heule, M., van Maaren, H., Walsh, T. (eds.) Handbook of Satisfiability, Frontiers in Artificial Intelligence and Applications, Chap. 26, vol. 185, pp.
   825–885. IOS Press, Amsterdam (2009)
7. Barrett, C., Stump, A., Tinelli, C.: The satisfiability modulo theories library (SMT-
   LIB) (2010). www.SMT-LIB.org
8. Biere, A., Biere, A., Heule, M., van Maaren, H., Walsh, T.: Handbook of Satisfiability, Frontiers in Artificial Intelligence and Applications, vol. 185. IOS Press,
   Amsterdam (2009)
9. Bixby, R.E.: Computational progress in linear and mixed integer programming. In:
   Presentation at ICIAM 2015 (2015)
10. Bobot, F., Conchon, S., Contejean, E., Iguernelala, M., Mahboubi, A., Mebsout,
    A., Melquiond, G.: A simplex-based extension of Fourier-Motzkin for solving linear
    integer arithmetic. In: Gramlich, B., Miller, D., Sattler, U. (eds.) IJCAR 2012.
    LNCS, vol. 7364, pp. 67–81. Springer, Heidelberg (2012)
11. Borralleras, C., Lucas, S., Navarro-Marset, R., Rodríguez-Carbonell, E., Rubio,
    A.: Solving non-linear polynomial arithmetic via SAT modulo linear arithmetic. In:
    Schmidt, R.A. (ed.) CADE-22. LNCS, vol. 5663, pp. 294–305. Springer, Heidelberg
    (2009)

12. Bosma, W., Cannon, J., Playoust, C.: The MAGMA algebra system I: the user language. J. Symbolic Comput. **24**(3–4), 235–265 (1997). Computational Algebra and Number Theory (London, 1993). http://dx.doi.org/10.1006/jsco.1996.0125
13. Bouton, T., Caminha, D., de Oliveira, B., Déharbe, D., Fontaine, P.: veriT: an open, trustable and efficient SMT-solver. In: Schmidt, R.A. (ed.) CADE-22. LNCS, vol. 5663, pp. 151–156. Springer, Heidelberg (2009)
14. Bradford, R., Chen, C., Davenport, J.H., England, M., Moreno Maza, M., Wilson, D.: Truth table invariant cylindrical algebraic decomposition by regular chains. In: Gerdt, V.P., Koepf, W., Seiler, W.M., Vorozhtsov, E.V. (eds.) CASC 2014. LNCS, vol. 8660, pp. 44–58. Springer, Heidelberg (2014)
15. Bradford, R., Davenport, J., England, M., McCallum, S., Wilson, D.: Truth table invariant cylindrical algebraic decomposition. J. Symbol. Comput. **76**, 1–35 (2016)
16. Bromberger, M., Sturm, T., Weidenbach, C.: Linear integer arithmetic revisited. In: Felty, A.P., Middeldorp, A. (eds.) CADE-25. LNCS, vol. 9195, pp. 623–637. Springer International Publishing, Switzerland (2015)
17. Brown, C.W.: QEPCAD B: a program for computing with semi-algebraic sets using CADs. ACM SIGSAM Bull. **37**(4), 97–108 (2003)
18. Brown, C.W., Davenport, J.H.: The complexity of quantifier elimination and cylindrical algebraic decomposition. In: Proceedings ISSAC 2007, pp. 54–60. ACM (2007)
19. Bruttomesso, R., Pek, E., Sharygina, N., Tsitovich, A.: The OpenSMT2 solver. In: Esparza, J., Majumdar, R. (eds.) TACAS 2010. LNCS, vol. 6015, pp. 150–153. Springer, Heidelberg (2010)
20. Buchberger, B.: Ein Algorithmus zum Auffinden des basiselemente des Restklassenringes nach einem nulldimensionalen Polynomideal. Ph.D. thesis, University of Innsbruck (1965). English translation: J. Symbolic Computation **41**, 475–511 (2006)
21. Chen, C., Moreno Maza, M., Xia, B., Yang, L.: Computing cylindrical algebraic decomposition via triangular decomposition. In: Proceedings ISSAC 2009, pp. 95–102. ACM (2009)
22. Cimatti, A., Griggio, A., Schaafsma, B., Sebastiani, R.: The MathSAT5 SMT solver. In: Piterman, N., Smolka, S.A. (eds.) TACAS 2013. LNCS, vol. 7795, pp. 93–107. Springer, Heidelberg (2013)
23. Codish, M., Fekete, Y., Fuhs, C., Giesl, J., Waldmann, J.: Exotic semi-ring constraints. In: Proceedings SMT 2013. EPiC Series, vol. 20, pp. 88–97. EasyChair (2013)
24. Collins, G.E.: The SAC-1 system: an introduction and survey. In: Proceedings SYMSAC 1971, pp. 144–152. ACM (1971)
25. Collins, G.E.: Quantifier elimination for real closed fields by cylindrical algebraic decomposition. In: Brakhage, H. (ed.) Automata Theory and Formal Languages. LNCS, vol. 33, pp. 134–183. Springer, Heidelberg (1975)
26. Conchon, S., Iguernelala, M., Mebsout, A.: A collaborative framework for nonlinear integer arithmetic reasoning in Alt-Ergo. In: Proceedings SYNASC 2013, pp. 161–168. IEEE (2013)
27. Cook, S.A.: The complexity of theorem-proving procedures. In: Proceedings STOC 1971, pp. 151–158. ACM (1971). http://doi.acm.org/10.1145/800157.805047
28. Corzilius, F., Kremer, G., Junges, S., Schupp, S., Ábrahám, E.: SMT-RAT: An open source C++ toolbox for strategic and parallel SMT solving. In: Heule, M., Weaver, S. (eds.) SAT 2015. LNCS, vol. 9340, pp. 360–368. Springer, Switzerland (2015)
29. Davenport, J.H., Heintz, J.: Real quantifier elimination is doubly exponential. J. Symbol. Comput. **5**, 29–35 (1988)

30. Davis, M., Logemann, G., Loveland, D.: A machine program for theorem-proving. Commun. ACM **5**(7), 394–397 (1962)
31. Davis, M., Putnam, H.: A computing procedure for quantification theory. J. ACM **7**(3), 201–215 (1960)
32. Decker, W., Greuel, G.M., Pfister, G., Schönemann, H.: `Singular` 4-0-2 – A computer algebra system for polynomial computations (2015). http://www.singular. uni-kl.de
33. Dolzmann, A., Sturm, T.: `Redlog`: computer algebra meets computer logic. ACM SIGSAM Bull. **31**(2), 2–9 (1997)
34. Dutertre, B., de Moura, L.: A fast linear-arithmetic solver for DPLL(T). In: Ball, T., Jones, R.B. (eds.) CAV 2006. LNCS, vol. 4144, pp. 81–94. Springer, Heidelberg (2006)
35. Eraşcu, M., Hong, H.: Synthesis of optimal numerical algorithms using real quantifier elimination (Case study: Square root computation). In: Proceedings ISSAC 2014, pp. 162–169. ACM (2014)
36. Fränzle, M., Herde, C., Teige, T., Ratschan, S., Schubert, T.: Efficient solving of large non-linear arithmetic constraint systems with complex Boolean structure. J. Satisfiability Boolean Model. Comput. **1**(3–4), 209–236 (2007)
37. Grayson, D.R., Stillman, M.E.: `Macaulay2`, a software system for research in algebraic geometry. http://www.math.uiuc.edu/Macaulay2/
38. Hearn, A.C.: `REDUCE`: The first forty years. In: Proceedings A3L, pp. 19–24. Books on Demand GmbH (2005)
39. Jenks, R.D., Sutor, R.S.: `AXIOM`: The Scientific Computation System. Springer, New York (1992)
40. Jovanović, D., de Moura, L.: Solving non-linear arithmetic. In: Gramlich, B., Miller, D., Sattler, U. (eds.) IJCAR 2012. LNCS(LNAI), vol. 7364, pp. 339–354. Springer, Heidelberg (2012)
41. Kahrimanian, H.G.: Analytic differentiation by a digital computer. Master's thesis, Temple University Philadelphia (1953)
42. Kroening, D., Strichman, O.: Decision Procedures: An Algorithmic Point of View. Springer, New York (2008)
43. Maple. http://www.maplesoft.com/
44. Marques-Silva, J.P., Sakallah, K.A.: `GRASP`: a search algorithm for propositional satisfiability. IEEE Trans. Comput. **48**, 506–521 (1999)
45. Martin, W.A., Fateman, R.J.: The `Macsyma` system. In: Proceedings SYMSAC 1971, pp. 59–75. ACM (1971)
46. Moses, J.: Symbolic integration. Ph.D. thesis, MIT & MAC TR-47 (1967)
47. de Moura, L., Passmore, G.O.: The strategy challenge in SMT solving. In: Bonacina, M.P., Stickel, M.E. (eds.) Automated Reasoning and Mathematics. LNCS, vol. 7788, pp. 15–44. Springer, Heidelberg (2013)
48. de Moura, L.M., Bjørner, N.: Z3: an efficient SMT solver. In: Ramakrishnan, C.R., Rehof, J. (eds.) TACAS 2008. LNCS, vol. 4963, pp. 337–340. Springer, Heidelberg (2008)
49. Nelson, G., Oppen, D.C.: Simplifications by cooperating decision procedures. ACM Trans. Program. Lang. Syst. **1**(2), 245–257 (1979)
50. Nolan, J.: Analytic differentiation on a digital computer. Master's thesis, MIT (1953)
51. Platzer, A., Quesel, J.-D., Rümmer, P.: Real world verification. In: Schmidt, R.A. (ed.) CADE-22. LNCS, vol. 5663, pp. 485–501. Springer, Heidelberg (2009)
52. Risch, R.H.: The problem of integration in finite terms. Trans. Am. Math. Soc. **139**, 167–189 (1969)

53. Scheibler, K., Kupferschmid, S., Becker, B.: Recent improvements in the SMT solver iSAT. In: Proceedings MBMV 2013, pp. 231–241. Institut für Angewandte Mikroelektronik und Datentechnik, Fakultät für Informatik und Elektrotechnik, Universität Rostock (2013)
54. Slagle, J.: A heuristic program that solves symbolic integration problems in freshman calculus. Ph.D. thesis, Harvard University (1961)
55. Strzeboński, A.: Solving polynomial systems over semialgebraic sets represented by cylindrical algebraic formulas. In: Proceedings ISSAC 2012, pp. 335–342. ACM (2012)
56. Weispfenning, V.: Comprehensive Gröbner bases. J. Symbol. Comput. **14**(1), 1–29 (1992)
57. Weispfenning, V.: Quantifier elimination for real algebra - the quadratic case and beyond. Appl. Algebra Eng. Commun. Comput. **8**(2), 85–101 (1997)
58. Wolfram Research, Inc.: Mathematica, version 10.4. Wolfram Research, Inc., Champaign, Illinois (2016)
59. Zankl, H., Middeldorp, A.: Satisfiability of non-linear (ir)rational arithmetic. In: Clarke, E.M., Voronkov, A. (eds.) LPAR-16 2010. LNCS, vol. 6355, pp. 481–500. Springer, Heidelberg (2010)

Formalization of Normal Random Variables in HOL

Muhammad Qasim[1]([⊠]), Osman Hasan[1], Maissa Elleuch[2,3], and Sofiène Tahar[1]

[1] Department of Electrical and Computer Engineering,
Concordia University, Montreal, QC, Canada
{m_qasi,o_hasan,tahar}@ece.concordia.ca
[2] CES Laboratory, Sfax University, Sfax, Tunisia
maissa.elleuch@ceslab.org
[3] Digital Research Center of Sfax, Sfax, Tunisia

Abstract. Many components of engineering systems exhibit random and uncertain behaviors that are normally distributed. In order to conduct the analysis of such systems within the trusted kernel of a higher-order-logic theorem prover, in this paper, we provide a higher-order-logic formalization of Lebesgue measure and Normal random variables along with the proof of their classical properties. To illustrate the usefulness of our formalization, we present a formal analysis of the probabilistic clock synchronization in wireless sensor networks.

1 Introduction

Many engineering systems exhibit *normally distributed* elements of randomness. Some notable examples include noise in communication channels, lengths and weights of manufactured goods, message arrival times in communication networks, blood pressure readings of a general population, lifetimes of an electric bulb and maximum speed of a car. The importance of normal distribution is also evident from its relationship with the central limit theorem [2], which states that, given certain conditions, the arithmetic mean of a sufficiently large number of iterations of independent random variables, each with a well-defined expected value and variance, is approximately normally distributed, regardless of the underlying distribution [20]. Therefore, if the sample size is large enough, the sample mean of other distributions may also be treated as normal.

Traditionally, paper-and-pencil based approaches are used for carrying out probabilistic analysis. This method, however, is prone to human error and is not scalable to deal with large systems. Similarly, simulation cannot provide accurate results due to approximations in numerical computations and its incompleteness, which is an outcome of enormous processing time requirements.

Given the safety-critical nature of present age engineering systems, these inaccuracies cannot be tolerated. Higher-order-logic theorem proving, which provides computerized mathematical proofs, can overcome the above-mentioned limitations and has been used to formalize probability theory [16], Markov

© Springer International Publishing Switzerland 2016
M. Kohlhase et al. (Eds.): CICM 2016, LNAI 9791, pp. 44–59, 2016.
DOI: 10.1007/978-3-319-42547-4_4

Chains [10,12] and discrete [8] and continuous [7] random variables. These foundations have been used to formally analyze many aspects of engineering applications, including the Stop-and-Wait protocol [9], wireless sensor networks [3], anonymity and confidentiality protocols [17], oil and gas pipelines [1], multiprocessor systems [13] and reconfigurable memory arrays [6]. However, to the best of our knowledge, no system, exhibiting the Normal random variables, has been reported in the literature. In Isabelle/HOL, there is a formalization of exponential, uniform and normal distributions [19], however, they lack the notion of probability density function and random variables, which play a vital role in analyzing real-world systems. To overcome this limitation, we ported Lebesgue-Borel measure from Isabelle/HOL [11] to HOL4 theorem prover and built upon Mhamdi's formalization of measure, Lebesgue and probability theories [16], available in the HOL4 theorem prover, to formalize probability density function and Normal random variables. We formally verify the correctness of our formalization of Normal random variables by verifying their various properties. These formalizations allow us to formally reason about the correctness of many engineering systems that involve Normal random variables. For illustration purposes, we present a formal analysis of the probabilistic clock synchronization in wireless sensor networks.

2   Preliminaries

2.1   Measure Theory

A measure assigns a number to a set corresponding to its size. Formally, a function defined on a set is a measure if it is positive and countably additive [16].

Definition 1 *(Measure Space).*
A triplet $(X, \mathcal{A}, \mu)$ is a measure space iff $(X, \mathcal{A})$ is a σ-field and $\mu : \mathcal{A} \to \overline{\mathbb{R}}$ (i.e., $\mathbb{R} \cup \{-\infty, +\infty\}$) is a non-negative and countably additive measure function.
$\vdash$ measure_space (X,A,μ) =
   sigma_algebra (X,A) $\wedge$ positive (X,A,μ) $\wedge$ countably_additive (X,A,μ)

The pair $(X, \mathcal{A})$ is called a σ-field or a measurable space and $\mathcal{A}$ is called a sigma algebra over X or a set of measurable sets.

Definition 2 *(Sigma Algebra).*
Let $\mathcal{A}$ be a collection of subsets (or subset class) of a space X. $\mathcal{A}$ defines a sigma algebra on X iff $\mathcal{A}$ contains the empty set $\{\}$, and is closed under countable unions and complementation within the space X.
$\vdash$ sigma_algebra (X,A) = subset_class X A $\wedge$ ($\forall$s. s $\in$A $\Rightarrow$ X DIFF s $\in$A) $\wedge$
   $\{\}$ $\in$ A $\wedge$ ($\forall$c. countable c $\wedge$ c $\subseteq$ A $\Rightarrow$ BIGUNION c $\in$A)

where subset_class and countable are defined as:

$\vdash$ subset_class X A = $\forall$s. s $\in$ A $\Rightarrow$ s $\subseteq$ X
$\vdash$ countable s = $\exists$f. $\forall$x. x $\in$s$\Rightarrow$ $\exists$(n:num). f n = x

For any collection G of subsets of X, there is at least one sigma algebra on X containing G, namely the powerset of X. The smallest sigma algebra on X containing G is an intersection of all those sigma algebras, and is called the sigma algebra on X generated by G. This notion is defined in HOL as:

⊢ sigma X G = (X, BIGINTER {s | G ⊆ s ∧ sigma_algebra (X,s)})

Some helper functions [16] for a σ-field or a measure space are

⊢ space (X,A) = X ∧subsets (X,A) = A
⊢ m_space (X,A,μ) = X ∧ measurable_sets (X,A,μ) = A ∧ measure (X,A,μ) = μ

For measurable functions, the inverse image of each measurable set is measurable.

Definition 3 *(Measurable Functions).*
Let $(X_1, \mathcal{A}_1)$ and $(X_2, \mathcal{A}_2)$ be two measurable spaces. A function $f : X_1 \to X_2$ is called measurable with respect to $(\mathcal{A}_1, \mathcal{A}_2)$ (or $(\mathcal{A}_1, \mathcal{A}_2)$ measurable) iff $f^{-1}(A) \in \mathcal{A}_1$ for all $A \in \mathcal{A}_2$.
⊢ f ∈measurable a b =
  sigma_algebra a ∧ sigma_algebra b ∧ f ∈(space a → space b) ∧
  ∀s. s ∈ subsets b ⇒ PREIMAGE f s ∩ space a ∈subsets a

2.2 Lebesgue Integration Theory

Similar to the way in which step functions are used in the development of the Riemann integral, the Lebesgue integral makes use of a special class of functions called positive simple functions. In HOL [15] a positive simple function g is represented by the triplet (s, a, α) as a finite linear combination of indicator functions of measurable sets (a_i) that form a partition of the space X.

$$\forall x \in X, \ g(x) = \sum_{i \in s} \alpha_i I_{a_i}(x), \quad \alpha_i \geq 0 \tag{1}$$

where s is a set of partition tags, a_i is a sequence of measurable sets, α_i is a sequence of real numbers and I_{a_i} is an indicator function on a_i:

⊢ indicator_fn A = (λx. if x ∈ A then 1 else 0)

The Lebesgue integral is first defined for positive simple functions and then extended to non-negative functions.

Definition 4 *(Lebesgue Integral of Positive Simple Functions).*
Let $(X, \mathcal{A}, \mu)$ be a measure space. The integral of the positive simple function g with respect to the measure μ is defined as $\int_X g \, d\mu = \sum_{i \in s} \alpha_i \mu(a_i)$.
⊢ pos_simple_fn_integral m s a α = SIGMA (λi. αi * measure m (a i)) s

Definition 5 *(Lebesgue Integral of Non-Negative Measurable Functions).*
Let $(X, \mathcal{A}, \mu)$ be a measure space. The integral of a non-negative measurable function f is defined as $\int_X f \, d\mu = \sup \{\int_X g \, d\mu \mid g \leq f \text{ and } g \text{ positive simple function}\}$.
⊢ pos_fn_integral m f = sup {r | ∃g. r ∈ psfis m g ∧ ∀x. g x ≤ f x}

where r ∈ `psfis` m g is equivalent to r = `pos_simple_fn_integral` m s a α and g is a positive simple function represented by (s, a, α).

2.3 Probability Theory

The probability space is defined in HOL [16] as a measure space, i.e., (Ω, F, p), where Ω is the sample space, F is a set of events and p is the probability measure such that $p(\Omega) = 1$. A random variable is defined as a measurable function.

Definition 6 *(Random Variable).*
⊢ `random_variable` X p s ⇔
    `prob_space` p ∧ X ∈ `measurable` (`p_space` p,`events` p) s

where `p_space` is a renaming of `m_space` and `events` is a renaming of `measurable_sets`. The probability distribution of a random variable X is defined as the function assigning to A the probability of the event $\{X \in A\}$.

$$\forall A \in \mathcal{B}(\overline{\mathbb{R}}), \ p(\{X \in A\}) = p(X^{-1}(A))$$

Definition 7 *(Probability Distribution).*
⊢ `distribution` p X = (λA. `prob` p (`PREIMAGE` X A ∩ `p_space` p))

3 Formalization of Lebesgue-Borel Measure

For evaluating an integral using the Lebesgue integral [16], a suitable Lebesgue measure is required. For this purpose, we have defined a Lebesgue measure based on the Gauge integral. Our formalization is greatly inspired from the formalizations of Lebesgue measure in Isabelle/HOL [11].

3.1 Gauge Integral

Definition 8 *(Gauge Integral).*
Let f:[a,b]→ ℝ be some function, and let y be some number. We say that y is the Gauge integral of f over i written $y = \int_i f(x) \, dx$, if for each number e > 0 there exists a Gauge d such that $| \sum_p f - y | < e$, where, p is a tagged division of i and p is δ-fine with respect to p.
⊢ (f `has_integral_compact_interval` y) i = ∀e. 0 < e ⇒ ∃d. `gauge` d ∧
    ∀p. p `tagged_division_of` i ∧ d `fine` p ⇒
        `abs` (`sum` p (λ(x,k). `content` (k) * f(x)) - y) < e

An alternate definition of the Gauge integral that simplifies the proof steps for integration over intervals is given as:

⊢ (f `has_integral` y) i =
    if ∃a b. i = `interval` [a,b] then (f `has_integral_compact_interval` y) i
    else ∀e. 0 < e ⇒ ∃B. 0 < B ∧ ∀a b. `ball` (0,B) `SUBSET` `interval` [a,b] ⇒
        ∃z. ((λx. if x ∈ i then f x else 0) `has_integral_compact_interval` z)
            (`interval` [a,b]) ∧ `abs` (z - y) < e

The functional form of the above definition, using the Hilbert choice operator (@), is as follows,

```
⊢ integral i f = @y. (f has_integral y) i
```

3.2 Borel Measurable Sets

A collection of all borel measurable sets on the real line forms a sigma algebra, called the Borel sigma algebra. It allows us to prove various properties of measurable functions. The Borel sigma algebra is defined as the smallest sigma algebra generated by the open sets of the real line. Mhamdi [16] formalized Borel sigma algebra in the Measure theory as a sigma algebra generated by open intervals of extended real numbers $\overline{\mathbb{R}}$. Because the Gauge integral is formalized for real numbers $\mathbb{R}$ and we are working with Borel measurable functions, we had to formalize real valued Borel sigma algebra in addition to extended real valued Borel sigma algebra. We formalize the real valued Borel sigma algebra in HOL with the help of the **sigma** function, defined in Sect. 2.1.

```
⊢ borel = sigma UNIV {s | open s}
```

where UNIV is the universal set of real numbers $\mathbb{R}$ and **open** is defined as:

Definition 9 *(Open Set).*
A set s is called open if, given any point $x \in s$, there exists a real number $\epsilon > 0$ such that, given any point $y \in \mathbb{R}$ whose distance from x is smaller than ϵ, $y \in s$.
```
⊢ open s = ∀x. x ∈ s ⇒ ∃ ε. ε> 0 ∧ ∀y. dist (y,x) < ε ⇒ y ∈s
```

Using the above definition of **borel**, we proved that all open and closed sets are in Borel sigma algebra.

Theorem 1. *All open and closed sets of $\mathbb{R}$ are in $\mathcal{B}(\mathbb{R})$.*
```
⊢ ∀s. {s | open s} ∈ subsets borel ∧{s | closed s} ∈subsets borel
```

In order to reuse the proof steps of Mhamdi for proving various properties of our Borel sigma algebra, generated by open sets of real numbers $\mathbb{R}$, we proved that our Borel sigma algebra can also be generated by open intervals of real numbers $\mathbb{R}$.

Theorem 2. *$\mathcal{B}(\mathbb{R})$ is also generated by open intervals of real numbers.*
```
⊢ borel = sigma UNIV (IMAGE (λ(a,b). interval (a,b)) UNIV)
```

Real-Valued Borel Measurable Functions: For a function to be integrable over a Borel measurable set, it has to be Borel measurable, i.e., the inverse image of the function should belongs to the Borel sigma algebra.

Theorem 3. *If f and g are $(\mathcal{A}, \mathcal{B}(\mathbb{R}))$ measurable and $c \in \overline{\mathbb{R}}$ then $c * f$, $|f|$, f^n, $f + g$, $f * g$ and $max(f, g)$ are $(\mathcal{A}, \mathcal{B}(\mathbb{R}))$ measurable.*

```
⊢ ∀a f g h c. sigma_algebra a ∧
    f ∈measurable a Borel ∧g ∈measurable a Borel ⇒
    ((λx. c * f x) ∈measurable a Borel) ∧
    ((λx. abs(f x)) ∈measurable a Borel) ∧
    ((λx. f x pow n) ∈measurable a Borel) ∧
    ((λx. f x + g x) ∈measurable a Borel) ∧
    ((λx. f x * g x) ∈measurable a Borel) ∧
    ((λx. max (f x) (g x)) ∈measurable a borel)
```

Theorem 4. *Every continuous functions is $(\mathcal{B}(\mathbb{R}), \mathcal{B}(\overline{\mathbb{R}}))$ measurable.*

```
⊢ ∀g. g continuous UNIV(:real) ⇒g ∈ measurable borel Borel
```

Notice that `borel` is our Borel sigma algebra generated by open sets of real numbers $\mathbb{R}$ and `Borel` is the Borel sigma algebra of Mhamdi [16] generated by open intervals of extended real numbers $\overline{\mathbb{R}}$.

3.3 Lebesgue Measure

The Lebesgue measure is defined as the supremum of Gauge integrals of X_a for all intervals $[-n,n]$ (or `line n`), where X_a is the indicator function of a set A. We define it as a triplet by pairing it with the Lebesgue space and Lebesgue measurable sets, i.e., all sets for which their indicator function is integrable with respect to the inertval $[-n,n]$.

Definition 10 *(Lebesgue Measure).*

```
⊢ lebesgue = (univ(:real), {A | ∀n. indicator A integrable_on line n},
    (λA. sup {Normal (integral (line n) (indicator A)) | n IN univ(:real)}))
```

where the function `Normal` is used to map real numbers to their corresponding extended real numbers. We prove that Borel measurable sets are also Lebesgue measurable.

Theorem 5. *borel $\subset$ lebesgue*

```
⊢ ∀s. s ∈subsets borel ⇒s ∈ measurable_sets lebesgue
```

3.4 Lebesgue-Borel Measure

A Lebesgue measure assigned to Borel measurable sets is called a Lebesgue-Borel measure. We work with the Lebesgue-Borel measure to leverage upon the available formally verified properties of Borel sigma algebra and Borel measurable functions. Thus, we define the triplet of Lebesgue-Borel measure by pairing Lebesgue measure with Borel space and Borel sigma algebra. Also, we prove that Lebesgue-Borel is a sigma finite measure.

Definition 11 *(Lebesgue-Borel Measure).*

```
⊢ lborel = (space borel, subsets borel, measure lebesgue)
```

Theorem 6. *Lebesgue-Borel measure is σ-finite.*
⊢ sigma_finite_measure lborel

where sigma_finite_measure is defined in HOL as:

⊢ sigma_finite_measure (X,A,u) =
    ∃s. countable s ∧ s SUBSET A ∧ (BIGUNION A = X) ∧
        (∀a. a ∈ A ⇒ (u a ≠ PosInf))

4   Formalization of Normal Random Variables

Like any other continuous distribution, normal distribution is generally defined by its probability distribution function (PDF) [20]:

$$N(\mu,\sigma) = \frac{1}{\sigma\sqrt{2\pi}} \exp^{\left(-\frac{(x-\mu)^2}{2\sigma^2}\right)} \tag{2}$$

where μ represents its mean and σ is the standard deviation.

4.1   Radon Nikodym Theorem

The Radon-Nikodym derivative of a measure ν with respect to the measure μ is defined as a non-negative measurable function f, satisfying the following formula [5], for any measurable set A:

$$\int_A f \, d\mu = \nu(A) \tag{3}$$

⊢ RN_deriv m v = @f. f IN measurable (X,S) Borel ∧ ∀x ∈ X, 0 ≤ f x ∧
                 ∀a ∈ S, integral m (λx. f x × I_a x) = v a

The existence of the Radon-Nikodym derivative is guaranteed for absolutely continuous measures by the Radon-Nikodym theorem stating that if ν is absolutely continuous with respect to μ, then there exists a non-negative measurable function f satisfying Eq. (3) for any measurable set A. Mhamdi [16] proved the Radon Nikodym theorem for finite measures. Our main objective is to define the probability density function as a Radon Nikodym derivative of probability measure with respect to the Lebesgue-Borel measure. However, since the Lebesgue-Borel measure is not finite so we have to first generalize the Radon-Nikodym theorem for sigma finite measures.

Theorem 7. *Given a measurable space (X,S), if a measure ν on (X,S) is absolutely continuous with respect to a sigma-finite measure μ on (X,S), then there is a measurable function f, such that for any measurable subset $A \subset X$, $\int_A f \, d\mu = \nu(A)$.*

⊢ ∀u v X S. sigma_finite_measure (X,S,u) ∧
    measure_space (X,S,u) ∧ measure_space (X,S,v) ∧
    measure_absolutely_continuous (X,S,u) (X,S,v) ⇒
        ∃f. f ∈ measurable (X,S) Borel ∧ ∀x ∈ X, 0 ≤ f x ∧
            ∀a ∈ S, pos_fn_integral u (λx. f x × I_a x) = v a

where `measure_absolutely_continuous` is defined in HOL as:

Definition 12 *(Absolutely Continuous Measures).*
If u and v are two measures on a measure space (X,S), then v is absolutely continuous with respect to u if v(A) = 0 for any A ∈ S such that u(A) = 0.
⊢ ∀u v. measure_absolutely_continuous u v =
  ∀A. A ∈ measurable_sets u ∧ (measure v A = 0) ⇒ (measure u A = 0)

4.2 Probability Density Function

The distribution of a continuous random variable is usually defined by its PDF:

$$P(x_1 < x < x_2) = \int_{x_1}^{x_2} p(x)\,dx$$

where $p(x)$ represents the PDF of the random variable x. Formally, the PDF can be defined as a Radon-Nikodym derivative. The distribution of random variables paired with Borel space and Borel sigma algebra gives the probability measure. The PDF of a random variable X is the derivative of the probability measure with respect to the Lebesgue-Borel measure.

Definition 13 *(Probability Density Function).*
⊢ PDF X p = RN_deriv lborel
  (space borel, subsets borel, measurable_distr p X)

where `measurable_distr` is the same as the distribution in the Probability theory but limited to sets measurable with respect to the Lebesgue-Borel measure. We introduced `measurable_distr` because it is not possible to find the distribution of non-measurable sets.

Definition 14 *(Measurable Distribution).*
⊢ measurable_distr p X =
  (λA. if A ∈ measurable_sets lborel then distribution p X A else 0)

With the help of the Radon-Nikodym Theorem, discussed in Sect. 4.1, the following properties of PDF were proved in HOL.

Theorem 8. *PDF of a random variable is always positive.*
⊢ ∀p X v. (v = (space borel, subsets borel, measurable_distr p X)) ∧
  measure_space v ∧ measure_absolutely_continuous v lborel ⇒
  ∀x. 0 ≤ PDF p X x

Theorem 9. *Integral of PDF over the whole space is equal to 1.*
⊢ ∀p X v. (v = (space borel, subsets borel, measurable_distr p X)) ∧
  prob_space v ∧ measure_absolutely_continuous v lborel ⇒
  (integral m (PDF p X) = 1)

4.3   Normal Random Variables

From Eq. (2), it is clear that the probability density of a Normal random variable, called normal density, is defined by its mean μ and variance σ^2.

Definition 15 *(Normal Density).*
⊢ normal_density $\mu\ \sigma$ x =
  1 / sqrt (2 * π * σ pow 2) * exp (- (x - μ) pow 2 / 2 * σ pow 2)

We verified the following useful properties of the normal density.

Theorem 10. *Normal density is always positive.*
⊢ ∀ $\mu\ \sigma$ x. 0 ≤ normal_density $\mu\ \sigma$ x

Theorem 11. *If $0 < \sigma$, then normal density is also greater than 0.*
⊢ ∀ $\mu\ \sigma$x. 0 < σ ⇒0 < normal_density $\mu\ \sigma$ x

Theorem 12. *Normal density is a Borel measurable function.*
⊢ ∀ $\mu\ \sigma$. (λx. Normal (normal_density $\mu\ \sigma$ x)) ∈
  measurable (m_space lborel, measurable_sets lborel) Borel

where the function Normal is used to map real numbers to their corresponding extended real numbers. To prove various properties of Normal random variables, it is required to perform Lebesgue integration on normal density and since the Lebesgue Integral is defined for extended real valued functions, we have to use the function Normal in our formalization of normal density.

Now we formalize the probability that an event A (i.e., $P(X \in A)$) will occur for a Normal random variable X.

Definition 16 *(Normal Probability Measure).*
⊢ normal_pmeasure $\mu\ \sigma$A =
  if A ∈ measurable_sets lborel
  then pos_fn_integral lborel
    (λx. Normal (normal_density $\mu\ \sigma$ x) * indicator_fn A x) else 0

Our definition is limited to measurable functions since it is not possible to evaluate the integral of a function over non-measurable sets.

Definition 17 *(Normal Random Variable).*
⊢ normal_rv X p $\mu\ \sigma$=
  random_variable X p borel ∧ (measurable_distr p X = normal_pmeasure $\mu\ \sigma$)

The first conjunct indicates that X is a real random variable, i.e., it is measurable from the probability space to Borel space and the second conjunct ensures that it is a Normal random variable.

4.4   Properties of Normal Random Variables

In this section, we prove some interesting properties of Normal random variables. These properties are going to be very useful in minimizing the formal reasoning effort while conducting the formal analysis of real-world applications involving Normal random variables.

Theorem 13. *PDF of a Normal random variable is non-negative.*
⊢ ∀X p μ σ. normal_rv X p μ σ ⇒ ∀x. 0 ≤ PDF p X x

Theorem 14. *PDF interval over the whole space is equal to 1*
⊢ ∀X p μ σ. normal_rv X p μ σ ⇒ (integral lborel (PDF p X) = 1)

Theorem 15. *For a Normal random variable X,*

$$\int_{\mu-a}^{\mu} PDF\ p\ X\ dx = \int_{\mu}^{\mu+a} PDF\ p\ X\ dx$$

⊢ ∀X p μ σ a. normal_rv X p μ σ ⇒
   pos_fn_integral lborel
    (λx. PDF p X x * indicator_fn {x | μ-a ≤ x ∧ x ≤ μ} x) =
   pos_fn_integral lborel
    (λx. PDF p X x * indicator_fn {x | μ ≤ x ∧ x ≤ μ+a } x)

Theorem 16. *For a normal random variable X with* $p(x) = N(\mu, \sigma)$,

$$\int_{-\infty}^{\infty} p(x)\, dx = \int_{-\infty}^{\mu} p(x)\, dx + \int_{\mu}^{\infty} p(x)\, dx$$

⊢ ∀X p μ σ. normal_rv X p μ σ ∧
   (A = {x | x ≤ μ}) ∧ (B = {x | μ ≤ x}) ⇒
   pos_fn_integral lborel (λx. PDF p X x) =
   pos_fn_integral lborel (λx. PDF p X x * indicator_fn A x) +
   pos_fn_integral lborel (λx. PDF p X x * indicator_fn B x)

Theorem 17. *For a normal random variable X with* $p(x) = N(\mu, \sigma)$,

$$\int_{-\infty}^{\mu} p(x)\, dx = \int_{\mu}^{\infty} p(x)\, dx = \frac{1}{2}$$

⊢ ∀X p μ σ. normal_rv X p μ σ ∧A = {x | x ≤ μ} ∧B = {x | μ ≤x} ⇒
   (pos_fn_integral lborel (λx. PDF p X x * indicator_fn A x) = 1 / 2) ∧
   (pos_fn_integral lborel (λx. PDF p X x * indicator_fn B x) = 1 / 2)

Theorem 18. *If X is a Normal random variable with mean* μ *and standard deviation* σ, *then* $Y = b + a * X$ *is also a Normal random variable with mean* $b + a * \mu$ *and standard deviation* | a | $* \sigma$.
⊢ ∀X p μ Y a b. normal_rv X p μ σ ∧ (∀x. Y x = b + a * X x) ∧
   a ≠ 0 ∧ 0 < σ ∧ ⇒ normal_rv Y p (b + a * μ) (abs a * σ)

Theorem 19. *Convolution of Normal density with mean $\mu = 0$.*
⊢ ∀ σ1 σ2 p X Y x. 0 < σ1 ∧0 < σ2 ∧ normal_rv X p 0 σ1 ⇒
  pos_fn_integral lborel
    (λy. Normal (normal_density 0 σ1 (x - y) *
        Normal (normal_density 0 σ2 y))) =
  Normal (normal_density 0 (sqrt (σ1 pow 2 + σ2 pow 2)) x)

Theorem 20. *If $X \sim N(\mu1, \sigma1^2)$ and $Y \sim N(\mu2, \sigma2^2)$ are two independent Normal random variables, then $Z = X + Y$ is also normal with mean $(\mu1 + \mu2)$ and variance $(\sigma1^2 + \sigma2^2)$.*
⊢ ∀p X Y μ1 μ2 σ1 σ2. prob_space p ∧0 < σ1 ∧0 < σ2 ∧
  indep_var p borel_triplet X borel_triplet Y ∧
  normal_rv X p μ1 σ1 ∧ normal_rv Y p μ2 σ2 ⇒
  normal_rv (λx. X x + Y x) p (μ1 + μ2) (sqrt (σ1 pow 2 + σ2 pow 2))

where `borel_triplet` represents `(borel space, subsets borel, (λx. 0))`.

Theorem 21. *If $X_i \sim N(\mu_i, \sigma_i^2)$ is a finite set of independent Normal random variables, and $Z = \Sigma\, X_i$ then, $Z \sim N(\Sigma\, \mu_i, \Sigma\, \sigma_i^2)$.*
⊢ ∀p X μ σ I. prob_space p ∧ FINITE I ∧ ∧ I ≠ {} ∧
  indep_vars p (λi. borel_triplet) X I ∧ (∀i, i ∈ I ⇒ 0 < σ i) ∧
  (∀i, i ∈ I ⇒ normal_rv (X i) p (μ i) (σ i)) ⇒
  normal_rv (λx. sum I (λx. X i x)) p (sum I μ)
        (sqrt (sum I (λi. (σ i) pow 2)))

where `indep_vars` and `indep_sets` are defined as:

⊢ indep_vars p M X I =
  (∀i. i ∈ I ⇒
    random_variable (X i) p (m_space (M i), measurable_sets (M i))) ∧
  indep_sets p
    (λi. PREIMAGE X A INTER p_space p | A ∈ measurable_sets (M i)) I

⊢ indep_sets p F I = prob_space p ∧
  (∀i. i ∈ I ⇒ F i SUBSET events p) ∧
  (∀J. J SUBSET I ∧ J ≠ {} ∧ FINITE J ⇒)
    ∀A. A ∈ (Pi J F) ⇒ (prob p (BIGINTER A j| j ∈ J) =
    Normal (product J (λj. real (prob p (A j)))))

where `Pi J F` represents $\{f \mid \forall x.\ x \in J \Rightarrow f(x) \in F(x)\}$. Using above definition of `indep_vars`, two independent random variables are defined as:

⊢ indep_var p M_a A M_b B =
  indep_vars p (λi. if i = 0 then M_a else M_b)
        (λi. if i = 0 then A else B) UNIV

In the proof of above properties, the theories of Extended Real, Measure, Lebesgue Integral and Probability from HOL4 along with the theory of Lebesgue measure ported from Isabelle/HOL were used. Also, the tactics SET_TAC and

Induct (on Borel measurable functions) proved to be very useful and were ported from HOL Light and Isabelle/HOL theorem provers. The proof script of the formalization and verification of the notions presented in this paper required around 17500 lines of HOL4 code.

5   Application: Probabilistic Clock Synchronization in Wireless Sensor Networks

Wireless sensor networks involve highly accurate clock synchronization protocols, which require more processing and hence more energy consumption. Due to these unique characteristics, it is difficult to apply traditional approaches for clock synchronization. Elson *et al.* [4] presented an analytical way to convert service specifications to protocol parameters, called Reference Broadcast Sychronization (RBS). PalChaudhuri *et al.* [18] extended this work and provided probabilistic bounds on clock synchronization error for single and multi-hop networks. We conduct the formal analysis for both of these cases as an illustrative example.

The main cause of error in clock synchronization is the non-determinism in message delivery latency. The RBS protocol entails synchronizing a set of receivers with each other, in contrast to synchronizing with the sender. For this reason, the time required to build the message at the sender node and the waiting time required to get access to the transmission channel are identical for all receivers. While the time required for the message to reach the receiver and the processing time required at the receiver may vary.

5.1   Single-Hop Network

Elson *et al.* [4] discovered the distribution of the synchronization error among receivers. Multiple pulses are sent from the sender to the set of receivers. The difference in actual reception time at the receivers is plotted. As each of these pulses are independently distributed, the difference in reception times gives a normal distribution with zero mean. PalChaudhuri *et al.* [18] extended this work and provided probabilistic bounds on clock synchronization error. If the maximum error that is allowed between two sensors is ϵ_{max}, then the probability of synchronization with an error $\epsilon \leq \epsilon_{max}$ is given as

$$P(|\epsilon| \leq \epsilon_{max}) = \frac{\int_{-\epsilon_{max}}^{\epsilon_{max}} \exp^{-\frac{x^2}{2}}}{\sqrt{2\pi}} \tag{4}$$

For n reference packets from the sender, the receivers exchange their observations. The slope of the skew between the receivers is found by a least square linear estimation using the n data points. The calculated slope of the skew has an associated error in it. This error is the difference in phase between the calculated slope and the actual slope. As the points have a normal distribution, this error can be calculated as

$$P(|\epsilon| \leq \epsilon_{max}) = 2 \, erf\left(\frac{\sqrt{n}\epsilon_{max}}{\sigma}\right) \tag{5}$$

where ϵ is the synchronization error, i.e., difference in packet reception time between two sensors, ϵ_{max} is the maximum allowable error, n is the minimum number of synchronization messages to guarantee the specified error, σ^2 is the variation of the distribution and *erf* is the error function given as

$$erf(z) = \frac{\int_0^z \exp^{-\frac{x^2}{2}} dx}{\sqrt{2\pi}} \qquad (6)$$

Definition 18 *(Error Function)*.
⊢ err_func z = pos_fn_integral lborel
  (λx. Normal (1 / sqrt (2 * π) * exp (-(x pow 2) / 2)) *
  indicator_fn {x | 0 ≤ x ∧ x ≤ z} x)

Now we formally verify the result of Eq. (5).

Theorem 22. *Probability of synchronization error for single hop network*
⊢ ∀p X μ σ n Emax. prob_space p ∧ (I = (1 .. n)) ∧
  (0 < σ) ∧ (0 < n) ∧ (∀i. i ∈ I ⇒ sync_error (X i) p μ σ) ∧
  (Z = (λx. sum I (λi. X i x) / n)) ∧ (μ = 0) ∧ 0 ≤ Emax ⇒
  (prob_sync_error p Z {x | abs (x) ≤ Emax} =
  2 * err_func (Emax * sqrt n / σ))

where sync_error is a Normal random variable, Z is the average error for n reference packets, prob_sync_error p Z represents the distribution of random variable Z, i.e., measurable_distr p Z and Emax is the maximum allowable synchronization error.

5.2   Multi-hop Network

For this protocol, the senders are considered at various levels. A sender which does not need any synchronization is called a sender at level 0. A sensor node which is within the broadcast region of a sender at level 0 can behave as a sender in order to synchronize sensor nodes, which are two hops away from the sender at level 0. Such a sender is called a sender at level 1. Receivers within the broadcast region of the sender at level 0 are synchronized using the same method discussed in the previous section. Once these receivers get synchronized, each receiver starts behaving as a sender at level 1. In the same manner, suitable time transformations can be performed all along the routing path of the message. We define the transformation for multi-hops in HOL as the sum of synchronization errors and find the maximum synchronization possible along with the probability that the error will stay within bounds for k hops.

Definition 19 *(Transformation)*.
⊢ transformation X k = (λx. sum (1 .. k) (λi. X i x))

Theorem 23. *If Emax is the max allowable error for a single hop, then the maximum error between two sensor nodes, k hops apart, is $k * Emax$.*
⊢ ∀X Emax k. 0 ≤ Emax ⇒
  (∀x. (∀i. (X i) x ∈ {x:real | abs (x) ≤ Emax}) ⇒
  transformation X k x ∈ {x:real | abs (x) ≤ Emax * &k})

Theorem 24. *If we consider the error over a single hop to Emax then the error over k hops will be sqrt (k) * Emax.*

⊢ ∀p X μ σ k Emax.
   prob_space p ∧ (I = (1 .. n)) ∧ (0 < σ) ∧
   indep_vars p (λi. borel_triplet) X I ∧
   (0 < k) ∧ (∀i. i ∈ I ⇒ sync_error (X i) p μ σ) ∧
   (Z = (λx. sum I (λi. X i x))) ∧ (μ = 0) ∧ (0 ≤ Emax) ⇒
   (prob_sync_error p Z {x | abs (x) ≤ Emax * sqrt(k)} =
   prob_sync_error p (X k) {x | abs (x) ≤ Emax})

5.3 Discussion

In this case study, we were able to formally reason about the probabilities of clock synchronization error in single-hop and multi-hop wireless sensor networks with universally quantified variables for various design. This is a novelty which is not available in the simulation based approaches. This added benefit comes at the cost of a significant amount of time and effort spent, while formalizing the systems behavior, by the user. However, the formalization of Normal random variables, presented in Sect. 4 of this paper, greatly facilitated the reasoning process and the proof script corresponding to the application, which only consists of 500 lines of HOL4 code. Besides simulation and testing, the analysis of clock synchronization algorithms for WSN has been sometimes performed using timed automata model checking (e.g. [14, 21, 22]). However, both probability modeling and scalability in these works were very limited. For example, only a 7 node network was analysed in [14], which is very restricting for wireless sensor networks.

6 Conclusion

The analysis of engineering systems used in safety critical domains, such as transportation and medicine, is usually done using informal techniques. The unreliable results produced using such techniques may lead to heavy financial loss, or even the loss of human lives. Therefore, in this paper we propose to conduct the probabilistic analysis of engineering systems exhibiting normally distributed randomness using higher-order-logic theorem proving. To do so, we have provided a formalization of Normal random variables along with the mathematical notions required to formalize them. Compared to the standard techniques of computer simulation and paper-and-pencil analysis, our approach provides more accurate and trusted results by exploiting the soundness of theorem proving. It also allows to provide generic results instead of proving the properties for specific instances of the system. To prove the usefulness of our formalization, we conducted the formal analysis of the probabilistic clock synchronization in wireless sensor networks. This application highlight the feasibility and benefits of conducting a formal probabilistic analysis using a higher-order-logic theorem prover. Our HOL4 proof script is available for download at http://hvg.ece.concordia.ca/projects/prob-it/pr7.html, and thus can be used for further developments and analysis of different engineering systems.

Acknowledgement. This publication was made possible by NPRP grant # [5 - 813 - 1 134] from the Qatar National Research Fund (a member of Qatar Foundation). The statements made herein are solely the responsibility of the author[s].

References

1. Ahmed, W., Hasan, O., Tahar, S., Hamdi, M.S.: Towards the formal reliability analysis of oil and gas pipelines. In: Watt, S.M., Davenport, J.H., Sexton, A.P., Sojka, P., Urban, J. (eds.) CICM 2014. LNCS, vol. 8543, pp. 30–44. Springer, Heidelberg (2014)
2. Billingsley, P.: Probability and Measure. Wiley, New York (2012)
3. Elleuch, M., Hasan, O., Tahar, S., Abid, M.: Formal probabilistic analysis of detection properties in wireless sensor networks. Formal Aspects Comput. **27**(1), 79–102 (2015)
4. Elson, J., Girod, L., Estrin, D.: Fine-grained network time synchronization using reference broadcasts. ACM SIGOPS Oper. Syst. Rev. **36**(SI), 147–163 (2002)
5. Goldberg, R.R.: Methods of Real Analysis. Wiley, New York (1976)
6. Hasan, O., Abbasi, N., Tahar, S.: Formal probabilistic analysis of stuck-at faults in reconfigurable memory arrays. In: Leuschel, M., Wehrheim, H. (eds.) IFM 2009. LNCS, vol. 5423, pp. 277–291. Springer, Heidelberg (2009)
7. Hasan, O., Tahar, S.: Formalization of continuous probability distributions. In: Pfenning, F. (ed.) CADE 2007. LNCS (LNAI), vol. 4603, pp. 3–18. Springer, Heidelberg (2007)
8. Hasan, O., Tahar, S.: Using theorem proving to verify expectation and variance for discrete random variables. Autom. Reasoning **41**(3–4), 295–323 (2008)
9. Hasan, O., Tahar, S.: Performance analysis and functional verification of the stop-and-wait protocol in HOL. Autom. Reasoning **42**(1), 1–33 (2009)
10. Hölzl, J.: Analyzing discrete-time Markov chains with countable state space in Isabelle/HOL (2013). http://home.in.tum.de/hoelzl/classifying/
11. Hölzl, J., Heller, A.: Three chapters of measure theory in Isabelle/HOL. In: van Eekelen, M., Geuvers, H., Schmaltz, J., Wiedijk, F. (eds.) ITP 2011. LNCS, vol. 6898, pp. 135–151. Springer, Heidelberg (2011)
12. Liu, L., Hasan, O., Tahar, S.: Formalization of finite-state discrete-time Markov chains in HOL. In: Bultan, T., Hsiung, P.-A. (eds.) ATVA 2011. LNCS, vol. 6996, pp. 90–104. Springer, Heidelberg (2011)
13. Liu, L., Hasan, O., Tahar, S.: Formal analysis of memory contention in a multi-processor system. In: Iyoda, J., de Moura, L. (eds.) SBMF 2013. LNCS, vol. 8195, pp. 195–210. Springer, Heidelberg (2013)
14. McInnes, A.I.: Model-checking the flooding time synchronization protocol. In: International Conference on Control and Automation, pp. 422–429. IEEE (2009)
15. Mhamdi, T., Hasan, O., Tahar, S.: On the formalization of the Lebesgue integration theory in HOL. In: Kaufmann, M., Paulson, L.C. (eds.) ITP 2010. LNCS, vol. 6172, pp. 387–402. Springer, Heidelberg (2010)
16. Mhamdi, T., Hasan, O., Tahar, S.: Formalization of entropy measures in HOL. In: van Eekelen, M., Geuvers, H., Schmaltz, J., Wiedijk, F. (eds.) ITP 2011. LNCS, vol. 6898, pp. 233–248. Springer, Heidelberg (2011)
17. Mhamdi, T., Hasan, O., Tahar, S.: Evaluation of anonymity and confidentiality protocols using theorem proving. Formal Methods Syst. Des. **47**(3), 265–286 (2015)

18. PalChaudhuri, S., Saha, A.K., Johnson, D.B.: Adaptive clock synchronization in sensor networks. In: Information Processing in Sensor Networks, pp. 340–348. ACM (2004)
19. Isabelle/HOL Probability Distribution Repository (2016). https://isabelle.in.tum. de/dist/library/HOL/HOL-Probability/Distributions.html
20. Rice, J.A.: Mathematical Statistics and Data Analysis. Duxbury Press, Pacific Grove (1995)
21. Schuts, M., Zhu, F., Heidarian, F., Vaandrager, F.: Modelling clock synchronization in the Chess gMAC WSN protocol. In: Quantitative Formal Methods: Theory and Applications. EPTCS, vol. 13, pp. 41–54 (2009)
22. Zhang, F., Bu, L., Wang, L., Zhao, J., Chen, X., Zhang, T., Li, X.: Modeling and evaluation of wireless sensor network protocols by stochastic timed automata. Electron. Notes Theoret. Comput. Sci. **296**, 261–277 (2013)

Digital Mathematics Libraries

Progress of Self-Archiving Within the DML Corpus, with a View Toward Community Dynamics

Fabian Müller and Olaf Teschke[(✉)]

FIZ Karlsruhe – Leibniz Institute for Information Infrastructure,
Franklinstr. 11, 10587 Berlin, Germany
olaf.teschke@fiz-karlsruhe.de

Abstract. Self-archiving has developed as a key component to realize Open Access within the DML framework, with the arXiv being by far the most widely used platform. Important features like full-text formula search are facilitated by the openly available LaTeX sources. However, despite the obvious growth of the arXiv corpus, it is not clear what share of the published mathematical literature is already openly accessible in this way, and whether it might eventually converge to full coverage. We present the methodology of the matching procedure of the zbMATH corpus (comprising most of the published math literature since 1868) to the arXiv, and derive from the granular zbMATH data a detailed analysis of the progress of self-archiving within the different mathematical communities, taking into account subject specifics, publication delays, peer review policies, and author networks, among other things. On this basis we give some projections of future developments.

Keywords: Green Open Access · Community behavior · Self-archiving · Corpus analysis

1 Introduction[1]

About 25 years ago, Paul Ginsparg started the central repository for physics preprints that would later develop into what is now widely known as the arXiv [1]. Even anticipating the *Self-Archiving Initiative* [12] (nowadays frequently termed *Green Open Access*), it is perhaps not surprising that since then the service prevailed as the dominating infrastructure for centralized self-archiving not just in physics, but also in other fields like mathematics. Indeed, though several alternatives exist (*e.g.*, the open archive HAL [11], which has an automated depositing agreement with arXiv), a heuristic analysis of about 16 million references from mathematical publications in the zbMATH database [22] indicates that the number of preprint citations pointing to the arXiv is significantly

---

[1] A short announcement of some results contained in this article has been published in [16].

© Springer International Publishing Switzerland 2016
M. Kohlhase et al. (Eds.): CICM 2016, LNAI 9791, pp. 63–74, 2016.
DOI: 10.1007/978-3-319-42547-4_5

higher than to the sum of all other preprint sources, including personal home-pages (which seems to coincide with public perception). Hence, when analysing the progress of self-archiving in mathematics, it is acceptable to restrict to the arXiv.

From a DML viewpoint, the arXiv has at least three key features: Its time-liness, its openness, and the availability of source files (especially LaTeX). The timeliness is naturally connected to the arXiv's initial main purpose of a quick dissemination and allows for a coverage of the most recent research (*cf.* Sect. 3 for an estimate of the head start caused by publication delay). Its openness provides a basis to apply DML tools to the content, though the arXiv's interop-erability is somewhat restricted in this regard by technical and legal limitations. Finally, the availability of source files (especially LaTeX files for mathematical content) distinguishes it from most other electronic libraries (though *e.g.* for a considerable fraction of the ELibM [7] such sources are available as well). For various advanced DML features for mathematical content analysis and retrieval, like formula search [14], the existence of appropriate LaTeX data is currently indispensable.

With these advantages in mind, a natural question arises: can a significant part of the research corpus relevant for a comprehensive DML be made available via community-based self-archiving efforts? Despite obviously being highly rele-vant for the architecture of the envisioned Global Digital Mathematics Library [4], answers so far have been at most roughly approximate and based on sheer magnitudes, an approach which omits key aspects like the scope definition, the actual overlap or the effects of publication delay. The overlap question has so far been addressed only for selected journals in physics by a tedious intellectual analysis of a sample of some thousand articles [13].[2]

The starting point of our analysis is the recent complete matching of the zbMATH database to the math set of the arXiv. zbMATH is a database aim-ing at the coverage of the complete mathematical peer-reviewed research liter-ature. It currently indexes almost 3.6 million documents published since 1755 (with an almost complete coverage since 1868), along with large amounts of additional information like reviews, author data, references, and classifications. Section 2 explains the methodology of the matching and gives an error estimate. In Sect. 3 we give a first application to explore the effects caused by publication and indexing delay. By evaluating the differences of publication and arXiv sub-mission years, we can also answer the question of feasibility of crowd-sourced *retroarchiving*, that is, self-archiving of papers published in the past. Unfortu-nately, current figures indicate that this happens only very rarely, which seems to emphasise the importance of establishing appropriate *moving wall* policies (*i.e.*, research publications becoming open access after a certain embargo period) on

---

[2] The generic approach of [9] has the immense methodological drawback of testing just accessibility, therefore mixing self-archiving, academic, gold and predatory open access, and relying on Google Scholar and Microsoft Academic Search related esti-mates, with their inherent high imprecision due to possibly inflated data and largely unsolved questions of scope and quality.

a comprehensive scale. Taking these effects into account, we give estimates of the overall progress of self-archiving in mathematics in Sect. 4. It becomes clear that after an enormous two-decade growth, there is now a natural slow-down, indicating that the potential might be partially exhausted. More detailed causes of such *saturation effects* can be given by analysing the community behaviour with respect to arXiv submission. For this purpose, we employ some zbMATH features – namely, author identification and MSC [15] indexing in Sects. 5 and 6, respectively – to give a more granular analysis of community dynamics with respect to self-archiving.

2   Matching the arXiv and zbMATH: Methodology and Precision

In this section we give a detailed description of the methodology for matching entries in the zbMATH database to arXiv submissions from the `arXiv:math` set. More precisely, bibliographic data for the published version of the paper as recorded in the zbMATH database is compared to the information available via the arXiv's OAI interface. Only the most recent arXiv version of an article is considered for this, since versions submitted earlier are not exposed via the OAI interface. The amount of information available for matching is rather limited, however, since DOIs are available for a large share of the data, there exists a natural evaluation dataset. It turns out that an algorithm originally developed for matching reference citation strings to zbMATH entries provides surprisingly good results, namely, a precision of 97.0 % on this evaluation set.

During the course of 2015, zbMATH released its new citation matching interface (at times affectionately called zbMATcH) [21]. It consists of a web interface and a REST API, where a user can submit a citation string that the algorithm will attempt to match with a bibliographic entry of the zbMATH database. Due to several factors such as the wealth of different citation formats and norms, the possibility of misspellings, and the existence of different competing transcription systems for non-English author names, this algorithm must be flexible enough to allow for a certain degree of variation.

Citation information can be supplied both in a structured fashion, *i.e.*, broken down by author, title, journal source, etc., or as a plain string containing all this information in a human-readable format. In the latter case, the structured semantic information first needs to be extracted from this string. For this we employ the machine learning library `Grobid` [10], which provides methods to analyse a citation string and return structured bibliographic metadata in the TEI XML format [20]. In either case, the extracted or supplied structured information can then be used to query a full-text search index built on the basis of the popular commercial open-source software `Elasticsearch` [6]. The query returns a number of matching documents, each of which is accompanied by a matching score that quantifies the extent to which it matches the search query. The matching score is computed according to the tf-idf algorithm together with a suitable weighting for different parts of the query.

The natural subsequent problem is to settle on an appropriate minimum threshold $s_{\min}$ that the matching result has to exceed in order to be accepted. We extracted an evaluation dataset consisting of about 4,800,000 references matched via DOI (Digital Object Identifier) – implying a large degree of confidence – as well as overlap with articles from the computer science bibliography dblp [5]. This dataset was split up into categories according to article type (journal article, book article or book), and from the results for each category, a weighted average according to the prevalence of the respective type in the zbMATH database was calculated. The metric used was *informedness*, computed as

$$\mathrm{Inf}_\beta = \mathrm{tpr} - \beta\mathrm{fpr},$$

where tpr and fpr are the true and false positive rates, respectively, and β is a weighting factor that quantifies the relative penalty from a false positive against the bonus obtained from a true positive. The more common F_β measure, defined as the weighted harmonic mean of precision and recall, was unsuitable in this case due to the varying rates of real positives versus real negatives in the evaluation datasets within the individual categories. For a factor of $\beta = 2$ we determined a minimum score of $s_{\min} = 5.0$ to be optimal with respect to the weighted average mentioned above (see Fig. 1).

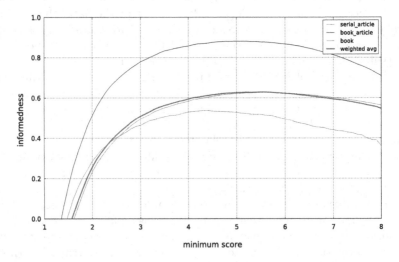

Fig. 1. Inf_2 metric for zbMATH/arXiv matching with varying $s_{\min}$ (Color figure online)

The same algorithm can be used to match zbMATH entries to corresponding preprints available on the arXiv. The arXiv provides an interface for harvesting metadata according to the OAI (Open Archives Initiative) standard, which is also supported by several other large institutional repository providers [3]. While the bibliographic information in this case is already split into author and title, the matching is made more difficult due to the common lack of journal source and pagination data. A subset of arXiv preprints from the math set contains DOI information supplied retroactively by authors after publication, or directly in the case of retroarchiving (*i.e.*, submission of already published papers). There are about 60,000 articles in the arXiv math set that contain a DOI, of which 45,000 have corresponding entries in zbMATH. This enabled us to create another reliable evaluation dataset and compute a new minimum matching score appropriate to this use case (this time it came out at $s_{min} = 8.0$ due to the less reliable information available for matching). In this way we were able to match more than 75,000 further zbMATH articles to their corresponding arXiv preprints with a precision of 97.0 %, bringing the total number of articles with an arXiv link to over 120,000.

3   Time Lag Effect: Retroarchiving and Publication/ Indexing Delay

In this section we analyse the time difference between arXiv submission and publication in a peer-reviewed journal or collection, especially from the viewpoint of identifying the amount of retroarchived papers and the time lag caused by publication delay. The data reflect the information contained in zbMATH as of March 14, 2016; however, the reader can easily reproduce more recent information from the database by searching for, *e.g.*, "arXiv:08*" (using arXiv identifiers in the new format in use since 2007), or "arXiv:math/06*", "arXiv:math-ph/06*", *etc.* (for the format used until 2007). The number of items in the respective publication years can then be read off from the filters in the right hand column.

In principle, a self-archiving structure like the arXiv has no limitations with respect to the covered time-frame: Though the initial main purpose had been the dissemination of recent results, it is in principle possible to submit adapted versions of published papers to the repository (a process generally referred to as retroarchiving). However, lacking the incentive of notifying other researchers about current developments, it is the question whether such a function can be achieved via a community effort.

Indeed, the data shows that the amount of retroarchived papers is negligible: The overall quota is smaller than 5 %, with no clear trend recognisable. Taking into account the matching imprecision, it becomes obvious that no clear development can be read off the data except for the fact that there is no sign that a comprehensive repository including historical publications can be achieved by individual self-archiving efforts.[3] Frameworks like the European Digital Mathematics Library [8], which rely on suitable moving wall policies, seem to be a more adequate solution for gathering the historical heritage of mathematics.

Figure 2 shows the delay between arXiv submission and publication year as recorded in zbMATH (*i.e.*, the year an article appeared in a peer-reviewed publication). The graph approximately follows a Poisson distribution, with a

---

[3] There are of course prominent exceptions like the famous [18], currently the arXiv:math document with the earliest publication year.

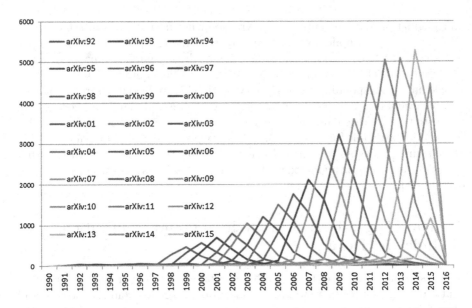

Fig. 2. Time lag between arXiv submission and zbMATH publication year for arXiv submission years 1992–2015 (Color figure online)

clear peak in the year following the submission, then the year after that and the submission year. On average the publication delay amounts to about 1.5 years. It might be noted that there is a significant bias here due to the Journal of High Energy Physics – its considerable bulk of papers (basically all of which are on the arXiv) in some years accounts for almost 10 % of the arXiv/zbMATH overlap and, for a large proportion of them, the time gap between submission and publication is only about two months. This accounts for a large share of the same-year publications and decreases the total average by almost two months overall. These figures ought to be kept in mind when doing a projection into the future. It should also be noted that this is an ongoing process, as some research might be published with a huge delay that is not yet visible.[4]

An additional effect that should be taken into account is the indexing delay. zbMATH aims to cover all peer-reviewed research literature in mathematics, which is quite diverse; a quite considerable fraction still exists only in print, and the selection process for publications from journals containing only partially mathematical content takes some time. Hence the most recent years will usually not be covered completely (in a scope sense), so the matching does not yet apply to the full corpus of published mathematics, and growth rates can only rely on estimates.

Naturally, the precise size of the indexing delay is unknown, but it can be estimated from Fig. 3 to be about 25,000 documents in the arXiv/zbMATH

---

[4] The most extreme case so far seems to be [17] with a delay of no less than 21 years.

overlap as the difference between the actual and projected overlaps under the assumption of a similar growth development.

4   General Coverage Figures and Dynamics

In this section we provide a first analysis of the zbMATH/arXiv overlap relative to the publication year as recorded in zbMATH, which allows for a discussion of the growth rate of self-archiving in mathematics. Several effects need to be taken into consideration: The time gap between arXiv submission and final publication (publication delay), the time gap between publication and indexing in zbMATH (indexing delay), the gap caused by a possibly different scope of the arXiv math set and zbMATH (scope gap), and the amount of arXiv submissions with do not make it into a peer-reviewed publication.

The number of zbMATH entries matched with an arXiv document is currently 119,881 out of 3,580,946, or about 3.3 %. Taking into account the low amount of retroarchiving (only 21 of these arXiv documents have been published before 1991), the fraction should be set into relation to the time frame: For publications since 1991, the figures are already 119,860 out of 1,443,305, or 8.3 %, despite the fact that the arXiv started very small. Figure 3 shows the growth of arXiv/zbMATH overlap since 1991 relative to publication years; the total decline of the figures for recent years is due to the already explained indexing delay.

One sees that the ratio is growing impressively; starting with an almost negligible ratio of 0.05 % in 1991, the overall share of mathematical publications available via the arXiv has recently approached almost 20 %. For a number of subject areas the ratio is even higher (see Sect. 6). While the growth of peer-reviewed research publications (without predatory publishing) has been just slightly less than 4 % every year for the last 25 years, the average growth of its arXiv fraction was on average about 32 % for the same period. Perhaps more interesting, even the last five years show a considerable growth by about 16 %, though the growth rates slow down naturally due to saturation effects in some areas (see also Sects. 5 and 6).

On the other hand, the growth of arXiv submission rates in mathematics has declined recently to about 10 % [2]. The difference is not surprising, since due to publication delay the 16 % mentioned above should rather be compared to the similar growth of arXiv submissions between 2008 and 2013. In any case, the growth will remain above the general publication growth during the next years even when it still declines due to saturation effects, probably pushing the ratio of recent publications available through self-archiving to above 25 % within the next five years; but getting significantly nearer to 100 % would require additional changes of attitude in the community.[5]

A further interesting question concerns the amount and character of arXiv submissions that do not make it into zbMATH indexed publications. At first

---

[5] The publication type plays a role as well: so far, only 331 math books are on the arXiv, a considerable part of which are derived from PhD theses.

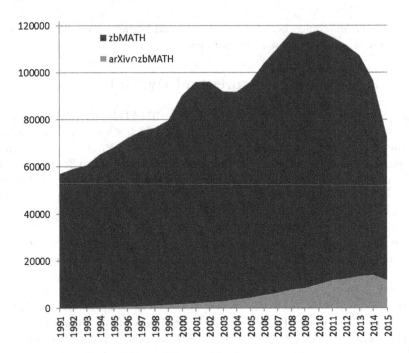

Fig. 3. Number of publications indexed in zbMATH and share having also been submitted to arXiv, relative to publication year recorded in zbMATH (Color figure online)

sight, the number seems to be surprisingly large – more than 280,000 submissions in the arXiv math set compared to only about 120,000 in the zbMATH overlap. But one has to take into account that some publications may be outside the zbMATH scope: this may concern some arXiv:math-ph submission for topical reasons, or publications by predatory publishers. The amount can be estimated by the DOI matching figures in Sect. 2: 60,000 articles with DOI in the arXiv set match to 45,000 in zbMATH. Of the gap, about 10,000 can be estimated to be caused by indexing delay (using a similar approach as indicated at the end of the previous section), so slightly less than 10 % are really outside the zbMATH scope; this would result in an overall gap of about 15,000 published papers. Even larger are the delay effects on the overall scale: By assuming the mentioned growth rates, one can estimate that about 40,000 submissions are missing due to publication delay, and 25,000 due to indexing delay. So, in total, there remain only about 80,000, or 30 %, arXiv math set submissions that do not seem to make it into publication at all (a rate that seems rather stable when one looks at specific submission years, and that corresponds to figures on individual author levels described in Sect. 5). The reasons for this are certainly quite varied – this set contains as diverse examples as Perelman's work on the Geometrisation Conjecture alongside frequent submissions in `arXiv:math.GM` of elementary proofs of Fermat's Last Theorem or the Riemann Hypothesis (though the latter may occasionally find their way into predatory publishers' journals).

A considerable part might just be the basis of further derivative publications, *e.g.* from merged or split arXiv submissions, which therefore do not match well to the published version.

5   Submission Behavior: An Author-Based Analysis

In this section we analyse the structure of submissions to the arXiv math set with respect to uniquely identified authors (as given by their zbMATH author identifiers). The main goal is to identify the number of authors who submit to the arXiv for the first time, and to obtain a first overview of the community dynamics of arXiv submitters.

Submitting to the arXiv is, after all, mainly an individual decision of the author(s). Hence it is natural to employ the zbMATH author database to obtain more details on submission behaviour and dynamics. So far, 60,441 authors are involved into the matched arXiv submissions; a fraction of the about 900,000 overall authors (more than half of them active after 1991) that roughly reflects the publication ratios. However, the distribution is even more extreme than for overall publications: 27,633 of these authors have only a single paper at the arXiv, while 7,345 make up for half of the submissions. A natural guess might be that the number of authors increases the chance that one of them posts an article – but in fact, the opposite holds: among the authors present in the arXiv math set, for the 8,354 authors with an average number of coauthors >2, only 30 % of their math papers since their first submission are on the arXiv, while this number rises to 40 % for the 18,826 authors with average number of coauthors <1. The explanation is given by the subjects: although the largest coauthors figures belong to submissions in high energy physics, which are very well covered, they cannot outweigh the numbers of relatively sparse participation in statistics or numerical and engineering mathematics, for which the arXiv coverage is significantly lower, and the coauthor number higher, than in other areas (see Sect. 6). In fact, though this cannot be checked on a large scale due to data protection issues, small samples indicate that for coauthor groups with several papers the author who submits to the arXiv might always be the same.

Hence it is not surprising that one cannot expect to have a full coverage for every single author of the set, even when restricting to subsequent arXiv submissions after their first. In fact, the overall ratio of self-archived published papers to all publications after the first arXiv submission is about 36.1 %. The diversity might be illustrated by the case of Saharon Shelah [19], currently the author with the most arXived publications in zbMATH: As an early adopter with 26 submissions in 1992 (23 of them later published), he has by now 981 publications in zbMATH, 706 since 1991, 390 of them matched to the arXiv, and 680 arXiv submissions overall – which can perhaps be considered as an almost optimal ratio (taking delay effects into account). This is rather typical – indeed, the 1,000 most prolific math submitters, which account for more than 20 % of the total corpus, also reach an average overlap of just slightly above 50 % with publications after their first submission.

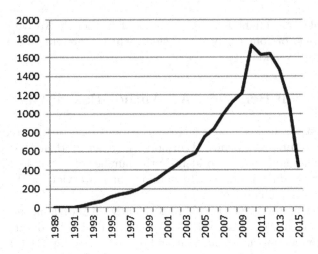

Fig. 4. Number of new actively self-archiving authors from arXiv/zbMATH overlap per year

Moreover, data show that frequent submitters usually stick to self-archiving during their whole research career. Hence, the growth of the arXiv depends at the moment mainly on a steady inflow of regular contributors. Figure 4 shows the number of authors having least two arXiv submissions who self-archive more than half of their zbMATH indexed publications, depending on the date of their first publication. While the decline after 2012 is certainly a delay effect, the diagram indicates some stagnation since the 2010 peak, which coincides with the decreasing growth rates. A possible explanation is offered in the following section.

6   Subject Specifics

Results from previous sections already indicate that the attitude towards self-archiving is highly dependent on the field of research. In this section we employ the information available from the Mathematical Subject Classification (MSC) in zbMATH to quantify the varying self-archiving rates within the 63 main fields of mathematics according to the MSC. This analysis also offers possible explanation for some of the saturation effects seen earlier, and helps to identify challenges which need to be addressed in the course of approaching virtually complete self-archiving for recent mathematical publications.

As we have already seen in the case of Saharon Shelah, logics was among the first mathematical areas to adopt the arXiv; but on a larger scale, the service was first adopted by algebraic geometers since 1998 (see also Fig. 2), probably due to the close connection of this field to high energy physics. In 2002, more than 20 % of the arXiv/math papers were from this area, which also indicated a self-archiving ratio of more than 20 % of the publications; and it remained the most numerous `arXiv:math` section until 2011 (much unlike for math publications in general).

Since the publications in zbMATH are classified by MSC 2010 [15], we can perform a granular analysis of subject dynamics. Figure 5 shows the self-archiving ratio for the main MSC areas.

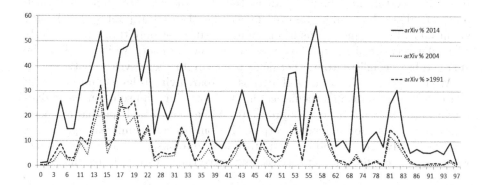

Fig. 5. arXiv ratio for zbMATH publications with publication year 2014, 2004, and total after 1991, depending on MSC main area

We can see that the proportion of publications with arXiv versions available varies dramatically with field: from almost a third of the publications in algebraic geometry since 1991 or almost 30 % in algebraic topology and K-Theory, to only about 2 % in numerical mathematics and less than 0.1 % in mathematics history (surprisingly, the total figures are rather close to the 2004 distribution). This pattern still prevails for recent publications, though some changes are certainly visible, *e.g.*, for the publication year 2014, about 55 % of research in algebraic geometry, algebraic topology and K-Theory is available through the arXiv, but only about 10 % in numerical mathematics and 1 % in mathematics history or mathematics education. This may also serve as an explanation of the saturation effects mentioned above: A look at the new frequent submitters reveals that they come in large number from fields that already have a high arXiv coverage. This helps to approach approximate completeness in these areas but will not improve the total figures significantly. The main challenge will be to establish in areas where self-archiving is less popular a similar culture like in those where it is already the de facto standard. There is no reason why this should not be possible – *e.g.*, the 10 % in numerical mathematics are similar to the situation in algebraic geometry in 1998, which turned out to be a sufficient critical mass for a following dynamic development. But as we have seen in the previous section, this relies on the efforts of a relatively small fraction of the mathematicians, a base which needs permanent stabilisation and enlargement to achieve at least approximate completeness for recent research.

7   Conclusions

Self-archiving via the arXiv has made impressive progress during the last 25 years, and constitutes an important component to preserve the mathematical research in the public domain.

It has already achieved a certain level of approximate completeness for recent research in certain mathematical areas. However, the proportion depends much on the field, so the total figure even for new mathematical publications is only about 30 %. Furthermore, this has been achieved so far only through the efforts of a relatively small group of very active mathematicians, which needs to be enlarged by specialists from other fields to ensure further development.

With respect to the total DML corpus, retroarchiving is largely unsuccessful; hence, to ensure public mathematical heritage, moving wall solutions as in digital libraries like EuDML seem appropriate. While there is no hope that a general solution will work for the whole corpus, the joint forces of different approaches may eventually prevail, and the main task will be to ensure a sustainable framework to connect the different services and make them work well together.

References

1. arXiv e-Print archive. http://arxiv.org/
2. arXiv Mathematics article statistics (2015). http://arxiv.org/year/math/15
3. arXiv bulk data. https://arxiv.org/help/bulk_data
4. The Global Digital Mathematics Library Working Group. https://blog.wias-berlin. de/imu-icm-panel-wdml/2014/08/28/the-global-digital-mathematical-library-wor king-group-gdml-wg/
5. dblp database. http://dblp.uni-trier.de/
6. Elasticsearch open source software. https://www.elastic.co/products/elasticsearch
7. Electronic Library of Mathematics. http://www.emis.de/elibm
8. European Digital Mathematics Library. https://eudml.org/
9. Giles, C.L., Khabsa, M.: The number of scholarly documents on the public web. PLoS ONE **9**(5), e93949 (2014)
10. Grobid Machine Learning Library. https://github.com/kermitt2/grobid
11. Hyper Articles en Ligne. https://hal.archives-ouvertes.fr/
12. Harnad, S.: The self-archiving initiative. Nature **410**(6832), 1024–1025 (2001)
13. Ingoldsby, T.: Physics journals and the arXiv: what is myth and what is reality? American Institute of Physics, Technical report (2009)
14. Kohlhase, M., Mihaljević-Brandt, H., Sperber, W., Teschke, O.: Mathematical formula search. Eur. Math. Soc. Newsl. **89**, 56–58 (2013)
15. Mathematics Subject Classification (2010). http://msc2010.org/
16. Müller, F., Teschke, O.: Will all mathematics be on the arXiv (soon)? Eur. Math. Soc. Newslett. **99**, 55–57 (2016)
17. Poirier, A.: Hubbard forests. Ergodic Theory Dyn. Syst. **33**(1), 303–317 (2013). arxiv:math/9208204
18. Grothendieck, A., Raynaud, M.: Séminaire de géométrie algébrique du Bois Marie 1960/1961 (SGA 1). Lect. Notes Math. **224**, xxii+447 pp. (1971). arXiv:math/0206203
19. Saharon Shelah author profile. https://zbmath.org/authors/shelah.saharon
20. TEI XML format. http://www.tei-c.org/index.xml
21. zbMATcH interface. https://zbmath.org/citationmatching/
22. zbMATH database (1755–). https://zbmath.org/

Mathematical Knowledge Management

Accessing the Mizar Library with a Weakly Strict Mizar Parser

Adam Naumowicz[1(✉)] and Radosław Piliszek[1,2]

[1] Institute of Informatics, University of Białystok, Konstantego Ciołkowskiego 1M,
15-245 Białystok, Poland
adamn@math.uwb.edu.pl, r.piliszek@uwb.edu.pl
[2] High Performance Computing Center, University of Białystok,
Konstantego Ciołkowskiego 1M, 15-245 Białystok, Poland

Abstract. Our work is focused on the Mizar proof assistant and accessing the contents of its library in a machine readable and easily accessible form. The main result of the work described here is the implementation of an independent parser of the Weakly Strict Mizar language (WS-Mizar) along with a formal specification of its grammar and a program simulating an existing Mizar utility but using the new parser. The WS-Mizar language is less complex than the original Mizar language from a programmer's point of view, while there is a software tool available that can translate any text written in Mizar into its WS-Mizar representation for easier access to the library. This is the key step towards developing various external utilities for processing mathematical data contained in Mizar articles.

1 Introduction

For over four decades [1], the Mizar project[1] has been geared towards designing a computer environment that supports writing traditional mathematical papers under strict control of computer programs that check syntactical, semantical and logical correctness of texts. The reader is kindly referred to a recent survey paper [2] documenting the project's state-of-the-art, in particular the proof-checking system, the underlying language and a vast collection of formalized mathematical data available as the Mizar Mathematical Library (MML).

The Mizar language has been devised to encode mathematical formulas and their proofs in a form that is as much as possible readable for humans, which makes its syntax rather complex (c.f. [3]). On the other hand, it has always been equally important that the texts written in the Mizar language should be effectively processed by the set of programs included in the Mizar system distribution. The complexity of the system grows as all sorts of new mechanisms are being continuously added to the system [4–6] to cater to more and more advanced developments formalized (e.g. [7–10]). At the same time, the effectiveness of former implementations is being steadily enhanced taking advantage of new methods and ideas (see e.g. [11,12]).

---

[1] http://mizar.org.

© Springer International Publishing Switzerland 2016
M. Kohlhase et al. (Eds.): CICM 2016, LNAI 9791, pp. 77–82, 2016.
DOI: 10.1007/978-3-319-42547-4_6

However, there is a lot of current research concerning the contents of the Mizar library that do not require in-depth understanding of the inner workings of the Mizar system. For example, categorizing and refactoring the library articles [13–15], detecting duplications [16] or improving the legibility [17,18] of available texts, etc. should be feasible, provided there are methods developed that allow more "shallow" processing of MML articles [19,20].

For this reason, it is an important task to implement new independent utilities for parsing Mizar texts, that can be done not only by Mizar developers. There have been several attempts to produce a working third party parser for the Mizar language based on its high-level grammar. A detailed analysis highlighting a number of difficulties posed by the complexity of the language was presented in a paper by Cairns and Gow [21]. To tackle such problems, a new language has been proposed – WS-Mizar (Weakly Strict Mizar, WSM) [22], which is less complex than the original Mizar language from a programmer's point of view, while there is a software tool available that can translate any text written in Mizar into its WS-Mizar representation. The goal of this paper is to present how the grammar of WS-Mizar was formally created based on the available grammar of the original Mizar language, which enabled the implementation of a dedicated parser independent from the one built into the Mizar system.

The Mizar language is described by its grammar available in the system's distribution (`syntax.txt` and `syntax.xml` files) as well as on the project's website[2]. This grammar, however, contains some ambiguities stemming from making the language as close as possible to the informal way of writing mathematical proofs, which must be solved by a working implementation [23]. These ambiguities make it practically difficult to implement an external utility for analyzing Mizar texts based only on this grammar, and so the WS-Mizar language was proposed.

The name "Weakly Strict Mizar" should indicate that the language is not completely strict in the sense of containing full semantic representation, but it is strict enough to enable parsing the text without any particular knowledge of how the text is internally processed by the Mizar system. It is also worthwhile to note another language mentioned in [22], namely MS-Mizar (More Strict Mizar, MSM), which is a next step in representing more semantic information contained in Mizar texts. Implementing a parser, however, does not require using MSM. It is important to note that both WS-Mizar and MS-Mizar can be used by the original Mizar utilities (after restoring the environment).

With the current Mizar system one can generate a WS-Mizar document from a Mizar article using the `wsmparser` tool. When the article is processed, the system creates also a WSX version of the file, which contains its WS-Mizar content represented in a directly corresponding XML-based format. Here we should note the difference between this format and the semantic internal XML representation of Mizar texts developed by Urban [24].

Formal specification of the WS-Mizar grammar was possible thanks to combining the original Mizar language's grammar with Mizar articles' representations stored in MIZ, WSX and WSM files.

---

[2] http://mizar.org/language/mizar-grammar.xml.

A parser for WS-Mizar, called `wsm-parser` (with a hyphen), based on that grammar was implemented using the popular open-source GNU parser generator suite: `flex` and `bison` [25] that gets in line with the free license on which the Mizar Mathematical Library is distributed [26]. The parser's source code is written in the C++ programming language and compiled with the GCC compiler. The underlying lexer generated by `flex` is augmented with the information extracted from the environment of a Mizar article which needed a separate ad-hoc parsing. The parser is to be used mainly in the GNU/Linux system, but it can also be used within MinGW or Cygwin environments under Windows.

2   WS-Mizar Grammar Specification

The first step to obtain a formal machine-readable specification of the WS-Mizar language informally introduced in [22] was the transformation from the available EBNF form into plain BNF, which resembles the input format accepted by GNU bison, by applying standard techniques (mainly eliminating optionality, disjunctions and lists).

Specifying the grammar of WS-Mizar as opposed to the original Mizar language, was aimed at normalization which should allow easy processing the texts with external tools. This normalization should reflect the internal representation of a Mizar article in an XML-based format stored in a *.wsx file generated by the current implementation of the original Mizar parser. Simply speaking, *WSX* is a representation of a Mizar article in an XML format reflecting the hierarchical structure of the article's elements, which corresponds to the WS-Mizar representation.

In the case of WS-Mizar, the article contains only the text proper, whereas the environment part is not mentioned at all. This part is not that relevant for the syntactic analysis, however the information about the vocabularies imported in the environment must be extra provided for the lexer to correctly qualify each identifier into a suitable category. These can be extracted from the `.dct` file generated by the `accom` program. The WSM file generated by the `wsmparser` on the basis of the WSX file immediately shows also other simple normalizations.

First of all, the file contains a number of extra white-space characters that physically split all tokens [22]. This is not directly reflected in the grammar, but significantly simplifies the lexer. All white-space characters are of course ignored.

The second main difference when we look at the two grammars is that WS-Mizar requires the use of parentheses in many contexts where they are not necessary in the original Mizar language. This is needed to compensate the lack of a dedicated scanning algorithm [27] that efficiently handles notation overloading commonly used in Mizar. See [22] for an example of how this disambiguation makes it evident which type a reserved variable should have and eliminates the need to refer to the overloaded notations to parse text correctly. In addition to the above transformation, the generated WS-Mizar introduces a split into several independent reservation blocks. A similar split is applied in the case of multiple type-qualified variable segments that in the standard Mizar appear in quantifiers, or follow the `let` keyword for loci declarations in definitions as well as generalizations within proofs.

3   Parser Implementation

Our complete WS-Mizar parser implementation consists of several modules: the lexer (which transforms the input stream into a sequence of tokens for the main parser), the parser proper (which is responsible for the syntax analysis), the module processing the vocabulary contained in the article's environment (which is necessary for the lexer), and the `main` function (which handles command line parameters and file input).

The WS-Mizar parser was implemented in the following programming environment: (operating system: GNU/Linux, C++ compiler: GCC 4.8.2, lexer generator: flex 2.5.35, parser generator: bison 3.0.2). For wider applicability, the tools were also tested on the Windows platform using Cygwin and MinGW.

The parser had been initially developed for the Mizar version 8.1.02 equipped with the Mizar Mathematical Library (MML) version 5.22.1191. The relevant updates within the Mizar grammar that stem from this development had been incorporated in the current official Mizar version 8.1.04 distributed with MML version 5.33.1254 (dated 16 Sep 2015). The parser code was written in the C++ language and complies with the ISO C++11 standard. It can be downloaded from a dedicated Git repository[3]. The distribution includes a simple Makefile for use with GNU make, which contains instructions to generate both the lexer and parser source code, and then build an executable called `wsm-parser`.

Additionally, the repository provides two shell scripts to automate the application of the parser to the whole Mizar library: `wsm-all.sh` which performs the translation of all articles (*.miz files) into *.wsm, and `parse-all.sh` which can be used to process all *.wsm files in a given directory with `wsm-parser`.

An example application also included in the Git repository imitates the `irrths` utility which Mizar users commonly use to eliminate unnecessary library references in an article being worked on (the Mizar system's user manual is available as the paper [28]). The utility is very simplistic, yet the complete grammar available for providing references (that can be split across several lines and apply different format for theorems, definitions and schemes as well as shortened reference lists of labels within a given article) make it rather impossible to implement it based only on simple regular expression search techniques without a proper grammar analysis. The implementation based on our WSM parser requires only a couple of additional input lines included for demonstration in two additional source files: `events.h` and `irrths.cpp` and the action implementation for three selected grammar rules concerning library references (included in the `wsm.y` file).

4   Conclusions

In this paper we presented a working parser for the WS-Mizar language, independent from the built-in parser of the original Mizar language. The parser can now

---

[3] https://github.com/MizarProject/wsm-tools.

be used to properly access the Mizar library on a syntactic level with a simple programming interface based on the popular open-source GNU parser generator suite: `flex` and `bison`. The parser can be used in the GNU/Linux system, but it can also be used within MinGW or Cygwin environments under Windows. This opens new possibilities for carrying out numerous experiments with the library that need syntactic processing. Using the provided parser, various experiments can easily be conducted not only by Mizar developers, but also without the need to have access to and recompiling the Mizar system's dependent utilities.

References

1. Grabowski, A., Korniłowicz, A., Naumowicz, A.: Four decades of Mizar. J. Autom. Reason. **55**(3), 191–198 (2015)
2. Bancerek, G., Byliński, C., Grabowski, A., Korniłowicz, A., Matuszewski, R., Naumowicz, A., Pąk, K., Urban, J.: Mizar: state-of-the-art and beyond. In: Kerber, M., et al. [29], pp. 261–279
3. Korniłowicz, A.: Flexary connectives in Mizar. Comput. Lang. Syst. Struct. **44**, 238–250 (2015)
4. Korniłowicz, A.: Definitional expansions in Mizar. J. Autom. Reason. **55**(3), 257–268 (2015)
5. Korniłowicz, A.: On rewriting rules in Mizar. J. Autom. Reason. **50**(2), 203–210 (2013)
6. Naumowicz, A.: Interfacing external CA systems for Gröbner bases computation in Mizar proof checking. Int. J. Comput. Math. **87**(1), 1–11 (2010)
7. Pąk, K.: Readable formalization of Euler's partition theorem in Mizar. In: Kerber, M., et al. [29], pp. 211–226
8. Grabowski, A.: Mechanizing complemented lattices within Mizar type system. J. Autom. Reason. **55**(3), 211–221 (2015)
9. Grabowski, A.: Efficient rough set theory merging. Fundamenta Informaticae **135**(4), 371–385 (2014)
10. Grabowski, A.: Automated discovery of properties of rough sets. Fundamenta Informaticae **128**(1–2), 65–79 (2013)
11. Grabowski, A., Korniłowicz, A., Schwarzweller, C.: Equality in computer proof-assistants. In: Ganzha, M., Maciaszek, L.A., Paprzycki, M. (eds.) Proceedings of the 2015 Federated Conference on Computer Science and Information Systems, pp. 45–54. IEEE (2015). doi:10.15439/2015F229
12. Naumowicz, A.: Automating Boolean set operations in Mizar proof checking with the aid of an external SAT solver. J. Autom. Reason. **55**(3), 285–294 (2015)
13. Grabowski, A., Schwarzweller, C.: Towards automatically categorizing mathematical knowledge. In: Ganzha, M., Maciaszek, L.A., Paprzycki, M. (eds.) Proceedings of Federated Conference on Computer Science and Information Systems - FedCSIS 2012, Wroclaw, 9–12 September 2012, pp. 63–68 (2012)
14. Grabowski, A., Schwarzweller, C.: Revisions as an essential tool to maintain mathematical repositories. In: Kauers, M., Kerber, M., Miner, R., Windsteiger, W. (eds.) MKM/CALCULEMUS 2007. LNCS (LNAI), vol. 4573, pp. 235–249. Springer, Heidelberg (2007)
15. Pąk, K.: Methods of lemma extraction in natural deduction proofs. J. Autom. Reason. **50**(2), 217–228 (2013)

16. Grabowski, A., Schwarzweller, C.: On duplication in mathematical repositories. In: Autexier, S., Calmet, J., Delahaye, D., Ion, P.D.F., Rideau, L., Rioboo, R., Sexton, A.P. (eds.) AISC 2010. LNCS, vol. 6167, pp. 300–314. Springer, Heidelberg (2010)
17. Pąk, K.: Improving legibility of formal proofs based on the close reference principle is NP-hard. J. Autom. Reason. **55**(3), 295–306 (2015)
18. Pąk, K.: Improving legibility of natural deduction proofs is not trivial. Log. Methods Comput. Sci. **10**(3), 1–30 (2014)
19. Alama, J.: Mizar-items: exploring fine-grained dependencies in the Mizar mathematical library. In: Davenport, J.H., Farmer, W.M., Urban, J., Rabe, F. (eds.) MKM 2011 and Calculemus 2011. LNCS, vol. 6824, pp. 276–277. Springer, Heidelberg (2011)
20. Naumowicz, A.: Tools for MML environment analysis. In: Kerber, M., et al. [29], pp. 348–352
21. Cairns, P.A., Gow, J.: Using and parsing the Mizar language. Electr. Notes Theor. Comput. Sci. **93**, 60–69 (2004)
22. Bylinski, C., Alama, J.: New developments in parsing Mizar. In: Jeuring, J., Campbell, J.A., Carette, J., Dos Reis, G., Sojka, P., Wenzel, M., Sorge, V. (eds.) CICM 2012. LNCS, vol. 7362, pp. 427–431. Springer, Heidelberg (2012)
23. Wenzel, M., Wiedijk, F.: A comparison of Mizar and Isar. J. Autom. Reason. **29**(3–4), 389–411 (2002)
24. Urban, J.: XML-izing Mizar: making semantic processing and presentation of MML easy. In: Kohlhase, M. (ed.) MKM 2005. LNCS (LNAI), vol. 3863, pp. 346–360. Springer, Heidelberg (2006)
25. Levine, J.: Flex & Bison. O'Reilly Media, Sebastopol (2009)
26. Alama, J., Kohlhase, M., Mamane, L., Naumowicz, A., Rudnicki, P., Urban, J.: Licensing the Mizar mathematical library. In: Davenport, J.H., Farmer, W.M., Urban, J., Rabe, F. (eds.) MKM 2011 and Calculemus 2011. LNCS, vol. 6824, pp. 149–163. Springer, Heidelberg (2011)
27. Trybulec, A.: Some features of the Mizar language. In: ESPRIT Workshop, Torino (1993)
28. Grabowski, A., Kornilowicz, A., Naumowicz, A.: Mizar in a nutshell. J. Formaliz. Reason. **3**(2), 153–245 (2010)
29. Kerber, M., Carette, J., Kaliszyk, C., Rabe, F., Sorge, V. (eds.): CICM 2015. LNCS, vol. 9150, pp. 261–279. Springer, Heidelberg (2015)

Incorporating Quotation and Evaluation into Church's Type Theory: Syntax and Semantics

William M. Farmer[✉]

Computing and Software, McMaster University, Hamilton, Canada
wmfarmer@mcmaster.ca

Abstract. CTT_{qe} is a version of Church's type theory that includes quotation and evaluation operators that are similar to quote and eval in the Lisp programming language. With quotation and evaluation it is possible to reason in CTT_{qe} about the interplay of the syntax and semantics of expressions and, as a result, to formalize syntax-based mathematical algorithms. We present the syntax and semantics of CTT_{qe} and give several examples that illustrate the usefulness of having quotation and evaluation in CTT_{qe}. We do not give a proof system for CTT_{qe}, but we do sketch what a proof system could look like.

1 Introduction

The Lisp programming language is famous for its use of *quotation* and *evaluation*. From code the Lisp quotation operator called *quote* produces meta-level data (i.e., S-expressions) that represents the code, and from this data the Lisp evaluation operator called *eval* produces the code that the data represents. In Lisp, *metaprogramming* (i.e., programming at the meta-level) is performed by manipulating S-expressions and is *reflected* (i.e., integrated) into object-level programming by the use of quote and eval.

Metaprogramming with reflection is a very powerful programming tool. Besides Lisp, several other programming languages employ quotation and evaluation mechanisms to enable metaprogramming with reflection. Examples include Agda [16,17], Archon [22], Elixir [18], F# [25], MetaML [23], MetaOCaml [20], reFLect [12], and Template Haskell [21].

Analogous to metaprogramming in a programming language, *metareasoning* is performed in a logic by manipulating meta-level values (e.g., syntax trees) that represent expressions in the logic and is *reflected* into object-level reasoning using quotation and evaluation[1] mechanisms [6]. In proof assistants like Coq and Agda, metareasoning with reflection is implemented in the logic by defining an infrastructure consisting of (1) an *inductive type of syntactic values* that represent certain object-level expressions, (2) an *informal quotation operator* that maps these object-level expressions to syntactic values, and (3) a *formal*

This research was supported by NSERC.

[1] Evaluation in this context is also called unquoting, interpretation, dereferencing, and dereification.

M. Kohlhase et al. (Eds.): CICM 2016, LNAI 9791, pp. 83–98, 2016.
DOI: 10.1007/978-3-319-42547-4_7

evaluation operator that maps syntactic values to the values of the object-level expressions that they represent [4, 10, 26]. Metareasoning with reflection is used for formalizing metalogical techniques and incorporating symbolic computation into proof assistants [4, 8, 10, 13, 26].

The metareasoning and reflection infrastructures that have been employed in today's proof assistants are *local* in the sense that the syntactic values of the inductive type represent only a subset of the expressions of the logic, the quotation operator can only be applied to these expressions, and the evaluation operator can only be applied to the syntactic values of the inductive type. Can metareasoning with reflection be implemented in a traditional logic like first-order logic or simple type theory using a *global* infrastructure with quotation and evaluation operators like Lisp's quote and eval? This is largely an open question. As far as we know, there is no readily implementable version of a traditional logic that admits global quotation and evaluation. We have proposed a version of NBG set theory named Chiron [7] and a version of Alonzo Church's type theory [5][2] named $\mathcal{Q}_0^{\mathrm{uqe}}$ [9] that include global quotation and evaluation operators, but these logics have a high level of complexity and are not easy to implement.

Many challenging problems face the logic engineer who seeks to incorporate global quotation and evaluation into a traditional logic. The three problems that most concern us are the following. We will write the quotation and evaluation operators applied to an expression e as $\ulcorner e \urcorner$ and $\llbracket e \rrbracket$, respectively.

1. *Evaluation Problem.* An evaluation operator is applicable to syntactic values that represent formulas and thus is effectively a truth predicate. Hence, by the proof of Alfred Tarski's theorem on the undefinability of truth [24], if the evaluation operator is total in the context of a sufficiently strong theory like first-order Peano arithmetic, then it is possible to express the liar paradox using the quotation and evaluation operators. Therefore, the evaluation operator must be partial and the law of disquotation cannot hold universally (i.e., for some expressions e, $\llbracket \ulcorner e \urcorner \rrbracket \neq e$). As a result, reasoning with evaluation is cumbersome and leads to undefined expressions.

2. *Variable Problem.* The variable x is not free in the expression $\ulcorner x + 3 \urcorner$ (or in any quotation). However, x is free in $\llbracket \ulcorner x + 3 \urcorner \rrbracket$ because $\llbracket \ulcorner x + 3 \urcorner \rrbracket = x + 3$. If the value of a constant c is $\ulcorner x + 3 \urcorner$, then x is free in $\llbracket c \rrbracket$ because $\llbracket c \rrbracket = \llbracket \ulcorner x + 3 \urcorner \rrbracket = x + 3$. Hence, in the presence of an evaluation operator, whether or not a variable is free in an expression may depend on the values of the expression's components. As a consequence, the substitution of an expression for the free occurrences of a variable in another expression depends on the semantics (as well as the syntax) of the expressions involved and must be integrated with the proof system of the logic. That is, a logic with quotation and evaluation requires a semantics-dependent form of substitution in which side conditions, like whether a variable is free in an expression, are proved within the proof system. This is a major departure from traditional logic.

---

[2] Church's type theory is a version of simple type theory with lambda notation.

3. *Double Substitution Problem.* By the semantics of evaluation, the value of $\llbracket e \rrbracket$ is the *value* of the expression whose syntax tree is represented by the *value* of e. Hence the semantics of evaluation involves a double valuation (see condition 6 of the definition of a model in Sect. 3.3). If the value of a variable x is $\ulcorner x \urcorner$, then $\llbracket x \rrbracket = \llbracket \ulcorner x \urcorner \rrbracket = x = \ulcorner x \urcorner$. Hence the substitution of $\ulcorner x \urcorner$ for x in $\llbracket x \rrbracket$ requires one substitution inside the argument of the evaluation operator and another substitution after the evaluation operator is eliminated. This double substitution is another major departure from traditional logic.

$\mathrm{CTT_{qe}}$ is a version of Church's type theory [5] with quotation and evaluation that overcomes these three problems. It is much simpler than $\mathcal{Q}_0^{\mathrm{uqe}}$ since (1) the quotation operator can only be applied to expressions that do not contain the evaluation operator and (2) substitution is not a logical constant (applied to syntactic values). Like $\mathcal{Q}_0^{\mathrm{uqe}}$, $\mathrm{CTT_{qe}}$ is based on $\mathcal{Q}_0$ [2], Peter Andrews' version of Church's type theory. In this paper, we present the syntax and semantics of $\mathrm{CTT_{qe}}$ and give several examples that illustrate the usefulness of having quotation and evaluation in $\mathrm{CTT_{qe}}$. We do not give a proof system for $\mathrm{CTT_{qe}}$, but we do sketch what a proof system could look like.

2 Syntax

The syntax of $\mathrm{CTT_{qe}}$ is very similar to the syntax of $\mathcal{Q}_0$ [2, pp. 210–211]. $\mathrm{CTT_{qe}}$ has the syntax of Church's type theory plus an inductive type of syntactic values, a quotation operator, and a typed evaluation operator. Like $\mathcal{Q}_0$, the propositional connectives and quantifiers are defined using function application, function abstraction, and equality. For the sake of simplicity, $\mathrm{CTT_{qe}}$ does not contain, as in $\mathcal{Q}_0$, a definite description operator or, as in the logic of HOL [11], an indefinite description (choice) operator or type variables.

2.1 Types

A *type* of $\mathrm{CTT_{qe}}$ is a string of symbols defined inductively by the following formation rules:

1. *Type of individuals*: ι is a type.
2. *Type of truth values*: o is a type.
3. *Type of constructions*: ϵ is a type.
4. *Function type*: If α and β are types, then $(\alpha \to \beta)$ is a type.[3]

Let $\mathcal{T}$ denote the set of types of $\mathrm{CTT_{qe}}$. $\alpha, \beta, \gamma, \ldots$ are syntactic variables ranging over types. When there is no loss of meaning, matching pairs of parentheses in types may be omitted. We assume that function type formation associates to the right so that a type of the form $(\alpha \to (\beta \to \gamma))$ may be written as $\alpha \to \beta \to \gamma$.

We will see in the next section that in $\mathrm{CTT_{qe}}$ types are directly assigned to variables and constants and thereby indirectly assigned to expressions.

---

[3] In Andrews' $\mathcal{Q}_0$ [2] and Church's original system [5], the function type $(\alpha \to \beta)$ is written as $(\beta\alpha)$.

2.2   Expressions

A *typed symbol* is a symbol with a subscript from $\mathcal{T}$. Let $\mathcal{V}$ be a set of typed symbols such that, for each $\alpha \in \mathcal{T}$, $\mathcal{V}$ contains denumerably many typed symbols with subscript α. A *variable of type* α of CTT$_{qe}$ is a member of $\mathcal{V}$ with subscript α. $\mathbf{f}_\alpha, \mathbf{g}_\alpha, \mathbf{h}_\alpha, \mathbf{u}_\alpha, \mathbf{v}_\alpha, \mathbf{w}_\alpha, \mathbf{x}_\alpha, \mathbf{y}_\alpha, \mathbf{z}_\alpha, \ldots$ are syntactic variables ranging over variables of type α. We will assume that $f_\alpha, g_\alpha, h_\alpha, u_\alpha, v_\alpha, w_\alpha, x_\alpha, y_\alpha, z_\alpha, \ldots$ are actual variables of type α of CTT$_{qe}$.

Let $\mathcal{C}$ be a set of typed symbols disjoint from $\mathcal{V}$ that includes the typed symbols in Table 1. A *constant of type* α of CTT$_{qe}$ is a member of $\mathcal{C}$ with subscript α. The typed symbols in Table 1 are the *logical constants* of CTT$_{qe}$. $\mathbf{c}_\alpha, \mathbf{d}_\alpha, \ldots$ are syntactic variables ranging over constants of type α.

Table 1. Logical constants

$=_{\alpha \to \alpha \to o}$ for all $\alpha \in \mathcal{T}$
is-var$_{\epsilon \to o}$
is-con$_{\epsilon \to o}$
app$_{\epsilon \to \epsilon \to \epsilon}$
abs$_{\epsilon \to \epsilon \to \epsilon}$
quo$_{\epsilon \to \epsilon}$
is-expr$_{\epsilon \to o}^{\alpha}$ for all $\alpha \in \mathcal{T}$

An *expression of type* α of CTT$_{qe}$ is a string of symbols defined inductively by the formation rules below. $\mathbf{A}_\alpha, \mathbf{B}_\alpha, \mathbf{C}_\alpha, \ldots$ are syntactic variables ranging over expressions of type α. An expression is *eval-free* if it is constructed using just the first five formation rules.

1. *Variable*: $\mathbf{x}_\alpha$ is an expression of type α.
2. *Constant*: $\mathbf{c}_\alpha$ is an expression of type α.
3. *Function application*: $(\mathbf{F}_{\alpha \to \beta}\, \mathbf{A}_\alpha)$ is an expression of type β.
4. *Function abstraction*: $(\lambda\, \mathbf{x}_\alpha \,.\, \mathbf{B}_\beta)$ is an expression of type $\alpha \to \beta$.
5. *Quotation*: $\ulcorner \mathbf{A}_\alpha \urcorner$ is an expression of type ϵ if $\mathbf{A}_\alpha$ is eval-free.
6. *Evaluation*: $\llbracket \mathbf{A}_\epsilon \rrbracket_{\mathbf{B}_\beta}$ is an expression of type β.

The purpose of the second component $\mathbf{B}_\beta$ in an evaluation $\llbracket \mathbf{A}_\epsilon \rrbracket_{\mathbf{B}_\beta}$ is to establish the type of the evaluation. A *formula* is an expression of type o. When there is no loss of meaning, matching pairs of parentheses in expressions may be omitted. We assume that function application formation associates to the left so that an expression of the form $((\mathbf{G}_{\alpha \to \beta \to \gamma}\, \mathbf{A}_\alpha)\, \mathbf{B}_\beta)$ may be written as $\mathbf{G}_{\alpha \to \beta \to \gamma}\, \mathbf{A}_\alpha\, \mathbf{B}_\beta$.

2.3   Constructions

A *construction* of CTT_{qe} is an expression of type ϵ defined inductively as follows:

1. $\ulcorner \mathbf{x}_\alpha \urcorner$ is a construction.
2. $\ulcorner \mathbf{c}_\alpha \urcorner$ is a construction.
3. If $\mathbf{A}_\epsilon$ and $\mathbf{B}_\epsilon$ are constructions, then $\mathsf{app}_{\epsilon \to \epsilon \to \epsilon} \mathbf{A}_\epsilon \mathbf{B}_\epsilon$, $\mathsf{abs}_{\epsilon \to \epsilon \to \epsilon} \mathbf{A}_\epsilon \mathbf{B}_\epsilon$, and $\mathsf{quo}_{\epsilon \to \epsilon} \mathbf{A}_\epsilon$ are constructions.

The set of constructions is thus an inductive type whose base elements are quotations of variables and constants and whose constructors are $\mathsf{app}_{\epsilon \to \epsilon \to \epsilon}$, $\mathsf{abs}_{\epsilon \to \epsilon \to \epsilon}$, and $\mathsf{quo}_{\epsilon \to \epsilon}$. We will call these three constants *syntax constructors*.

Let $\mathcal{E}$ be the function mapping eval-free expressions to constructions that is defined inductively as follows:

1. $\mathcal{E}(\mathbf{x}_\alpha) = \ulcorner \mathbf{x}_\alpha \urcorner$.
2. $\mathcal{E}(\mathbf{c}_\alpha) = \ulcorner \mathbf{c}_\alpha \urcorner$.
3. $\mathcal{E}(\mathbf{F}_{\alpha \to \beta} \mathbf{A}_\alpha) = \mathsf{app}_{\epsilon \to \epsilon \to \epsilon} \mathcal{E}(\mathbf{F}_{\alpha \to \beta}) \mathcal{E}(\mathbf{A}_\alpha)$.
4. $\mathcal{E}(\lambda \mathbf{x}_\alpha . \mathbf{B}_\beta) = \mathsf{abs}_{\epsilon \to \epsilon \to \epsilon} \mathcal{E}(\mathbf{x}_\alpha) \mathcal{E}(\mathbf{B}_\beta)$.
5. $\mathcal{E}(\ulcorner \mathbf{A}_\alpha \urcorner) = \mathsf{quo}_{\epsilon \to \epsilon} \mathcal{E}(\mathbf{A}_\alpha)$.

$\mathcal{E}$ is clearly injective. When $\mathbf{A}_\alpha$ is eval-free, $\mathcal{E}(\mathbf{A}_\alpha)$ is a construction that represents the syntax tree of $\mathbf{A}_\alpha$. That is, $\mathcal{E}(\mathbf{A}_\alpha)$ is a syntactic value that represents how $\mathbf{A}_\alpha$ is syntactically constructed. For every eval-free expression, there is a construction that represents its syntax tree, but not every construction represents the syntax tree of an eval-free expression. For example, $\mathsf{app}_{\epsilon \to \epsilon \to \epsilon} \ulcorner \mathbf{x}_\alpha \urcorner \ulcorner \mathbf{x}_\alpha \urcorner$ represents the syntax tree of $(\mathbf{x}_\alpha \mathbf{x}_\alpha)$ which is not an expression of CTT_{qe} since the types are mismatched. A construction is *proper* if it is in the range of $\mathcal{E}$, i.e., it represents the syntax tree of an eval-free expression.

The five kinds of eval-free expressions and the syntactic values that represent their syntax trees are given in Table 2.

Table 2. Five kinds of eval-free expressions

Kind	Syntax	Syntactic values
Variable	$\mathbf{x}_\alpha$	$\ulcorner \mathbf{x}_\alpha \urcorner$
Constant	$\mathbf{c}_\alpha$	$\ulcorner \mathbf{c}_\alpha \urcorner$
Function application	$\mathbf{F}_{\alpha \to \beta} \mathbf{A}_\alpha$	$\mathsf{app}_{\epsilon \to \epsilon \to \epsilon} \mathcal{E}(\mathbf{F}_{\alpha \to \beta}) \mathcal{E}(\mathbf{A}_\alpha)$
Function abstraction	$\lambda \mathbf{x}_\alpha . \mathbf{B}_\beta$	$\mathsf{abs}_{\epsilon \to \epsilon \to \epsilon} \mathcal{E}(\mathbf{x}_\alpha) \mathcal{E}(\mathbf{B}_\beta)$
Quotation	$\ulcorner \mathbf{A}_\alpha \urcorner$	$\mathsf{quo}_{\epsilon \to \epsilon} \mathcal{E}(\mathbf{A}_\alpha)$

2.4   Definitions and Abbreviations

As Andrews does in [2, p. 212], we introduce in Table 3 several defined logical constants and abbreviations. The former includes constants for true and false and the propositional connectives. The latter includes notation for equality, the propositional connectives, universal and existential quantification, and a simplified notation for evaluations.

Table 3. Definitions and abbreviations

$(\mathbf{A}_\alpha = \mathbf{B}_\alpha)$	stands for	$=_{\alpha \to \alpha \to o} \mathbf{A}_\alpha \mathbf{B}_\alpha$
T_o	stands for	$=_{o \to o \to o} \, = \, =_{o \to o \to o}$
F_o	stands for	$(\lambda x_o \, . \, T_o) = (\lambda x_o \, . \, x_o)$
$(\forall \mathbf{x}_\alpha \, . \, \mathbf{A}_o)$	stands for	$(\lambda \mathbf{x}_\alpha \, . \, T_o) = (\lambda \mathbf{x}_\alpha \, . \, \mathbf{A}_o)$
$\wedge_{o \to o \to o}$	stands for	$\lambda x_o \, . \, \lambda y_o \, . \, ((\lambda g_{o \to o \to o} \, . \, g_{o \to o \to o} \, T_o \, T_o) = (\lambda g_{o \to o \to o} \, . \, g_{o \to o \to o} \, x_o \, y_o))$
$(\mathbf{A}_o \wedge \mathbf{B}_o)$	stands for	$\wedge_{o \to o \to o} \mathbf{A}_o \mathbf{B}_o$
$\supset_{o \to o \to o}$	stands for	$\lambda x_o \, . \, \lambda y_o \, . \, (x_o = (x_o \wedge y_o))$
$(\mathbf{A}_o \supset \mathbf{B}_o)$	stands for	$\supset_{o \to o \to o} \mathbf{A}_o \mathbf{B}_o$
$\neg_{o \to o}$	stands for	$=_{o \to o \to o} F_o$
$(\neg \mathbf{A}_o)$	stands for	$\neg_{o \to o} \mathbf{A}_o$
$\vee_{o \to o \to o}$	stands for	$\lambda x_o \, . \, \lambda y_o \, . \, \neg(\neg x_o \wedge \neg y_o)$
$(\mathbf{A}_o \vee \mathbf{B}_o)$	stands for	$\vee_{o \to o \to o} \mathbf{A}_o \mathbf{B}_o$
$(\exists \mathbf{x}_\alpha \, . \, \mathbf{A}_o)$	stands for	$\neg(\forall \mathbf{x}_\alpha \, . \, \neg \mathbf{A}_o)$
$[\![\mathbf{A}_\epsilon]\!]_\beta$	stands for	$[\![\mathbf{A}_\epsilon]\!]_{\mathbf{B}_\beta}$

3   Semantics

The semantics of $\mathrm{CTT}_{\mathrm{qe}}$ extends the semantics of $\mathcal{Q}_0$ [2, pp. 238–239] by defining the domain of the type ϵ and what quotations and evaluations mean.

3.1   Frames

A *frame* of $\mathrm{CTT}_{\mathrm{qe}}$ is a collection $\{D_\alpha \mid \alpha \in \mathcal{T}\}$ of domains such that:

1. D_ι is a nonempty set of values (called *individuals*).
2. $D_o = \{\mathrm{T}, \mathrm{F}\}$, the set of standard *truth values*.
3. D_ϵ is the set of *constructions* of $\mathrm{CTT}_{\mathrm{qe}}$.
4. For $\alpha, \beta \in \mathcal{T}$, $D_{\alpha \to \beta}$ is the set of *total functions* from D_α to D_β.

3.2   Interpretations

An *interpretation* of $\mathrm{CTT}_{\mathrm{qe}}$ is a pair $(\{D_\alpha \mid \alpha \in \mathcal{T}\}, I)$ consisting of a frame and an interpretation function I that maps each constant in $\mathcal{C}$ of type α to an element of D_α such that:

1. For all $\alpha \in \mathcal{T}$, $I(=_{\alpha\to\alpha\to o})$ is the function $f \in D_{\alpha\to\alpha\to o}$ such that, for all $d_1, d_2 \in D_\alpha$, $f(d_1)(d_2) = \text{T}$ iff $d_1 = d_2$. That is, $I(=_{\alpha\to\alpha\to o})$ is the identity relation on D_α.
2. $I(\text{is-var}_{\epsilon\to o})$ is the function $f \in D_{\epsilon\to o}$ such that, for all $\mathbf{A}_\epsilon \in D_\epsilon$, $f(\mathbf{A}_\epsilon) = \text{T}$ iff $\mathbf{A}_\epsilon = \ulcorner \mathbf{x}_\alpha \urcorner$ for some variable $\mathbf{x}_\alpha \in \mathcal{V}$.
3. $I(\text{is-con}_{\epsilon\to o})$ is the function $f \in D_{\epsilon\to o}$ such that, for all $\mathbf{A}_\epsilon \in D_\epsilon$, $f(\mathbf{A}_\epsilon) = \text{T}$ iff $\mathbf{A}_\epsilon = \ulcorner \mathbf{c}_\alpha \urcorner$ for some constant $\mathbf{c}_\alpha \in \mathcal{C}$.
4. $I(\text{app}_{\epsilon\to\epsilon\to\epsilon})$ is the function $f \in D_{\epsilon\to\epsilon\to\epsilon}$ such that, for all $\mathbf{A}_\epsilon, \mathbf{B}_\epsilon \in D_\epsilon$, $f(\mathbf{A}_\epsilon)(\mathbf{B}_\epsilon)$ is the construction $\text{app}_{\epsilon\to\epsilon\to\epsilon} \, \mathbf{A}_\epsilon \, \mathbf{B}_\epsilon$.
5. $I(\text{abs}_{\epsilon\to\epsilon\to\epsilon})$ is the function $f \in D_{\epsilon\to\epsilon\to\epsilon}$ such that, for all $\mathbf{A}_\epsilon, \mathbf{B}_\epsilon \in D_\epsilon$, $f(\mathbf{A}_\epsilon)(\mathbf{B}_\epsilon)$ is the construction $\text{abs}_{\epsilon\to\epsilon\to\epsilon} \, \mathbf{A}_\epsilon \, \mathbf{B}_\epsilon$.
6. $I(\text{quo}_{\epsilon\to\epsilon})$ is the function $f \in D_{\epsilon\to\epsilon}$ such that, for all $\mathbf{A}_\epsilon \in D_\epsilon$, $f(\mathbf{A}_\epsilon)$ is the construction $\text{quo}_{\epsilon\to\epsilon} \, \mathbf{A}_\epsilon$.
7. For all $\alpha \in \mathcal{T}$, $I(\text{is-expr}^\alpha_{\epsilon\to o})$ is the function $f \in D_{\epsilon\to o}$ such that, for all $\mathbf{A}_\epsilon \in D_\epsilon$, $f(\mathbf{A}_\epsilon) = \text{T}$ iff $\mathbf{A}_\epsilon = \mathcal{E}(\mathbf{B}_\alpha)$ for some (eval-free) expression $\mathbf{B}_\alpha$.

Remark 3.21 (Domain of Constructions). We would prefer to define D_ϵ to be the set of proper constructions because we need only proper constructions to represent the syntax trees of eval-free expressions. However, then the natural interpretations of the three syntax constructors — $\text{app}_{\epsilon\to\epsilon\to\epsilon}$, $\text{abs}_{\epsilon\to\epsilon\to\epsilon}$, and $\text{quo}_{\epsilon\to\epsilon}$ — would be partial functions. Since CTT_{qe} admits only total functions, it is more convenient to allow D_ϵ to include improper constructions than to interpret the syntax constructors as total functions that represent partial functions.

An *assignment* into a frame $\{D_\alpha \mid \alpha \in \mathcal{T}\}$ is a function φ whose domain is $\mathcal{V}$ such that, for each variable $\mathbf{x}_\alpha$, $\varphi(\mathbf{x}_\alpha) \in D_\alpha$. Given an assignment φ, a variable $\mathbf{x}_\alpha$, and $d \in D_\alpha$, let $\varphi[\mathbf{x}_\alpha \mapsto d]$ be the assignment ψ such that $\psi(\mathbf{x}_\alpha) = d$ and $\psi(\mathbf{y}_\beta) = \varphi(\mathbf{y}_\beta)$ for all variables $\mathbf{y}_\beta \neq \mathbf{x}_\alpha$. Given an interpretation $\mathcal{M} = (\{D_\alpha \mid \alpha \in \mathcal{T}\}, I)$, $\text{assign}(\mathcal{M})$ is the set of assignments into the frame of $\mathcal{M}$.

3.3   Models

An interpretation $\mathcal{M} = (\{D_\alpha \mid \alpha \in \mathcal{T}\}, I)$ is a *model* for CTT_{qe} if there is a binary valuation function $V^{\mathcal{M}}$ such that, for all assignments $\varphi \in \text{assign}(\mathcal{M})$ and expressions $\mathbf{C}_\gamma$, $V^{\mathcal{M}}_\varphi(\mathbf{C}_\gamma) \in D_\gamma$ and each of the following conditions is satisfied:

1. If $\mathbf{C}_\gamma \in \mathcal{V}$, then $V^{\mathcal{M}}_\varphi(\mathbf{C}_\gamma) = \varphi(\mathbf{C}_\gamma)$.
2. If $\mathbf{C}_\gamma \in \mathcal{C}$, then $V^{\mathcal{M}}_\varphi(\mathbf{C}_\gamma) = I(\mathbf{C}_\gamma)$.
3. If $\mathbf{C}_\gamma$ is $\mathbf{F}_{\alpha\to\beta} \, \mathbf{A}_\alpha$, then $V^{\mathcal{M}}_\varphi(\mathbf{C}_\gamma) = V^{\mathcal{M}}_\varphi(\mathbf{F}_{\alpha\to\beta})(V^{\mathcal{M}}_\varphi(\mathbf{A}_\alpha))$.
4. If $\mathbf{C}_\gamma$ is $\lambda \mathbf{x}_\alpha \cdot \mathbf{B}_\beta$, then $V^{\mathcal{M}}_\varphi(\mathbf{C}_\gamma)$ is the function $f \in D_{\alpha\to\beta}$ such that, for each $d \in D_\alpha$, $f(d) = V^{\mathcal{M}}_{\varphi[\mathbf{x}_\alpha \mapsto d]}(\mathbf{B}_\beta)$.
5. If $\mathbf{C}_\gamma$ is $\ulcorner \mathbf{A}_\alpha \urcorner$, then $V^{\mathcal{M}}_\varphi(\mathbf{C}_\gamma) = \mathcal{E}(\mathbf{A}_\alpha)$.
6. If $\mathbf{C}_\gamma$ is $\llbracket \mathbf{A}_\epsilon \rrbracket_\beta$ and $V^{\mathcal{M}}_\varphi(\text{is-expr}^\beta_{\epsilon\to o} \, \mathbf{A}_\epsilon) = \text{T}$, then

$$V^{\mathcal{M}}_\varphi(\mathbf{C}_\gamma) = V^{\mathcal{M}}_\varphi(\mathcal{E}^{-1}(V^{\mathcal{M}}_\varphi(\mathbf{A}_\epsilon))).$$

Proposition 3.31. *Models for* CTT$_{qe}$ *exist.*

Proof. It is easy to construct an interpretation $\mathcal{M} = (\{\mathcal{D}_\alpha \mid \alpha \in \mathcal{T}\}, I)$ that is a model for CTT$_{qe}$. Note that, if $V^{\mathcal{M}}_\varphi(\text{is-expr}^\beta_{\epsilon \to o} \mathbf{A}_\epsilon) = \text{F}$, then $V^{\mathcal{M}}_\varphi(\llbracket \mathbf{A}_\epsilon \rrbracket_\beta)$ can be any value in D_β. $\qquad\square$

Remark 3.32 (Standard vs. General Models). The notion of a model defined here is a *standard model* in which each function domain $D_{\alpha \to \beta}$ is the set of *all* total functions from D_α to D_β. Andrews' semantics for $\mathcal{Q}_0$ is based on the notion of a *general model*, introduced by Henkin [15], in which each function domain $D_{\alpha \to \beta}$ is a set of *some* total functions from D_α to D_β. General models can be easily defined for CTT$_{qe}$. The definition of a frame, however, has to be changed so that the domain D_ϵ may include "nonstandard constructions".

Remark 3.33 (Semantics of Evaluations). When $V^{\mathcal{M}}_\varphi(\text{is-expr}^\beta_{\epsilon \to o} \mathbf{A}_\epsilon) = \text{T}$, the semantics of $V^{\mathcal{M}}_\varphi(\llbracket \mathbf{A}_\epsilon \rrbracket_\beta)$ involves a double valuation as mentioned in the Double Substitution Problem described in the Introduction.

Remark 3.34 (Undefined Evaluations). Suppose $V^{\mathcal{M}}_\varphi(\mathbf{A}_\epsilon)$ is an improper construction. Then $V^{\mathcal{M}}_\varphi(\mathcal{E}^{-1}(V^{\mathcal{M}}_\varphi(\mathbf{A}_\epsilon)))$ is undefined and $V^{\mathcal{M}}_\varphi(\llbracket \mathbf{A}_\epsilon \rrbracket_\beta)$ has no natural value. Since CTT$_{qe}$ does not admit undefined expressions, $V^{\mathcal{M}}_\varphi(\llbracket \mathbf{A}_\epsilon \rrbracket_\beta)$ is defined but its value is unspecified. Similarly, if $V^{\mathcal{M}}_\varphi(\mathbf{A}_\epsilon)$ is a proper construction of the form $\mathcal{E}(\mathbf{B}_\gamma)$ with $\gamma \neq \beta$, $V^{\mathcal{M}}_\varphi(\llbracket \mathbf{A}_\epsilon \rrbracket_\beta)$ is unspecified.

Let $\mathcal{M}$ be a model for CTT$_{qe}$. $\mathbf{A}_o$ is *valid* in $\mathcal{M}$, written $\mathcal{M} \models \mathbf{A}_o$, if $V^{\mathcal{M}}_\varphi(\mathbf{A}_o) = \text{T}$ for all assignments $\varphi \in \text{assign}(\mathcal{M})$.

Proposition 3.35. *Let* $\mathcal{M}$ *be a model for* CTT$_{qe}$, $\mathbf{A}_\epsilon$ *be a construction, and* $\varphi \in \text{assign}(\mathcal{M})$. *Then* $V^{\mathcal{M}}_\varphi(\mathbf{A}_\epsilon) = \mathbf{A}_\epsilon$.

Proof. Follows immediately from conditions 4–6 of the definition of an interpretation and condition 5 of the definition of a model. $\qquad\square$

Theorem 3.36 (Law of Quotation). $\ulcorner \mathbf{A}_\alpha \urcorner = \mathcal{E}(\mathbf{A}_\alpha)$ *is valid in every model of* CTT$_{qe}$.

Proof. Let $\mathcal{M}$ be a model of CTT$_{qe}$ and $\varphi \in \text{assign}(\mathcal{M})$. Then

$$V^{\mathcal{M}}_\varphi(\ulcorner \mathbf{A}_\alpha \urcorner) \tag{1}$$

$$= \mathcal{E}(\mathbf{A}_\alpha) \tag{2}$$

$$= V^{\mathcal{M}}_\varphi(\mathcal{E}(\mathbf{A}_\alpha)) \tag{3}$$

(2) follows from condition 5 of the definition of a model, and (3) follows from Proposition 3.35. Hence $V^{\mathcal{M}}_\varphi(\ulcorner \mathbf{A}_\alpha \urcorner) = V^{\mathcal{M}}_\varphi(\mathcal{E}(\mathbf{A}_\alpha))$ for all $\varphi \in \text{assign}(\mathcal{M})$ which implies $\ulcorner \mathbf{A}_\alpha \urcorner = \mathcal{E}(\mathbf{A}_\alpha)$ is valid in $\mathcal{M}$. $\qquad\square$

Theorem 3.37 (Law of Disquotation). $\llbracket \ulcorner \mathbf{A}_\alpha \urcorner \rrbracket_\alpha = \mathbf{A}_\alpha$ *is valid in every model of* CTT$_{qe}$.

Proof. Let $\mathcal{M}$ be a model of CTT_{qe} and $\varphi \in \mathsf{assign}(\mathcal{M})$. Then

$$\mathcal{V}_\varphi^{\mathcal{M}}(\llbracket \ulcorner \mathbf{A}_\alpha \urcorner \rrbracket_\alpha) \tag{4}$$

$$= \mathcal{V}_\varphi^{\mathcal{M}}(\mathcal{E}^{-1}(\mathcal{V}_\varphi^{\mathcal{M}}(\ulcorner \mathbf{A}_\alpha \urcorner))) \tag{5}$$

$$= \mathcal{V}_\varphi^{\mathcal{M}}(\mathcal{E}^{-1}(\mathcal{E}(\mathbf{A}_\alpha))) \tag{6}$$

$$= \mathcal{V}_\varphi^{\mathcal{M}}(\mathbf{A}_\alpha) \tag{7}$$

Since $V_\varphi^{\mathcal{M}}(\text{is-expr}_{\epsilon \to o}^\alpha \ulcorner \mathbf{A}_\alpha \urcorner) = \mathsf{T}$, (5) follows from condition 6 of the definition of a model. $\mathcal{V}_\varphi^{\mathcal{M}}(\ulcorner \mathbf{A}_\alpha \urcorner) = \mathcal{E}(\mathbf{A}_\alpha)$ by condition 5 of the definition of a model. (6) and (7) are then immediate. Hence $\mathcal{V}_\varphi^{\mathcal{M}}(\llbracket \ulcorner \mathbf{A}_\alpha \urcorner \rrbracket_\alpha) = \mathcal{V}_\varphi^{\mathcal{M}}(\mathbf{A}_\alpha)$ for all $\varphi \in \mathsf{assign}(\mathcal{M})$ which implies $\llbracket \ulcorner \mathbf{A}_\alpha \urcorner \rrbracket_\alpha = \mathbf{A}_\alpha$ is valid in $\mathcal{M}$. $\square$

Remark 3.38 (Evaluation Problem). Theorem 3.37 shows that disquotation holds universally in CTT_{qe} contrary to the Evaluation Problem described in the Introduction. We have avoided the Evaluation Problem in CTT_{qe} by admitting only quotations of eval-free expressions. If quotations of non-eval-free expressions were allowed in CTT_{qe}, the logic would be significantly more expressive, but also much more complicated, as seen in $\mathcal{Q}_0^{\mathrm{uqe}}$ [9].

Remark 3.39 (Quotation Restricted to Closed Expressions). If quotation is restricted to closed eval-free expressions in CTT_{qe}, then the Variable Problem and Double Substitution Problem disappear. However, most of the usefulness of having quotation and evaluation in CTT_{qe} would also disappear — which is illustrated by the examples in the next section.

4 Examples

We will present in this section four examples that illustrate the utility of the quotation and evaluation facility in CTT_{qe}.

4.1 Reasoning About Syntax

Reasoning about the syntax of expressions is normally performed in the metalogic, but in CTT_{qe} reasoning about the syntax of eval-free expressions can be performed in the logic itself. This is done by reasoning about constructions (which represent the syntax trees of eval-free expressions) using quotation and the machinery of constructions. Algorithms that manipulate eval-free expressions can be formalized as functions that manipulate constructions. The functions can be executed using beta-reduction, rewriting, and other kinds of simplification.

As an example, consider the constant make-implication$_{\epsilon \to \epsilon \to \epsilon}$ defined as

$$\lambda\, x_\epsilon \,.\, \lambda\, y_\epsilon \,.\, (\mathsf{app}_{\epsilon \to \epsilon \to \epsilon}\, (\mathsf{app}_{\epsilon \to \epsilon \to \epsilon}\, \ulcorner \supset_{o \to o \to o} \urcorner\, x_\epsilon)\, y_\epsilon).$$

It can be used to build constructions that represent implications. As another example, consider the constant is-app$_{\epsilon \to o}$ defined as

$$\lambda\, x_\epsilon \,.\, \exists\, y_\epsilon \,.\, \exists\, z_\epsilon \,.\, x_\epsilon = (\mathsf{app}_{\epsilon \to \epsilon \to \epsilon}\, y_\epsilon\, z_\epsilon).$$

It can be used to test whether a construction represents a function application.

Reasoning about syntax is a two-step process: First, a construction is built using quotation and the machinery of constructions, and second, the construction is employed using evaluation. Continuing the example above,

$$\text{make-implication}_{\epsilon \to \epsilon \to \epsilon} \ulcorner \mathbf{A}_o \urcorner \ulcorner \mathbf{B}_o \urcorner$$

builds a construction equivalent to the quotation $\ulcorner \mathbf{A}_o \supset \mathbf{B}_o \urcorner$ and

$$\llbracket \text{make-implication}_{\epsilon \to \epsilon \to \epsilon} \ulcorner \mathbf{A}_o \urcorner \ulcorner \mathbf{B}_o \urcorner \rrbracket_o$$

employs the construction as the implication $\mathbf{A}_o \supset \mathbf{B}_o$. Using this mixture of quotation and evaluation, it is possible to express the interplay of syntax and semantics that is needed to formalize syntax-based algorithms that are commonly used in mathematics [8]. See Sect. 4.4 for an example.

4.2 Quasiquotation

Quasiquotation is a parameterized form of quotation in which the parameters serve as holes in a quotation that are filled with expressions that denote syntactic values. It is a very powerful syntactic device for specifying expressions and defining macros. Quasiquotation was introduced by Willard Van Orman Quine in 1940 in the first version of his book *Mathematical Logic* [19]. It has been extensively employed in the Lisp family of programming languages [3].[4]

In CTT_{qe}, constructing a large quotation from smaller quotations can be tedious because it requires many applications of syntax constructors. Quasiquotation provides a convenient way to construct big quotations from little quotations. It can be defined straightforwardly in CTT_{qe}.

A *quasi-expression* of CTT_{qe} is defined inductively as follows:

1. $\lfloor \mathbf{A}_\epsilon \rfloor$ is a quasi-expression called an *antiquotation*.
2. $\mathbf{x}_\alpha$ is a quasi-expression.
3. $\mathbf{c}_\alpha$ is a quasi-expression.
4. If M and N are quasi-expressions, then $(M\, N)$, $(\lambda \mathbf{x}_\alpha \,.\, N)$, $(\lambda \lfloor \mathbf{A}_\epsilon \rfloor \,.\, N)$, and $\ulcorner M \urcorner$ are quasi-expressions.

A quasi-expression is thus an expression where one or more subexpressions have been replaced by antiquotations. For example, $\neg(\mathbf{A}_o \wedge \lfloor \mathbf{B}_\epsilon \rfloor)$ is a quasi-expression. Obviously, every expression is a quasi-expression.

Let $\mathcal{E}'$ be the function mapping quasi-expressions to expressions of type ϵ that is defined inductively as follows:

1. $\mathcal{E}'(\lfloor \mathbf{A}_\epsilon \rfloor) = \mathbf{A}_\epsilon$.
2. $\mathcal{E}'(\mathbf{x}_\alpha) = \ulcorner \mathbf{x}_\alpha \urcorner$.
3. $\mathcal{E}'(\mathbf{c}_\alpha) = \ulcorner \mathbf{c}_\alpha \urcorner$.

---

[4] In Lisp, the standard symbol for quasiquotation is the backquote (') symbol, and thus in Lisp, quasiquotation is usually called *backquote*.

4. $\mathcal{E}'(M\,N) = \mathsf{app}_{\epsilon\to\epsilon\to\epsilon}\,\mathcal{E}'(M)\,\mathcal{E}'(N)$.
5. $\mathcal{E}'(\lambda\,M\,.\,N) = \mathsf{abs}_{\epsilon\to\epsilon\to\epsilon}\,\mathcal{E}'(M)\,\mathcal{E}'(N)$.
6. $\mathcal{E}(\ulcorner M\urcorner) = \mathsf{quo}_{\epsilon\to\epsilon}\,\mathcal{E}'(M)$.

Notice that $\mathcal{E}'(M) = \mathcal{E}(M)$ when M is an expression. Continuing our example above, $\mathcal{E}'(\neg(\mathbf{A}_o \wedge \lfloor \mathbf{B}_\epsilon \rfloor)) =$

$$\mathsf{app}_{\epsilon\to\epsilon\to\epsilon}\,\ulcorner\neg_{o\to o}\urcorner(\mathsf{app}_{\epsilon\to\epsilon\to\epsilon}\,(\mathsf{app}_{\epsilon\to\epsilon\to\epsilon}\,\ulcorner\wedge_{o\to o\to o}\urcorner\mathcal{E}'(\mathbf{A}_o))\,\mathbf{B}_\epsilon).$$

A *quasiquotation* is an expression of the form $\ulcorner M\urcorner$ where M is a quasi-expression. Thus every quotation is a quasiquotation. The quasiquotation $\ulcorner M\urcorner$ serves as an alternate notation for the expression $\mathcal{E}'(M)$. So $\ulcorner\neg(\mathbf{A}_o \wedge \lfloor \mathbf{B}_\epsilon \rfloor)\urcorner$ stands for the significantly more verbose expression in the previous paragraph. It represents the syntax tree of a negated conjunction in which the part of the tree corresponding to the second conjunct is replaced by the syntax tree represented by $\mathbf{B}_\epsilon$. If $\mathbf{B}_\epsilon$ is a quotation $\ulcorner \mathbf{C}_o\urcorner$, then the quasiquotation $\ulcorner\neg(\mathbf{A}_o \wedge \lfloor \ulcorner \mathbf{C}_o\urcorner \rfloor)\urcorner$ is equivalent to the quotation $\ulcorner\neg(\mathbf{A}_o \wedge \mathbf{C}_o)\urcorner$.

4.3 Schemas

A *schema* is a metalogical expression containing syntactic variables. An instance of a schema is a logical expression obtained by replacing the syntactic variables with appropriate logical expressions. In $\mathrm{CTT}_{\mathrm{qe}}$, a schema can be formalized as a single logical expression.

For example, consider the *law of excluded middle (LEM)* that is expressed as the formula schema $A \vee \neg A$ where A is a syntactic variable ranging over all formulas. LEM can be formalized in $\mathrm{CTT}_{\mathrm{qe}}$ as the universal statement

$$\forall x_\epsilon \,.\, \mathsf{is\text{-}expr}^o_{\epsilon\to o}\,x_\epsilon \supset [\![x_\epsilon]\!]_o \vee \neg[\![x_\epsilon]\!]_o.$$

An instance of this formalization of LEM is any instance of the universal statement. Using quasiquotation, LEM could also be formalized in $\mathrm{CTT}_{\mathrm{qe}}$ as

$$\forall x_\epsilon \,.\, \mathsf{is\text{-}expr}^o_{\epsilon\to o}\,x_\epsilon \supset [\![\ulcorner\lfloor x_\epsilon\rfloor \vee \neg\lfloor x_\epsilon\rfloor\urcorner]\!]_o.$$

If we assume that the domain of the type ι is the natural numbers and $\mathcal{C}$ includes the usual constants of natural number arithmetic (including a constant $\mathsf{S}_{\iota\to\iota}$ representing the successor function), then the (first-order) *induction schema for Peano arithmetic* can be formalized in $\mathrm{CTT}_{\mathrm{qe}}$ as

$$\forall f_\epsilon \,.\, \mathsf{is\text{-}expr}^{\iota\to o}_{\epsilon\to o}\,f_\epsilon \supset$$
$$((\![f_\epsilon]\!]_{\iota\to o}\,0 \wedge (\forall x_\iota \,.\, [\![f_\epsilon]\!]_{\iota\to o}\,x_\iota \supset [\![f_\epsilon]\!]_{\iota\to o}\,(\mathsf{S}_{\iota\to\iota}\,x_\iota))) \supset \forall x_\iota \,.\, [\![f_\epsilon]\!]_{\iota\to o}\,x_\iota).$$

Hence it is possible to directly formalize first-order Peano arithmetic in $\mathrm{CTT}_{\mathrm{qe}}$.

Notice that there is no restriction on which formulas can be used to produce instances of this schema. If we want to restrict the formulas, e.g., to formalized the induction schema for Presburger arithmetic, we can do this by introducing a new family of constants $\mathsf{is\text{-}expr}^\alpha_{\epsilon\to(\epsilon\to o)\to o}$ such that $\mathsf{is\text{-}expr}^\alpha_{\epsilon\to(\epsilon\to o)\to o}\,\ulcorner\mathbf{A}_\alpha\urcorner\mathbf{B}_{\epsilon\to o}$ is true iff $\mathbf{B}_{\epsilon\to o}\,\ulcorner\mathbf{c}_\gamma\urcorner$ is true for each constant $\mathbf{c}_\gamma$ occurring in $\mathbf{A}_\alpha$. $\mathbf{B}_{\epsilon\to o}$ represents here a signature or language as a set of constants.

4.4 Meaning Formulas

Many symbolic algorithms work by manipulating mathematical expressions in a mathematically meaningful way. A *meaning formula* for such an algorithm is a statement that captures the mathematical relationship between the input and output expressions of the algorithm. For example, consider a symbolic differentiation algorithm that takes as input an expression (say x^2), repeatedly applies syntactic differentiation rules to the expression, and then returns as output the final expression ($2x$) that is produced. The intended meaning formula of this algorithm states that the function $(\lambda x : \mathbb{R} \, . \, 2x)$ represented by the output expression is the derivative of the function $(\lambda x : \mathbb{R} \, . \, x^2)$ represented by the input expression.

Meaning formulas are difficult to express in a traditional logic like first-order logic or simple type theory since there is no way to directly refer to the syntactic structure of the expressions in the logic [8]. However, meaning formulas can be easily expressed in $\mathrm{CTT_{qe}}$.

Consider the following example. Assume that the domain of the type ι is the real numbers and $\mathcal{C}$ includes the usual constants of real number arithmetic plus (1) is-poly$_{\epsilon \to o}$ such that is-poly$_{\epsilon \to o}\, \mathbf{A}_\epsilon = \mathsf{T}$ iff $\mathbf{A}_\epsilon$ represents a syntax tree of an expression of type ι that is a polynomial, (2) deriv$_{(\iota \to \iota) \to (\iota \to \iota)}$ such that deriv$_{(\iota \to \iota) \to (\iota \to \iota)}\, \mathbf{F}_{\iota \to \iota}$ is the derivative of the function $\mathbf{F}_{\iota \to \iota}$, and (3) poly-diff$_{\epsilon \to \epsilon \to \epsilon}$ such that, if is-poly$_{\epsilon \to o}\, \mathbf{A}_\epsilon$ holds, then poly-diff$_{\epsilon \to \epsilon \to \epsilon}\, \mathbf{A}_\epsilon \ulcorner \mathbf{x}_\iota \urcorner$ is the result of applying the usual differentiation rules for polynomials to $\mathbf{A}_\epsilon$ with respect to $\mathbf{x}_\iota$. Then the meaning formula for poly-diff$_{\epsilon \to \epsilon \to \epsilon}$ is[5]

$$\forall u_\epsilon \, . \, \forall v_\epsilon \, . \, (\text{is-var}_{\epsilon \to o}\, u_\epsilon \wedge \text{is-poly}_{\epsilon \to o}\, v_\epsilon) \supset$$
$$\text{deriv}_{(\iota \to \iota) \to (\iota \to \iota)}(\llbracket \text{abs}_{\epsilon \to \epsilon \to \epsilon}\, u_\epsilon\, v_\epsilon \rrbracket_{\iota \to \iota}) =$$
$$\llbracket \text{abs}_{\epsilon \to \epsilon \to \epsilon}\, u_\epsilon\, (\text{poly-diff}_{\epsilon \to \epsilon \to \epsilon}\, v_\epsilon\, u_\epsilon) \rrbracket_{\iota \to \iota}.$$

The string of equations

$$\text{deriv}_{(\iota \to \iota) \to (\iota \to \iota)}(\lambda x_\iota \, . \, x_\iota^2) \tag{8}$$

$$= \text{deriv}_{(\iota \to \iota) \to (\iota \to \iota)}(\llbracket \ulcorner \lambda x_\iota \, . \, x_\iota^2 \urcorner \rrbracket_{\iota \to \iota}) \tag{9}$$

$$= \text{deriv}_{(\iota \to \iota) \to (\iota \to \iota)}(\llbracket \text{abs}_{\epsilon \to \epsilon \to \epsilon} \ulcorner x_\iota \urcorner \ulcorner x_\iota^2 \urcorner \rrbracket_{\iota \to \iota}) \tag{10}$$

$$= \llbracket \text{abs}_{\epsilon \to \epsilon \to \epsilon} \ulcorner x_\iota \urcorner (\text{poly-diff}_{\epsilon \to \epsilon \to \epsilon} \ulcorner x_\iota^2 \urcorner \ulcorner x_\iota \urcorner) \rrbracket_{\iota \to \iota} \tag{11}$$

$$= \llbracket \text{abs}_{\epsilon \to \epsilon \to \epsilon} \ulcorner x_\iota \urcorner \ulcorner 2 * x_\iota \urcorner \rrbracket_{\iota \to \iota} \tag{12}$$

$$= \llbracket \ulcorner \lambda x_\iota \, . \, 2 * x_\iota \urcorner \rrbracket_{\iota \to \iota} \tag{13}$$

$$= \lambda x_\iota \, . \, 2 * x_\iota \tag{14}$$

proves (informally) the desired result where the equation given by (10) and (11) results from instantiating the meaning formula for poly-diff$_{\epsilon \to \epsilon \to \epsilon}$ with $\ulcorner x_\iota \urcorner$ and $\ulcorner x_\iota^2 \urcorner$.

---

[5] We restrict this example to polynomials since polynomial functions and their derivatives are always total. Thus issues of undefinedness do not arise in the formulation of the meaning formula for poly-diff$_{\epsilon \to \epsilon \to \epsilon}$.

5   A Sketch of a Simple Proof System

At first glance, it would appear that a proof system for $\mathrm{CTT_{qe}}$ could be straightforwardly developed by extending Andrews' proof system for $\mathcal{Q}_0$ [2, p. 213]. We can define is-var$_{\epsilon \to o}$ (and is-con$_{\epsilon \to o}$ in a similar way) by the axiom schemas is-var$_{\epsilon \to o}$ $\ulcorner \mathbf{x}_\alpha \urcorner$ and $\neg$is-var$_{\epsilon \to o}$ $\mathbf{A}_\epsilon$ where $\mathbf{A}_\epsilon$ is any construction that is not a quoted variable. We can recursively define is-expr$_{\epsilon \to o}^\alpha$ using a set of axiom schemas that say how expressions are constructed. We can specify that the type ϵ of constructions is an inductive type using a set of axioms that say (8) the constructions are distinct from each other and (9) induction holds for constructions. We can specify quotation using the Law of Quotation $\ulcorner \mathbf{A}_\alpha \urcorner = \mathcal{E}(\mathbf{A}_\alpha)$ (Theorem 3.36). And we can specify evaluation using the Law of Disquotation $\llbracket \ulcorner \mathbf{A}_\alpha \urcorner \rrbracket_\alpha = \mathbf{A}_\alpha$ (Theorem 3.37).

Andrews' proof system with these added axioms would enable simple theorems involving quotation and evaluation to be proved, but the proof system would not be able to substitute expressions for free variables occurring in the argument of an evaluation. Hence schemas and meaning formulas could be expressed in $\mathrm{CTT_{qe}}$, but they would be useless because they could not be instantiated. Clearly, a useful proof system for $\mathrm{CTT_{qe}}$ requires some form of substitution that is applicable to evaluations.

Due to the Variable Problem, substitution involving evaluations cannot be purely syntactic as in a traditional logic. It must be a semantics-dependent operation in which side conditions, like whether a variable is free in an expression, are proved within the proof system. Since $\mathrm{CTT_{qe}}$ supports reasoning about syntax, an obvious way forward is to add to $\mathcal{C}$ a logical constant sub$_{\epsilon \to \epsilon \to \epsilon \to \epsilon}$ such that, if $\mathbf{C}_\beta$ is the result of substituting $\mathbf{A}_\alpha$ for each free occurrence of $\mathbf{x}_\alpha$ in $\mathbf{B}_\beta$ without any variable captures, then

$$\widetilde{\mathrm{sub}}_{\epsilon \to \epsilon \to \epsilon \to \epsilon} \ulcorner \mathbf{A}_\alpha \urcorner \ulcorner \mathbf{x}_\alpha \urcorner \ulcorner \mathbf{B}_\beta \urcorner = \ulcorner \mathbf{C}_\beta \urcorner.$$

sub$_{\epsilon \to \epsilon \to \epsilon \to \epsilon}$ thus plays the role of an explicit substitution operator [1].

This approach, however, does not work in $\mathrm{CTT_{qe}}$ since $\mathbf{B}_\beta$ may contain evaluations, but quotations in $\mathrm{CTT_{qe}}$ may not contain evaluations. Although the approach does work in $\mathcal{Q}_0^{\mathrm{uqe}}$ [9] in which quotations in $\mathrm{CTT_{qe}}$ may contain evaluations, it is extremely complicated due to the Evaluation Problem.

A more promising approach is to add some axiom schemas to the five beta-reduction axiom schemas used by Andrews' in his proof system for $\mathcal{Q}_0$ [2, p. 213] that specify beta-reduction of an application of the form $(\lambda \mathbf{x}_\alpha . \llbracket \mathbf{B}_\epsilon \rrbracket_\beta) \mathbf{A}_\alpha$. But how do we overcome the Double Substitution Problem? There seems to be no easy way of emulating a double substitution with beta-reduction, so the best approach appears to be to consider only cases that do not require a second substitution, as formalized by the following axiom schema:

$$(\mathrm{is\text{-}expr}_{\epsilon \to o}^\beta ((\lambda \mathbf{x}_\alpha . \mathbf{B}_\epsilon) \mathbf{A}_\alpha) \wedge \neg(\mathrm{is\text{-}free\text{-}in}_{\epsilon \to \epsilon \to o} \ulcorner \mathbf{x}_\alpha \urcorner ((\lambda \mathbf{x}_\alpha . \mathbf{B}_\epsilon) \mathbf{A}_\alpha))) \supset$$
$$(\lambda \mathbf{x}_\alpha . \llbracket \mathbf{B}_\epsilon \rrbracket_\beta) \mathbf{A}_\alpha = \llbracket (\lambda \mathbf{x}_\alpha . \mathbf{B}_\epsilon) \mathbf{A}_\alpha \rrbracket_\beta.$$

Here is-free-in$_{\epsilon\to\epsilon\to o}$ would be a new logical constant in $\mathcal{C}$, and the second condition would say that $\mathbf{x}_\alpha$ is not free in the expression whose syntax tree is represented by $(\lambda \mathbf{x}_\alpha . \mathbf{B}_\epsilon) \mathbf{A}_\alpha$. As a result, there would be no free occurrences of $\mathbf{x}_\alpha$ in the right-hand side of the conclusion after the evaluation is eliminated. Details of this approach will be given in a future paper that presents the proof system for CTT$_{qe}$ that we have sketched.

6   Conclusion

Quotation and evaluation provide a basis for metaprogramming as seen in Lisp and other programming languages. We believe that these mechanisms can also provide a basis for metareasoning in traditional logics like first-order logic or simple type theory. However, incorporating quotation and evaluation into a traditional logic is much more challenging than incorporating them into a programming language due to the three problems we described in the Introduction.

In this paper we have introduced CTT$_{qe}$, a logic based on $\mathcal{Q}_0$ [2], Andrews' version of Church's type theory, that includes quotation and evaluation. We have presented the syntax and semantics of CTT$_{qe}$, sketched a proof system for it, and given examples that show the practical benefit of having quotation and evaluation in a logic.

CTT$_{qe}$ is a simpler version of $\mathcal{Q}_0^{uqe}$ [9], a richer, but more complicated, version of $\mathcal{Q}_0$ with undefinedness, quotation, and evaluation. In $\mathcal{Q}_0^{uqe}$, quotation may be applied to expressions containing evaluations, expressions may be undefined and functions may be partial, and substitution is implemented explicitly as a logical constant. Allowing quotation to be applied to all expressions makes $\mathcal{Q}_0^{uqe}$ much more expressive than CTT$_{qe}$ but also much more difficult to implement since substitution in the presence of evaluations is highly complex. We believe that CTT$_{qe}$ would not be hard to implement. Since it is a version of Church's type theory, it could be implemented by extending an implementation of HOL [11] such as HOL Light [14].

Our approach for incorporating quotation and evaluation into Church's type theory — introducing an inductive type of constructions, a quotation operator, and a typed evaluation operator — can be applied to other logics including many-sorted first-order logic. We have shown that developing the needed syntax and semantics is relatively straightforward, while developing a proof system for the logic is fraught with difficulties.

Acknowledgments. The author thanks the reviewers for their helpful comments and suggestions.

References

1. Abadi, M., Cardelli, L., Curien, P.-L., Lévy, J.-J.: Explicit substitution. J. Funct. Program. **1**, 375–416 (1991)
2. Andrews, P.B.: An Introduction to Mathematical Logic and Type Theory: To Truth through Proof, 2nd edn. Kluwer, Dordrecht (2002)
3. Bawden, A.: Quasiquotation in Lisp. In: Danvy, O. (ed.) Proceedings of the 1999 ACM SIGPLAN Symposium on Partial Evaluation and Semantics-Based Program Manipulation, pp. 4–12, 1999. Technical report BRICS-NS-99-1, University of Aarhus (1999)
4. Chlipala, A.: Certified Programming with Dependent Types: A Pragmatic Introduction to the Coq Proof Assistant. MIT Press, Cambridge (2013)
5. Church, A.: A formulation of the simple theory of types. J. Symb. Log. **5**, 56–68 (1940)
6. Costantini, S.: Meta-reasoning: a survey. In: Kakas, A.C., Sadri, F. (eds.) Computational Logic: Logic Programming and Beyond. LNCS (LNAI), vol. 2408, pp. 253–288. Springer, Heidelberg (2002)
7. Farmer, W.M.: Chiron: a set theory with types, undefinedness, quotation, and evaluation. Computing Research Repository, abs/1305.6206, 154 p. (2013)
8. Farmer, W.M.: The formalization of syntax-based mathematical algorithms using quotation and evaluation. In: Carette, J., Aspinall, D., Lange, C., Sojka, P., Windsteiger, W. (eds.) CICM 2013. LNCS, vol. 7961, pp. 35–50. Springer, Heidelberg (2013)
9. Farmer, W.M.: Simple type theory with undefinedness, quotation, and evaluation. Computing Research Repository, abs/1406.6706 (87 p.) (2014)
10. Gonthier, G., Mahboubi, A., Tassi, E.: A Small Scale Reflection Extension for the Coq system. Research Report RR-6455, Inria Saclay Ile de France (2015)
11. Gordon, M.J.C., Melham, T.F.: Introduction to HOL: A Theorem Proving Environment for Higher Order Logic. Cambridge University Press, Cambridge (1993)
12. Grundy, J., Melham, T., O'Leary, J.: A reflective functional language for hardware design and theorem proving. J. Funct. Program. **16**, 157–196 (2006)
13. Harrison, J.: Metatheory and reflection in theorem proving: a survey and critique. Technical report CRC-053, SRI Cambridge (1995). http://www.cl.cam.ac.uk/~jrh13/papers/reflect.ps.gz
14. Harrison, J.: HOL light: an overview. In: Berghofer, S., Nipkow, T., Urban, C., Wenzel, M. (eds.) TPHOLs 2009. LNCS, vol. 5674, pp. 60–66. Springer, Heidelberg (2009)
15. Henkin, L.: Completeness in the theory of types. J. Symb. Log. **15**, 81–91 (1950)
16. Norell, U.: Towards a practical programming language based on dependent type theory. PhD thesis, Chalmers University of Technology (2007)
17. Norell, U.: Dependently typed programming in Agda. In: Kennedy, A., Ahmed, A. (eds.) TLDI, pp. 1–2. ACM (2009)
18. Plataformatec. Elixir (2015). http://elixir-lang.org/
19. Quine, W.V.O.: Mathematical Logic. Harvard University Press, Cambridge (2003). Revised Edition
20. Rice University Programming Languages Team. Metaocaml: a compiled, type-safe, multi-stage programming language (2011). http://www.metaocaml.org/
21. Sheard, T., Jones, S.P.: Template meta-programming for Haskell. ACM SIGPLAN Not. **37**, 60–75 (2002)

22. Stump, A.: Directly reflective meta-programming. High. Order Symb. Comput. **22**, 115–144 (2009)
23. Taha, W., Sheard, T.: MetaML and multi-stage programming with explicit annotations. Theor. Comput. Sci. **248**, 211–242 (2000)
24. Tarski, A.: The concept of truth in formalized languages. In: Corcoran, J. (ed.) Logic, Semantics, Meta-Mathematics, 2nd edn., pp. 152–278. Hackett (1983)
25. The F# Software Foundation. F# (2015). http://fsharp.org/
26. van der Walt, P., Swierstra, W.: Engineering proof by reflection in Agda. In: Hinze, R. (ed.) IFL 2012. LNCS, vol. 8241, pp. 157–173. Springer, Heidelberg (2013)

Extracting Higher-Order Goals from the Mizar Mathematical Library

Chad E. Brown and Josef Urban$^{(\boxtimes)}$

Czech Technical University, Prague, Czech Republic
Josef.Urban@gmail.com

Abstract. Certain constructs allowed in Mizar articles cannot be represented in first-order logic but can be represented in higher-order logic. We describe a way to obtain higher-order theorem proving problems from Mizar articles that make use of these constructs. In particular, higher-order logic is used to represent schemes, a global choice construct and set level binders. The higher-order automated theorem provers Satallax and LEO-II have been run on collections of these problems and the results are discussed.

Keywords: Formalized mathematics · Set theory · Higher-order logic · Automated theorem proving

1 Introduction

The Mizar Problems for Theorem Proving (MPTP) system has been developed and used to extract first-order theorem proving problems from the Mizar Mathematical Library (MML) [14–16]. However, some aspects of the Mizar language cannot be directly represented in first-order. In particular, Mizar provides supports for *Schemes* (allowing some degree of quantification over predicates and functions), *Fraenkel terms* (allowing sets to be specified using term level binders such as $\{f(x)|x \in A, p(x)\}$) and a *global choice operator* the on types [6]. In order to obtain first-order problems, the MPTP has dealt with schemes used in a proof by exporting the first-order instances of the scheme used in the proof. Additionally, Fraenkel terms and global choice have been made first-order by a process of deanonymization [14].

We describe an extension of MPTP targeting higher-order logic. Schemes can be represented directly in higher-order logic since quantifiers over predicates and functions are allowed. Instead of giving the instances of schemes used in a proof, schemes are exported as second-order formulas (relying on the problem solver to find appropriate instances). Global choice can be represented by a selection operator on the type of individuals and a corresponding choice axiom. We also give a method for representing Fraenkel terms, though these are more challenging both to represent and to reason about.

J. Urban—This work was supported by ERC Consolidator grant nr. 649043 *AI4REASON*.

© Springer International Publishing Switzerland 2016
M. Kohlhase et al. (Eds.): CICM 2016, LNAI 9791, pp. 99–114, 2016.
DOI: 10.1007/978-3-319-42547-4_8

The resulting system has been used to extract a collection of higher-order theorem proving problems in THF0 format [9]. As in [14] we can partition the problem set into simple justifications (the Mizar **by** steps – or sometimes no explicit justification), scheme justifications (the Mizar **from** steps indicating application of a scheme) and theorems (including schemes proven in the MML). There are roughly 10192 scheme justifications throughout Mizar proofs in the MML, and we consider the higher-order problems corresponding to all of them. For simple justifications, we focus only on those involving global choice or Fraenkel terms and restrict ourselves to such steps in only four Mizar articles, giving 245 higher-order problems involving Fraenkel terms and 47 problems involving the global choice operator. For theorems, we focus only on 610 proven schemes whose proof in the MML requires a scheme justification. We describe some examples and results from running the higher-order automated theorem provers Satallax [3] and LEO-II [2] on some collections of these problems.

In Sect. 2 we give a short description of the syntax of higher-order logic. In Sect. 3 we define M-types, M-terms and M-propositions corresponding to an idealized version of the Mizar language. In Sect. 4 we describe the mapping of M-types, M-terms and M-propositions into higher-order terms, with a focus on the higher-order aspects. Section 5 describes experiments using Satallax and LEO-II on the resulting higher-order problems.

2   Syntax of Higher-Order Logic

We give a short introduction to the syntax of higher-order logic (in the form of Church's simple type theory [4]) so that we can describe the mapping in Sect. 4. In order to present higher-order problems to theorem provers, the THF0 format is used [9], but we mostly restrict ourselves to mathematical presentations of higher-order terms here.

There are two base types o (for propositions) and ι (for individuals, which will always be sets for us). The remaining types are function types $\alpha\beta$ where α and β are types. The type $\alpha\beta$ is the type of functions from α to β (and is sometimes written $\alpha \rightarrow \beta$).

We assume there are infinitely many variables x at each type α. We sometimes write the type as a subscript to make it clear, as in x_α. Likewise, there may be arbitrarily many constants c at each type α. We freely generate the set of typed terms as follows:

- A variable x of type α is a term of type α.
- A constant c of type α is a term of type α.
- If s is a term of type $\alpha\beta$ and t is a term of type α, then (st) is a term of type β.
- If x is a variable of type α and s is a term of type β, then $(\lambda x.s)$ is a term of type $\alpha\beta$.
- $\top$ is a term of type o.
- If s and t are terms of type α, then $(s =_\alpha t)$ is a term of type o.
- If s is a term of type o, then $(\neg s)$ is a term of type o.

- If s and t are terms of type o, then $(s \wedge t)$, $(s \vee t)$, $(s \to t)$ and $(s \leftrightarrow t)$ are terms of type o.
- If x is a variable of type α and s is a term of type o, then $(\forall x.s)$ and $(\exists x.s)$ are terms of type o.

Terms of type o are also called propositions.

We omit parentheses with the following conventions:

- Application associates to the left, e.g., stu means $((st)u)$.
- Binders have as large a scope as possible, e.g., both x are bound in $\forall x_o.x \vee \neg x$.
- The connectives $\to$, $\wedge$ and $\vee$ are considered right associative.
- The precedence of the binary and unary connectives are $=_\alpha$, $\neg$, $\wedge$, $\vee$, $\to$ and finally $\leftrightarrow$.

In addition, we omit the type subscript on $=$ when it is clear, and we write $s \neq t$ for $\neg(s = t)$. Likewise we may write several binders together, as in $\forall xyz_\alpha.s$ for $\forall x.\forall y.\forall z.s$ where x, y and z should all have type α.

3   Idealized Mizar

In order to describe the translation from Mizar to Higher-Order Logic we first give a short presentation of an idealized subset of the Mizar language. For a full presentation of the Mizar language, we direct the reader to [6].

To simplify the presentation, we assume that some variables and constants of higher-order logic are also variables and constants of Mizar, and that the translation will simply map variables and constants to themselves. The language of Mizar is restricted in a way that only variables and constants of certain types can be used:

- We call variables of type ι *object variables* and call constants of type ι *object constants*.
- For each $n \geq 1$, we call variables of simple type $\underbrace{\iota \ldots \iota\iota}_{n}$ *function variables (of arity n)*. Likewise, we call constants of this type *function constants (of arity n)*. We use F and G to range over function variables and f and g to range over function constants.
- For each $n \geq 0$, we call variables of simple type $\underbrace{\iota \ldots \iota o}_{n}$ *predicate variables (of arity n)*. Likewise, we call constants of this type *predicate constants (of arity n)*. We use P and Q to range over predicate variables and p and q to range over predicate constants.

Mizar quantifiers only bind object variables. Predicate variables and function variables only appear in schemes and are listed (with typing information) in the prefix of a scheme.

Mizar articles typically consist of definitions and theorems (some of which are schemes). A definition may be of an object constant, a function constant or a predicate constant. Predicate constants are sometimes defined as *modes* or *attributes*, which can then be used to construct Mizar types. Mizar types can be thought of as predicates over the universe of discourse. Mizar insists that types are nonempty and that all types, terms and propositions are well-typed (in Mizar's typing system).

In our idealized version of Mizar, we can ignore these restrictions and define more liberal sets of M-types, M-terms and M-propositions by mutual recursion. The intention is that Mizar types, terms and propositions (at least within the subset of Mizar considered in this article) will give M-types, M-terms and M-propositions, although not all M-types, M-terms and M-propositions would be accepted by Mizar.

M-types $A, B, \ldots$ are generated as follows:

- `set` is an M-type.
- If p is an $n + 1$-ary predicate constant and $T_1, \ldots T_n$ are M-terms, then $p(\cdot, T_1, \ldots, T_n)$ is an M-type. (Here p is playing the role of a Mizar *mode*.)
- If q is a unary predicate constant and A is an M-type, then $q\ A$ and `non` $q\ A$ are M-types. (Here q is playing the role of a Mizar *attribute*.)

M-terms $S, T, \ldots$ are generated as follows:

- An object variable x is an M-term.
- An object constant c is an M-term.
- If F is a function variable of arity n and $T_1, \ldots T_n$ are M-terms, then $F(T_1, \ldots, T_n)$ is an M-term.
- If f is a function constant of arity n and $T_1, \ldots T_n$ are M-terms, then $f(T_1, \ldots, T_n)$ is an M-term.
- If A is an M-type, then (`the` A) is an M-term. (The `the` is called a *global choice operator*.)
- If $x_1, \ldots, x_n$ are object variables, $A_1, \ldots, A_n$ are M-types, T is an M-term and Φ is an M-proposition, then $\{T$ `where` x_1 `is` $A_1, \ldots x_n$ `is` $A_n : \Phi\}$ is an M-term. (These are called *Fraenkel terms*.)

M-propositions $\Phi, \Psi, \ldots$ are generated as follows:

- If P is an n-ary predicate variable of arity n and $T_1, \ldots T_n$ are M-terms, then $P(T_1, \ldots, T_n)$ is an M-proposition.
- If p is an n-ary predicate constant of arity n and $T_1, \ldots T_n$ are M-terms, then $p(T_1, \ldots, T_n)$ is an M-proposition.
- If S and T are M-terms, then $(S = T)$ and $(S$ `in` $T)$ are M-propositions.
- If Φ is an M-proposition, then (`not` Φ) is an M-proposition.
- If Φ and Ψ are M-propositions, then $(\Phi$ `&` $\Psi)$, $(\Phi$ `or` $\Psi)$, $(\Phi$ `implies` $\Psi)$ and $(\Phi$ `iff` $\Psi)$ are M-propositions.
- If x is an object variable, A is an M-type and Φ is an M-proposition, then (`for` x `being` A `holds` Φ) and (`ex` x `being` A `st` Φ) are M-propositions.

Most Mizar theorems correspond to M-propositions. However, in some cases (namely, schemes) there are function variables or predicate variables which cannot be bound by quantifiers. We now define the notion of a prefix to list such variables. When translating to higher-order propositions, the prefix will determine the outermost quantifiers.

A variable declaration is one of the following:

- $x : A$ where x is an object variable and A is an M-type.
- $F(A_1, \ldots, A_n) : B$ where F is a function variable of arity n and $A_1, \ldots, A_n, B$ are M-types.
- $P[A_1, \ldots, A_n]$ where P is a predicate variable of arity n and $A_1, \ldots, A_n$ are M-types.

A prefix is a list of variable declarations.

An M-statement (Γ, Φ) is a prefix Γ and an M-proposition Φ. For Mizar theorems other than schemes, the prefix Γ will always be empty. Some Mizar schemes will declare what appears to be a function variable of arity 0. In such a case, we use object variables instead. (This is why object variable declarations are allowed in a prefix.)

An example of a scheme is Separation: for each set A and predicate P, there is a set X such that $x \in X$ iff $x \in A$ and $P(x)$ [5].

```
scheme Separation { A()-> set, P[set] } :
    ex X being set st for x being set holds x in X iff x in A() & P[x]
```

The M-statement in this case is (Γ, Φ) where Γ is the prefix A : set, $P[\text{set}]$ (declaring an object variable A of type set and a predicate variable P of arity 1) and Φ is the M-proposition

ex X being set st for x being set holds x in X iff x in A & $P(x)$

corresponding to the body of the scheme.

4   Mapping Mizar to Higher-Order Logic

We now describe a mapping from M-types, M-terms, M-propositions and M-statements to higher-order terms, concentrating on the aspects that require higher-order constructs. The base type ι will correspond to Mizar objects (sets). We will use $\ulcorner - \urcorner$ to denote the image of an M-type, M-term, M-proposition or M-statement as a term in higher-order logic under the translation. The intention is that mapping $\ulcorner - \urcorner$ should send M-statements corresponding to Mizar theorems to provable propositions in higher-order logic. To be precise about this would require giving details about the proof theory of Mizar, which is beyond the scope of this paper.

In order to specify the translation, we need to declare a family of constants the higher-order problems may make use of. A special relation in Mizar is set membership (in), translated as r2_hidden by the MPTP system. For this reason, we include a declared constant r2_hidden of type $\iota\iota o$ in the higher-order setting. For readability, we will write $s \in t$ for the term r2_hidden $s\ t$. (We will also write $s \notin t$ for $\neg(s \in t)$.) This allows us to translate an M-proposition S in T simply as $\ulcorner S \urcorner \in \ulcorner T \urcorner$. We also declare a constant ε of type $(\iota o)\iota$. This allows use to translate an M-term (**the** A) as $\varepsilon \ulcorner A \urcorner$. Finally, we need a family of constants for translating Fraenkel terms. For this purpose we declare a constant $\texttt{replSep}_n$ of type

$$(\iota o)(\iota\iota o) \cdots \underbrace{(\iota \cdots \iota o)}_{n}\underbrace{(\iota \cdots \iota\iota)}_{n}\underbrace{(\iota \cdots \iota o)}_{n}\iota$$

for each n. (In practice only a finite number of these can be declared in a single problem, and we declare them up to the maximum n required to translate the problem. When translating the MML the maximum required n was 6.) We can use $\texttt{replSep}_n$ to translate $\{T \text{ where } x_1 \text{ is } A_1, \ldots x_n \text{ is } A_n : \Phi\}$ as

$$\texttt{replSep}_n \ulcorner A_1 \urcorner (\lambda x_1. \ulcorner A_2 \urcorner) \cdots (\lambda x_1 \cdots x_{n-1}. \ulcorner A_n \urcorner)(\lambda x_1 \cdots x_n. \ulcorner T \urcorner)(\lambda x_1 \cdots x_n. \ulcorner \Phi \urcorner).$$

Before giving the translation, let us also remark on the intended semantics of these new constants. The constant ε is a choice operator so that εp satisfies p unless p is empty. The remaining constants are set theory related, and are required since the Mizar language targets set theory. In particular, the MML is based on Tarski-Grothendieck Set Theory (TG). For this reason, we take the intended interpretation of ι as a model of TG. The constant $\texttt{r2\_hidden}$ is intended to be membership on this model. The $\texttt{replSep}_n$ constants give ways to specify sets. For simplicity, we consider only the $n = 1$ case. A first approximation would be to think of $\texttt{replSep}_1 \ s \ (\lambda x.t) \ (\lambda x.u)$ as a set $\{t | x \in s, u\}$. However, s has type ιo, not type ι, so we should write $\{t | x : sx \wedge u\}$. In general, if s is a predicate that corresponds to a class instead of a set, $\{t | x : sx \wedge u\}$ will not be a set. Mizar avoids this problem by enforcing an extra condition when Fraenkel terms are used: all the types $A_1, \ldots, A_n$ must satisfy a "sethood" condition: that the collection of all elements of the type are contained in a bounding set. In the higher-order problems we define a corresponding constant $\texttt{sethood}$ of type $(\iota o)o$ as follows:

$$\lambda p_{\iota o}. \exists y_\iota. \forall x_\iota. px \to x \in y.$$

Then we can interpret $\texttt{replSep}_1 \ s \ (\lambda x.t) \ (\lambda x.u)$ to be $\{t | x : sx \wedge u\}$ if $\texttt{sethood} \ s$ holds and interpret $\texttt{replSep}_1 \ s \ (\lambda x.t) \ (\lambda x.u)$ to be the empty set otherwise. The new constants and corresponding axioms for the higher-order problems are given in Fig. 1. For each n there are two axioms for $\texttt{replSep}_n$: an introduction axiom $\texttt{replSepI}_n$ and an elimination axiom $\texttt{replSepE}_n$. The sethood conditions are only required for $\texttt{replSepI}_n$ since the intended interpretation of $\texttt{replSep}_n$ is the empty set when applied to an argument for which the sethood condition is violated. In practice, $\texttt{sethood}$ and $\texttt{replSep}_n$ (for $n \geq 1$) are only included if the problem contains a Fraenkel term.

Each M-type A will map to a term $\ulcorner A \urcorner$ of type ιo (a predicate or class), each M-term T will map to a term $\ulcorner T \urcorner$ of type ι (a set) and each M-proposition Φ will map to a term $\ulcorner \Phi \urcorner$ of type o (a proposition). Note that Mizar has dependent types and so an M-type A and the corresponding predicate $\ulcorner A \urcorner$ may contain free variables. The mapping is defined by recursion as given in Fig. 2. Note that while we take $\ulcorner x \urcorner = x$ and $\ulcorner c \urcorner = c$ in principle, variables and constants are

$$\varepsilon : (\iota o)\iota \qquad \textbf{epsax} : \forall p_{\iota o}.\forall x_\iota.px \rightarrow p(\varepsilon p) \qquad \textbf{r2\_hidden} : \iota\iota o$$

$$\textbf{sethood} : (\iota o)o := \lambda p_{\iota o}.\exists y_\iota.\forall x_\iota.px \rightarrow x \in y \qquad \textbf{replSep}_1 : (\iota o)(\iota\iota)(\iota o)\iota$$

$$\textbf{replSepI}_1 : \forall A_{\iota o}.\forall f_{\iota\iota}.\forall P_{\iota o}.\forall x_\iota.\textbf{sethood}\ A \rightarrow Ax \rightarrow Px \rightarrow fx \in \textbf{replSep}_1\ A\ f\ P$$

$$\textbf{replSepE}_1 : \forall A_{\iota o}.\forall f_{\iota\iota}.\forall P_{\iota o}.\forall y_\iota.y \in \textbf{replSep}_1\ A\ f\ P \rightarrow \exists x_\iota.Ax \wedge Px \wedge y = fx$$

$$\textbf{replSep}_2 : (\iota o)(\iota o)(\iota\iota\iota)(\iota o)\iota$$

$$\textbf{replSepI}_2 : \forall A_{\iota o}.\forall B_{\iota\iota o}\forall f_{\iota\iota\iota}.\forall P_{\iota\iota o}.\forall xy_\iota.\textbf{sethood}\ A \rightarrow (\forall x_\iota.Ax \rightarrow \textbf{sethood}\ (Bx)) \rightarrow$$

$$Ax \rightarrow Bxy \rightarrow Pxy \rightarrow fxy \in (\textbf{replSep}_2\ A\ B\ f\ P)$$

$$\cdots$$

$$\textbf{replSep}_n : (\iota o)(\iota\iota o)\cdots(\underbrace{\iota\cdots\iota o}_{n})(\underbrace{\iota\cdots\iota\iota}_{n})(\underbrace{\iota\cdots\iota o}_{n})\iota$$

$$\cdots$$

Fig. 1. Higher-order declarations

$$\ulcorner\textbf{set}\urcorner = \lambda x.\top \qquad \ulcorner p(\cdot, T_1, \ldots, T_n)\urcorner = \lambda x.p\ x\ \ulcorner T_1\urcorner \ldots \ulcorner T_n\urcorner^*$$

$$\ulcorner q\ A\urcorner = \lambda x.q\ x \wedge \ulcorner A\urcorner x^* \qquad \ulcorner \textbf{non}\ q\ A\urcorner = \lambda x.\neg q\ x \wedge \ulcorner A\urcorner x^* \qquad \ulcorner x\urcorner = x \qquad \ulcorner c\urcorner = c$$

$$\ulcorner F(T_1, \ldots, T_n)\urcorner = F\ \ulcorner T_1\urcorner \ldots \ulcorner T_n\urcorner \qquad \ulcorner f(T_1, \ldots, T_n)\urcorner = f\ \ulcorner T_1\urcorner \ldots \ulcorner T_n\urcorner$$

$$\ulcorner \textbf{the}\ A\urcorner = \varepsilon\ulcorner A\urcorner \qquad \ulcorner\{T\ \text{where}\ x_1\ \text{is}\ A_1, \ldots x_n\ \text{is}\ A_n : \varPhi\}\urcorner =$$

$$\textbf{replSep}_n\ \ulcorner A_1\urcorner\ (\lambda x_1.A_2)\cdots(\lambda x_1 \cdots x_{n-1}.\ulcorner A_n\urcorner)\ (\lambda x_1 \cdots x_n.\ulcorner T\urcorner)\ (\lambda x_1 \cdots x_n.\ulcorner\varPhi\urcorner)$$

$$\ulcorner P(T_1, \ldots, T_n)\urcorner = P\ \ulcorner T_1\urcorner \ldots \ulcorner T_n\urcorner \qquad \ulcorner p(T_1, \ldots, T_n)\urcorner = p\ \ulcorner T_1\urcorner \ldots \ulcorner T_n\urcorner$$

$$\ulcorner S = T\urcorner = \ulcorner S\urcorner =_\iota \ulcorner T\urcorner \qquad \ulcorner S\ \textbf{in}\ T\urcorner = \ulcorner S\urcorner \in \ulcorner T\urcorner \qquad \ulcorner \textbf{not}\ \varPhi\urcorner = \neg\ulcorner\varPhi\urcorner$$

$$\ulcorner\varPhi\ \&\ \varPsi\urcorner = \ulcorner\varPhi\urcorner \wedge \ulcorner\varPsi\urcorner \qquad \ulcorner\varPhi\ \textbf{or}\ \varPsi\urcorner = \ulcorner\varPhi\urcorner \vee \ulcorner\varPsi\urcorner \qquad \ulcorner\varPhi\ \textbf{implies}\ \varPsi\urcorner = \ulcorner\varPhi\urcorner \rightarrow \ulcorner\varPsi\urcorner$$

$$\ulcorner\varPhi\ \textbf{iff}\ \varPsi\urcorner = \ulcorner\varPhi\urcorner \leftrightarrow \ulcorner\varPsi\urcorner \qquad \ulcorner \textbf{for}\ x\ \textbf{being}\ A\ \textbf{holds}\ \varPhi\urcorner = \forall x.\ulcorner A\urcorner x \rightarrow \ulcorner\varPhi\urcorner$$

$$\ulcorner \textbf{ex}\ x\ \textbf{being}\ A\ \textbf{st}\ \varPhi\urcorner = \exists x.\ulcorner A\urcorner x \wedge \ulcorner\varPhi\urcorner$$

$$^*\ \text{where}\ x\ \text{is a fresh variable of type}\ \iota$$

Fig. 2. Definition of the translation

mapped to THF0 compliant names in practice. In order to map Mizar schemes we define $\ulcorner(\Gamma,\Phi)\urcorner$ for M-statements by a final recursion over the prefix Γ:

- $\ulcorner(\cdot,\Phi)\urcorner = \ulcorner\Phi\urcorner$.
- $\ulcorner((x:A,\Gamma),\Phi)\urcorner = \forall x.\ulcorner A\urcorner\, x \to \ulcorner(\Gamma,\Phi)\urcorner$.
- $\ulcorner((F(A_1,\ldots,A_n):B,\Gamma),\Phi)\urcorner = \forall F.(\forall x_1.\ulcorner A_1\urcorner\, x_1 \to \ldots \to \forall x_n.\ulcorner A_n\urcorner\, x_n \to \ulcorner B\urcorner\,(Fx_1\cdots x_n)) \to \ulcorner(\Gamma,\Phi)\urcorner$.
- $\ulcorner((P[A_1,\ldots,A_n],\Gamma),\Phi)\urcorner = \forall P.\ulcorner(\Gamma,\Phi)\urcorner$.

As a Mizar development is processed, new definitions are processed and the corresponding higher-order information must be declared in the problems which use this new information. We consider a few examples from early in the MML.

A simple example of a definition of an attribute is `empty` given in `xboole_0` [5]:

```
definition
  let X be set;
  attr X is empty means
  :Def1:
  not ex x being set st x in X;
end;
```

MPTP creates a name `v1_xboole_0` of type ιo. Note that simply due to its type, `v1_xboole_0` can be used as an attribute and mode to form M-types. It can also be used to form M-propositions. In the Mizar development, `empty` the proposition X `is empty` corresponds to the M-proposition `v1_xboole_0`(X) which translates to the higher-order proposition `v1_xboole_0` X. For particular problems, MPTP also exports relevant axioms about `v1_xboole_0`. For example, its definition translates to $\neg\exists x.\top \land x \in X$ (or, equivalently, $\neg\exists x.x \in X$).

The most common example of a mode used in this paper is `Element of` from the Mizar article `subset_1` [13]:

```
definition
  let X;
  mode Element of X means :Def1:
  it in X if X is non empty otherwise it is empty;
  ...
```

Since this is the first mode definition in the article, the corresponding name created by MPTP is `m1_subset_1`, declared to have type $\iota\iota o$. That is, `m1_subset_1` expects two arguments of type ι and yields a proposition. The Mizar type `Element of` X corresponds to the M-type `m1_subset_1`$(\cdot, X)$ which maps to the term $\lambda x_\iota.$`m1_subset_1` $x\, X$. Note that the dependent Mizar type `Element of` X maps to a term of type ιo with a free variable X (making the dependency explicit). For the sake of readability, we will write $s\hat{\in}t$ for `m1_subset_1` $s\ t$. Note that since Mizar requires all types to be nonempty, the `Element of` mode is defined so that $x\hat{\in}X$ if and only if either X is nonempty and $x \in X$ or both X and x are empty. That is, if X is nonempty, then $x\hat{\in}X$ if and only if $x \in X$, as expected. However, $x\hat{\in}\emptyset$ if and only if $x = \emptyset$, which may be surprising when it is first encountered.

Finally, we examine examples of schemes to see how M-statements are translated in practice.

The MML includes Fraenkel's Replacement axiom scheme as an axiom of TG. As formulated in Mizar, the scheme asserts that for each set A and each binary relation P on sets, if P is functional, then there is a set X such that $x \in X$ iff there is a $y \in A$ such that $P(y, x)$ [11]. In Mizar's syntax, the scheme is specified as follows:

```
scheme Fraenkel { A()-> set, P[set, set] }:
  ex X st for x holds x in X iff ex y st y in A() & P[y,x]
  provided for x,y,z st P[x,y] & P[x,z] holds y = z
```

This can be seen as an M-statement with prefix $A : \mathsf{set}, P[\mathsf{set}, \mathsf{set}]$ and an M-proposition corresponding to the body. The M-statement translates to the higher-order proposition

$$\forall A_\iota.\forall P_{\iota\iota o}.(\forall x y z_\iota.Pxy \wedge Pxz \rightarrow y = z) \rightarrow \exists X_\iota.\forall x_\iota.x \in X \leftrightarrow \exists y.y \in A \wedge Pyx.$$

An early application of the Fraenkel scheme is to prove Zermelo's Separation scheme discussed at the end of Sect. 3, where the corresponding M-statement is given. The M-statement translates to the following higher-order proposition:

$$\forall A_\iota.\forall P_{\iota o}.\exists X_\iota.\forall x_\iota.x \in X \leftrightarrow x \in A \wedge Px.$$

For each scheme proven in the MML, the MPTP system has generated a corresponding higher-order problem in THF0 format [9]. For example, the problem corresponding to the separation scheme is s1_xboole_0. In order to prove s1_xboole_0 automatically, a prover would need to synthesize the appropriate relation to use with Replacement, e.g., $\lambda x y_\iota.x = y \wedge Py$ where P is the predicate from Separation. At the moment, neither Satallax nor LEO-II can prove this automatically.

The Mizar proof begins by defining a predicate Q and then applying Replacement with Q.

```
  defpred Q[set,set] means $1 = $2 & P[$2];
A1: for x,y,z st Q[x,y] &Q[x,z] holds y = z;
  consider X such that
A2: for x holds x in X iff ex y st y in A() & Q[y,x]
                                   from TARSKI:sch 1(A1);
```

In λ-notation, the definition of Q is $\lambda x y_\iota.x = y \wedge Py$. Line A1 justifies $y = z$ whenever Qxy and Qxz. When schemes are used to justify Mizar proof steps, the keyword **from** is used. These are the steps we classify as *scheme justifications*. In this case, the Replacement scheme is used to justify the existence of a set X such that $x \in X$ iff $\exists y.y \in A \wedge Qyx$. A higher-order problem can be extracted from each such scheme justification. For this particular example, the conjecture to prove is $\exists X.\forall x.x \in X \leftrightarrow \exists y.y \in A \wedge y = x \wedge Px$. This follows from Replacement and A1, but requires instantiating the higher-order variable in the Replacement axiom with Q. Note that Q is not explicitly given in the problem, but can easily be recovered using pattern unification [7], as we now demonstrate. Suppose we replace the outermost quantifiers in the Replacement axiom with existential variables $\mathcal{A}$ of type ι and $\mathcal{R}$ of type $\iota\iota o$. The conclusion of the implication has the following form:

$$\exists X_\iota.\forall x_\iota.x \in X \leftrightarrow \exists y.y \in \mathcal{A} \wedge \mathcal{R}yx.$$

Since the subterm $\mathcal{R}yx$ is the higher-order existential variable $\mathcal{R}$ applied to distinct bound variables (y and x), we can use pattern unification (in this case pattern matching) to obtain solutions for $\mathcal{A}$ and $\mathcal{R}$. That is, when we match against

$$\exists X.\forall x.x \in X \leftrightarrow \exists y.y \in A \wedge y = x \wedge Px$$

we obtain the disagreement pairs $X, x, y | \mathcal{A} =^? A$ and $X, x, y | \mathcal{R}yx =^? y = x \wedge Px$ which has the unique (desired) solution: A for $\mathcal{A}$ and $\lambda yx.y = x \wedge Px$ for $\mathcal{R}$. Neither Satallax nor LEO-II re-prove this scheme justification within 5 min with the default strategy schedule. However, Satallax is able to prove the problem corresponding to this scheme justification under certain flag settings that encourage pattern unification.

5   Experiments

We now report on the results of running two higher-order automated theorem provers (Satallax and LEO-II) on some of the problems resulting from the translation described in the previous section. We consider four problem sets:[1]

- **SimpGC**: Simple justifications where the conclusion includes a global choice operator. From four Mizar articles [1,10,12,13] 47 problems were extracted.
- **SimpFr**: Simple justifications where the problem contains a Fraenkel term. We consider 245 such problems arising from three Mizar articles [1,10,12]. Since these proved to be surprisingly difficult, we also considered "pruned" versions of the problems in which the first-order theorem prover E [8] indicated which axioms it used to find a corresponding first-order proof.
- **SchJust**: For each scheme justifications (using `from`) in a Mizar proof in the MML, a corresponding problem was created. There are 10192 such problems.
- **SchPfs**: Out of 787 schemes proven in the MML, 610 have a proof making use of a scheme justification. For each of these 610 we have created a corresponding problem. Note that solving these problems requires finding a full proof, not justifying a single Mizar step in a proof. Hence these should be harder than the previous problem sets.

The results of running Satallax and LEO-II on the problem sets with the default settings and a time limit of 5 min are shown in Table 1. In addition, we note the

---

[1] The THF versions of the problems discussed here are available from http://147.32.69.25/~chad/mptp_thf.tgz.

estrogen. This last section will briefly outline methods for and challenges to testing the hypothesis that estrus and estrogen-mimicking compounds increase breast cancer risk by inducing macrophages to stiffen the extracellular matrix, which then feeds back to alter macrophage behavior. There are two ways of testing this hypothesis. First is the direct way of experimentally mimicking the effect of estrus-regulated, macrophage-dependent stiffening of the mammary gland microenvironment. The second and indirect way is to make verifiable predictions of altered breast biology in human populations that is consistent with the theoretical framework outlined by the hypothesis.

Experimental Approaches to Directly Testing the Hypothesis

A direct way of testing this hypothesis is to implant a gel substrate or actual human breast fragment into a mouse for an extended period of time, allowing many estrus cycles to occur, and then measuring the physical properties of the implant, the structural arrangement of the implant's matrix, and the degree of ROS production of macrophages associated with the implant. A number of materials are commonly used as gels that carry cells or molecules for implanting into mice (reviewed in (Frantz et al. 2010)), but since macrophages are known to promote the formation of and to digest collagen I, a major component of the mammary gland ECM, a collagen I gel would a good candidate substrate. It should be considered, however, that the type of collagen I used should be those that are extracted in a way that preserves their terminal ends, which contain the moieties required for crosslinking individual molecules into a fibril (Sabeh et al. 2009). Since reconstituted collagen gels do not fully replicate the in vivo ECM (Sabeh et al. 2009), intact explanted fragments from human reduction mammoplasties would be closer to the ideal model system. It is important to keep in mind that the human mammary gland has major structural differences compared to the mouse mammary gland. In humans, the ductal epithelia is surrounded by two thick layers of fibrous stroma, whereas the epithelia of mice only have a thin layer of fibroblasts that separate the ductal compartment from the adipose compartment. The scarring that results from the transplantation procedure may confound measures of stiffness in a xenografted tissue, so considerations should be taken to minimize this effect. But regardless of impeded physical measures, histological and immunohistological features can still be measured via the physical properties of fibrillar collagen and the use of antibodies that are specific to human collagen. Immunohistochemistry would be particularly useful in studying the arrangement of human collagen in human explants that were placed into the mouse mammary gland, since it is known that the prevalence of fibrillar collagen is associated with increased tissue stiffness. Xenografted human explants should be placed into the intact mammary glands of adult female mice, as opposed to mouse mammary glands in which the epithelial compartment has been previously removed. This is because the circuitry that recruits macrophages to the mammary gland during each estrus cycle involves complex feedback between multiple compartments (epithelial cells, fibroblasts, adipocytes, etc.). Human mammary fragments would have to be implanted into the mammary glands of immunocompromised mice

(Sheffield and Welsch 1988), which have intact mammary glands (Militzer and Schwalenstocker 1996). The length of time and window of time for implantation should also be considered. As female mice mature and then age, their menstrual cycles begin to slow down (Nelson et al. 1982). The varied aspects of the estrus cycle are likely dependent on the genetic background of the mouse strain.

Another method of testing this hypothesis is to measure physical forces, ECM structure, and macrophage phenotype in intact mammary glands of groups of mice that have different estrus rates. Mice that have a shorter cycle length would naturally have more cycles within their lifetime than those that have longer cycles. A genetically engineered BRCA1 mutant mouse model has been reported to exhibit shortened estrus cycles (Hong et al. 2010). Other BRCA1 mutant models may exhibit the same ovarian effect. It is possible to remove the endogenous ovaries of a mouse and then replace them with the over-active ovaries of a syngeneic donor. This approach would allow the endogenous mammary glands to be controlled by a highly active donor ovary.

Indirectly Testing the Hypothesis by Making Verifiable Predictions

The Effect of Aging

The hypothesis and theory—depending on how one uses the idea—developed in this chapter can be indirectly tested by making predictions in human populations. Regarding this estrus-regulated, macrophage-dependent ECM stiffening theory of risk from lifelong estrogen exposure, one of the most straightforward questions to ask is whether the breasts of older women are denser with ECM compared to those in younger women. Women with denser breasts have four to six times the risk of breast cancer than those with less dense breasts (Bertrand et al. 2013; Boyd et al. 2007; Byng et al. 1998; Pinsky and Helvie 2010). A study by Checka and colleagues (2012) analyzed the mammograms of 7007 women and showed that in general breast density decreases as women age, and that density was highest in women who were pre-menopausal (the average age of menopause is generally considered to be 50). 81 % of women less than 40 years-old had dense breasts, while 74 % of women between 40 and 49 years had dense breasts. The percentage drops to 57 % for those between 50 and 59, then to 44 % for those between 60 and 69, then to 36 % for those between 70 and 79, and finally rising to 41 % for those above 80 years. These data are consistent with the hypothesis that the more menstrual cycles a women undergoes, the more dense her breast tissue will be.

It should be noted that the Checka study examined the percentage of women characterized as having dense breasts across continuous age groups, but does not examine the increase in breast density within individual women across their lifetimes. This study did not address whether certain groups of women develop dense breasts early in life and then maintain that level of density up to and beyond number of problems both provers solved. For the remainder of the section, we discuss the results and describe some concrete examples.

One of the first uses of the global choice operator in Mizar is to define a (first-order) choice operator on sets called choose [13].

```
definition
  let S be set;
  func choose S -> Element of S equals
  the Element of S;
  correctness;
end;
```

Table 1. Results on problem sets with 5 min time limit

	Total problems	Satallax	LEO-II	Either
SimpGC	47	24 (51 %)	28 (60 %)	30 (64 %)
SimpFr	245	126 (52 %)	88 (36 %)	165 (67 %)
SimpFr pruned	245	159 (65 %)	155 (63 %)	192 (78 %)
SchJust	10192	5608 (55 %)	1524 (15 %)	6072 (60 %)
SchPfs	610	31 (5 %)	67 (11 %)	81 (13 %)

Note that no proof is given for correctness, as Mizar recognizes that the Element of S has type Element of S. Let us consider the corresponding higher-order simple justification problem. The higher-order problem would include the declaration of ε from Fig. 1. In addition, the fact that types of the form Element of A are nonempty is given: $\forall A_\iota.\exists B_\iota.B\hat{\in}A$. The conjecture to justify is

$$\varepsilon(\lambda A_\iota.A\hat{\in}c)\hat{\in}c$$

for a fixed c. This, of course, follows immediately from the two axioms and both Satallax and LEO-II can easily re-prove this simple justification.

Note that simply because a simple justification has a conclusion with a global choice operator does not mean that the choice axiom plays a role in the justification. Indeed, for the two examples from the problem set **SimpGC** Satallax proves but LEO-II does not, the proofs Satallax finds do not use the axiom about ε. Furthermore, upon inspection it became clear that some problems neither prover could solve also do not require the axiom about ε. Consider the following fragment of a Mizar proof about group theory [12].

```
    set a = the Element of G;
    ...
    consider b such that
A4: H * a = {b} by A1;
    h * a in H * a by A3,Th104;
    then
A5: h * a = b by A4,TARSKI:def 1;
```

The final justification is essentially the definition of singleton. The only reason the corresponding higher-order problem falls into class **SimpGC** is because a is $\varepsilon(\lambda x.x \hat{\in} (c\ G))$ (where c is a function taking a group to its carrier set, left implicit in the Mizar text). The fact that neither Satallax nor LEO-II could solve this problem was due to the fact that there are too many extra (unnecessary) axioms given in the generated problem. After pruning away the unnecessary axioms (with the help of E prover on a corresponding first-order problem), both Satallax and LEO-II can prove the pruned problem. LEO-II proves the pruned problem within 8 s and Satallax proves the pruned problem in less than a second.

We now turn to the problem set **SimpFr**: simple justifications involving at least one Fraenkel term, either in the conclusion or in one of the assumptions MPTP included in the problem. There were 640 such examples in the four Mizar articles we considered, but with experimentation it became clear that often the Fraenkel term was in an assumption that was unnecessary for the proof. In order to obtain a reasonable problem set, we used E on corresponding first-order problems to obtain pruned versions of the 640 problems. (In cases where E could not find the proof, we omitted the problem.) After pruning, there were 245 problems that still included a Fraenkel term. On each of these 245 problems, we ran Satallax and LEO-II on both the original and pruned problems. On the original versions, only 20 % of the problems could be solved by both provers, whereas on the pruned versions, 50 % could be solved by both provers. This suggests that better relevance filtering would be one of the most important potential improvements.

We briefly examine two small examples involving Fraenkel terms. Consider the following proof fragment from [10].

```
assume a in { x1 : x1 in A1 & not x1 in B1 or not x1 in A1 & x1 in B1 };
then ex x1 st a = x1 &
                (x1 in A1 & not x1 in B1 or not x1 in A1 & x1 in B1);
```

In the context of this fragment, x1 ranges over elements of a nonempty set X1. Mizar is able to verify the correctness of the last line from the first line without any explicit references as this is simply the property of membership in a Fraenkel term. In the corresponding higher-order problem, the elimination principle `replSepE`$_1$ is required for the justification. Satallax can prove the corresponding problem in less than a second. The first mode in the default strategy schedule that finds the proof is one making use of pattern unification. In particular, after replacing the outermost quantifiers of `replSepE`$_1$ with existential variables $\mathcal{A}$, $\mathcal{F}$, $\mathcal{P}$ and $\mathcal{Y}$, the proposition has the form:

$$\mathcal{Y} \in \texttt{replSep}_1\ \mathcal{A}\ \mathcal{F}\ \mathcal{P} \rightarrow \exists x_\iota . \mathcal{A}x \wedge \mathcal{P}x \wedge \mathcal{Y} = \mathcal{F}x.$$

All the occurrences of the existential variables are pattern occurrences, and so pattern matching can be used to find the appropriate instances. In particular, one axiom of the problem is

$$a \in \texttt{replSep}_1\ (\lambda x_\iota . x \hat{\in} X)\ (\lambda x_\iota . x)\ (\lambda x_\iota . x \in A \wedge x \notin B \vee x \notin A \wedge x \in B).$$

When the antecedent of the implication above is matched against this axiom, the following instantiations result:

- $\mathcal{Y} := a$
- $\mathcal{A} := \lambda x_\iota . x \hat{\in} X$
- $\mathcal{F} := \lambda x_\iota . x$
- $\mathcal{P} := \lambda x_\iota . x \in A \wedge x \notin B \vee x \notin A \wedge x \in B$

Given these instantiations, the solution is immediate. Satallax can prove both the pruned and unpruned version of this example in less than a second. LEO-II timed out after five minutes on both versions.

We consider a simple justification requiring the $\mathtt{replSepI}_1$. Consider the following proof fragment from [10]:

```
A2: a = x1 and
A3: P[x1];
  Q[x1] by A1,A3;
  hence thesis by A2;
```

where the thesis in the last step is

```
a in { z1 where z1 is Element of X1: Q[z1] }
```

As in the previous example, x1 ranges over elements of a nonempty set X1. In the higher-order problem corresponding to the final simple justification (by A2), the conjecture has the form $a \in \mathtt{replSep}_1 \ (\lambda x_\iota . x \hat{\in} X) \ (\lambda x_\iota . x) \ (\lambda x_\iota . Qx)$. In addition $\mathtt{replSepI}_1$, the axioms needed for the proof are $x_1 \hat{\in} X$ (using the type of x1 in the Mizar article), $a = x_1$ (from A2 in the proof fragment above), $Q x_1$ (from the previous step in the proof fragment above) and the extra axiom $\forall X_\iota . \mathtt{sethood} \ (\lambda x_\iota . x \hat{\in} X)$. Satallax requires roughly 6 s before reaching a mode in the default strategy schedule that can solve this problem. The successful mode requires less than a second to find the proof. Again, the mode makes use of pattern unification to find the proper instantiations. LEO-II can also find the proof in this example, and takes just under 6 s.

Lastly we turn to scheme justifications (**SchJust**) and full proofs of schemes (**SchPfs**). In Sect. 4 we have already discussed an example of a scheme that cannot be automatically proven (Separation from Replacement) by either prover. In addition we saw that neither prover could even re-prove the relevant scheme justification in the Mizar proof of Separation from Replacement within 5 min using the default settings.

Satallax performed significantly better than LEO-II on scheme justifications, while LEO-II performed significantly better than Satallax on proofs of full schemes. We consider one example of a scheme justification that Satallax solved but LEO-II did not. We then consider an example of a full scheme that LEO-II solved but Satallax did not.

The set operation $X \setminus Y$ is defined in an early Mizar article [5], and the following required existence proof is given:

```
defpred P[set] means not $1 in Y;
thus ex Z being set st for x holds x in Z iff x in X &P[x]
                                                    from Separation;
```

Note that the scheme justification makes use of the Separation scheme using the set X and the predicate $\lambda x.x \notin Y$. Again, the higher-order instantiation $\lambda x.x \notin Y$ can be determined using pattern matching, and Satallax can re-prove this in a fraction of a second using such a mode. With the default strategy schedule, Satallax tries such a mode and solves the problem in 37 s. LEO-II times out after 5 min.

A scheme LEO-II can fully prove but Satallax cannot is the following Mizar scheme [13]:

```
scheme SubsetEx { A() -> non empty set, P[set] } :
   ex B being Subset of A() st
   for x being Element of A() holds x in B iff P[x]
```

This is again a form of Separation and is proven using the Separation scheme already considered. The primary difference between the schemes is that the new scheme SubsetEx asserts that the set has type Subset of A (notation for Element of $\wp A$) and restricts the inner universal quantifier to Element of A. In the corresponding higher-order problem, we must prove the formula

$$\exists B.B \hat{\in} \wp A \wedge \forall x.x \hat{\in} A \rightarrow (x \in B \leftrightarrow Px)$$

from the higher-order formula

$$\forall Q_\iota \forall X_\iota.\exists B.\forall x.x \in B \leftrightarrow x \in X \wedge Qx.$$

The solution is simple: instantiate the assumption with the $Q := P$ and $X := A$ giving an appropriate witness B for the conjecture. Some minor first-order reasoning completes the proof. LEO-II can find the proof by doing some clause normalization and calling E. It is E that does the "higher-order" instantiation of P for Q and completes the proof. This is possible since the higher-order problem, after being encoded into first-order, is still provable. (In particular, the proof does not require β-reductions.) Satallax, on the other hand, does not solve the problem and times out after 5 min. The minor structural differences between the assumption and conclusion prevents pattern matching from suggesting the instantiation P for Q. While P is among the possible instantiations considered for Q, other possible instantiations are considered as well. The combination of multiple possible instantiations and required first-order reasoning makes the problem out of reach for the current version of Satallax.

6   Conclusion

We have described an extension of MPTP that creates higher-order theorem proving problems from the MML. The resulting problems seem to present challenges for higher-order theorem provers. For example, even some of the easiest problems become difficult if there are too many axioms, so better relevance filtering is necessary. Even simple reasoning about Fraenkel terms seems to be more difficult than one would expect, and so these examples may provide insights into improvements that can be made to automated provers.

There are multiple possibilities for the translation of Fraenkel terms that bind more than one set variable. We have implemented one way and suggested another. Further experimentation will likely be helpful for determining a good way to handle these cases.

The problems generated from scheme justifications and full proofs of schemes turned out to show the different strengths and weaknesses of Satallax and LEO-II. Hopefully such problem sets will lead to improvements in higher-order automated theorem provers. Given enough improvement on such problems, perhaps higher-order automated provers could provide help to Mizar authors who make use of the features of Mizar that go beyond first-order. In order to serve this purpose, care would have to be taken that the automated provers do not search for proofs that go beyond Mizar's logic (e.g., make use of higher-order quantifiers within instantiations). We leave such concerns to future work.

References

1. Bancerek, G.: On the characteristic and weight of a topological space. Formalized Math. **13**(1), 163–169 (2005)
2. Benzmüller, C., Paulson, L.C., Sultana, N., Theiß, F.: The higher-order prover LEO-II. J. Autom. Reasoning **55**(4), 389–404 (2015)
3. Brown, C.E.: Reducing higher-order theorem proving to a sequence of SAT problems. J. Autom. Reasoning **51**(1), 57–77 (2013)
4. Church, A.: A formulation of the simple theory of types. J. Symbol. Logic **5**, 56–68 (1940)
5. Committee, L.: Boolean properties of sets – definitions, April 2002. http://mizar. org/JFM/EMM/xboole_0.html
6. Grabowski, A., Kornilowicz, A., Naumowicz, A.: Mizar in a nutshell. J. Formalized Reasoning **3**(2), 153–245 (2010)
7. Miller, D., Nadathur, G.: A logic programming approach to manipulating formulas and programs. In: IEEE Symposium on Logic Programming. Salt Lake City (1987)
8. Schulz, S.: E - A Brainiac theorem prover. J. AI Commun. **15**(2/3), 111–126 (2002)
9. Sutcliffe, G., Benzmüller, C.: Automated reasoning in higher-order logic using the TPTP THF infrastructure. J. Formalized Reasoning **3**(1), 1–27 (2010)
10. Trybulec, A.: Domains and their Cartesian products. Formalized Math. **1**(1), 115–122 (1990)
11. Trybulec, A.: Tarski Grothendieck set theory. Formalized Math. **1**(1), 9–11 (1990)
12. Trybulec, W.A.: Subgroup and cosets of subgroups. Formalized Math. **1**(5), 855–864 (1990)

13. Trybulec, Z.: Properties of subsets. Formalized Math. **1**(1), 67–71 (1990)
14. Urban, J.: MPTP 0.2: design, implementation, and initial experiments. J. Autom. Reasoning **37**(1–2), 21–43 (2006)
15. Urban, J.: Translating Mizar for first order theorem provers. In: Asperti, A., Buchberger, B., Davenport, J.H. (eds.) MKM 2003. LNCS, vol. 2594, pp. 203–215. Springer, Heidelberg (2003). doi:10.1007/3-540-36469-2_16
16. Urban, J.: MPTP - motivation, implementation, first experiments. J. Autom. Reasoning **33**(3), 319–339 (2005). http://dx.org/10.1007/s10817-004-6245-1

Surveys and Projects

Interoperability in the OpenDreamKit Project: The Math-in-the-Middle Approach

Paul-Olivier Dehaye[1](✉), Mihnea Iancu[2], Michael Kohlhase[2],
Alexander Konovalov[3], Samuel Lelièvre[4], Dennis Müller[2], Markus Pfeiffer[3],
Florian Rabe[2], Nicolas M. Thiéry[4], and Tom Wiesing[2]

[1] University of Zürich, Zürich, Switzerland
`paul-olivier.dehaye@math.uzh.ch`
[2] Jacobs University, Bremen, Germany
[3] University of St Andrews, St Andrews, Scotland
[4] Université Paris-Sud, Orsay, France

Abstract. OPENDREAMKIT – "Open Digital Research Environment Toolkit for the Advancement of Mathematics" – is an H2020 EU Research Infrastructure project that aims at supporting, over the period 2015–2019, the ecosystem of open-source mathematical software systems. OPENDREAMKIT will deliver a flexible toolkit enabling research groups to set up Virtual Research Environments, customised to meet the varied needs of research projects in pure mathematics and applications.

An important step in the OPENDREAMKIT endeavor is to foster the interoperability between a variety of systems, ranging from computer algebra systems over mathematical databases to front-ends. This is the mission of the integration work package. We report on experiments and future plans with the *Math-in-the-Middle* approach. This architecture consists of a central mathematical ontology that documents the domain and fixes a joint vocabulary, or even a language, going beyond existing systems such as OpenMath, combined with specifications of the functionalities of the various systems. Interaction between systems can then be enriched by pivoting around this architecture.

1 Introduction

From their earliest days, computers have been used in pure mathematics to make tables, prove theorems (famously the four colour theorem) or, as with the astronomer's telescope, to explore new theories. Computer-aided experiments, and the use of databases relying on computer calculations such as the Small Groups Library in GAP, the Modular Atlas in group and representation theory, or the *L*-functions and Modular Forms Database (LMFDB, see later), are part of the standard toolbox of the pure mathematician. Certain areas of mathematics completely depend on these libraries. Computers are also increasingly used to support collaborative work and education.

In the last decades we witnessed the emergence of a wide ecosystem of open-source tools to support research in pure mathematics. This ranges from specialized to general purpose computational tools such as GAP, PARI/GP, LinBox,

© Springer International Publishing Switzerland 2016
M. Kohlhase et al. (Eds.): CICM 2016, LNAI 9791, pp. 117–131, 2016.
DOI: 10.1007/978-3-319-42547-4_9

MPIR, SAGE, or SINGULAR, via online databases like the LMFDB or online services like Wikipedia, ARXIV, to webpages like MathOverflow. A great opportunity is the rapid emergence of key technologies, in particular the JUPYTER (previously IPYTHON) platform for interactive and exploratory computing which targets all areas of science.

This has proven the viability and power of collaborative open-source development models, by users and for users, even for delivering general purpose systems targeting large audiences such as researchers, teachers, engineers, amateurs, and others. Yet some critical long term investments, in particular on the technical side, are in order to boost the productivity and lower the entry barrier:

- Streamlining access, distribution, portability on a wide range of platforms, including High Performance Computers or cloud services.
- Improving user interfaces, in particular in the promising area of collaborative workspaces as those provided by SAGEMATHCLOUD.
- Lowering barriers between research communities and promoting dissemination. For example make it easy for a specialist of scientific computing to use tools from pure mathematics, and vice versa.
- Bringing together the developer communities to promote tighter collaboration and symbiosis, accelerate joint development, and share best practices.
- Structure the development to outsource as much of it as possible to larger communities, and focus manpower on core specialities: the implementation of mathematical algorithms and databases.
- And last but not least: Promoting collaborations at all scales to further improve the productivity of researchers in pure mathematics and applications.

OPENDREAMKIT – "Open Digital Research Environment Toolkit for the Advancement of Mathematics" [ODK] – is a project funded under the European H2020 Infrastructure call [EI] on *Virtual Research Environments*, to work on many of these problems.

In Sect. 2, we will introduce the OPENDREAMKIT project to establish the context for the "Math-in-the-Middle" (MitM) integration approach described in Sect. 3. The remaining sections then elucidate the approach by presenting first experiments and refinements of the chosen integration paradigm: Sect. 4 details how existing knowledge representation and data structures can be represented as MitM interface theories with a case study of equipping the LMFDB with a MitM-based programming interface. Section 5 discusses system integration between GAP and SAGE and how this can be routed through a MitM ontology. Section 6 concludes the paper and discusses future work.

2   The OPENDREAMKIT Project (2015–2019)

The OPENDREAMKIT project runs for four years, starting in September 2015, and involves about 50 people spread over 15 sites in Europe, with a total budget of 7.6 million euros. The largest portion of that is devoted to employing an average of 11 researchers and developers working full time on the project, while the other participants contribute the equivalent of six people working full time.

OPENDREAMKIT's goal is to develop *Virtual Research Environments* (VRE), that is online services enabling groups of researchers, typically spread across many countries, to work collaboratively on a per project basis. Rather than constructing a large monolithic VRE, we have designed our proposal around the long-term investments listed in the previous section, working on the large scale yet modular integration of mathematical software. Our goal is a modular, interoperable, and customisable VRE toolkit built out of relatively modest components, interfaced through our approach to work on the grease to make this work. According to the funding scheme, the project addresses, besides its technical goals, aspects such as outreach, dissemination, or tools to support teaching.

An innovative aspect of the OPENDREAMKIT project is that its preparation and management happens, as much as is practical and without infringing on privacy, in the open. For example, most documents, including the proposal itself, are version controlled on public repositories and progress on tasks and deliverables is tracked using public issues (see [ODK]). This has proven a strong feature to collaborate tightly with the community and get early feedback.

In practice, OPENDREAMKIT's work plan consists of several work packages: component architecture (modularity, packaging, distribution, deployment), user interfaces (JUPYTER interactive notebook interfaces, 3D visualization, documentation tools), high performance mathematical computing (especially on multi-core/parallel architectures), a study of social aspects of collaborative software development, and a package on data/knowledge/software-bases.

The latter package focuses on the identification and extension of ontologies and standards to facilitate safe and efficient storage, reuse, interoperation and sharing of rich mathematical data, whilst taking provenance and citability into account. Its outcome will be a component architecture for semantically sound data archival and sharing, and integrate computational software and databases. The aim is to enable researchers to seamlessly manipulate mathematical objects across computational engines (e.g. switch algorithm implementations from one computer algebra system to another), front end interaction modes (database queries, notebooks, web, etc.) and even backends (e.g. distributed vs. local).

In this paper, we discuss the general approach chosen to develop this semantically aware component architecture.

3   Integrating Mathematical Software Systems via the Math-in-the-Middle Approach

As discussed before, we aim to make our components interoperable at a mathematical level. In particular, we have to establish a common meaning space that will allow us to share computation, visualization of the mathematical concepts, objects, and models between the respective systems. This mediation problem is well understood in information systems [Wie92], and has for instance been applied to natural language translation via a hub language [KW03]. Here, our hub is mathematics itself, and the vocabulary (or even language) admits further formalisation that translates into direct gains in interoperability. For this reason, neither OpenMath [Bus+04] nor MathML [Aus+03] have the practical expressivity needed for our intended applications.

3.1   A Common Meaning Space for Interoperability

One problem is that the software systems in OPENDREAMKIT cover different mathematical concepts, and if there are overlaps, their models for them differ, and the implementing objects have different functionalities. This starts with simple naming issues (*e.g.* elliptic curves are named ec in the LMFDB, and as EllipticCurve in SAGE), persists through the underlying data structures and in differing representations in the various tables of the LMFDB, and becomes virulent at the level of algorithms, their parameters, and domains of applicability.

To obtain a common meaning space for a VRE, we have the three well-known approaches in Fig. 1.

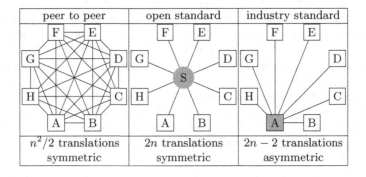

peer to peer	open standard	industry standard
$n^2/2$ translations symmetric	$2n$ translations symmetric	$2n - 2$ translations asymmetric

Fig. 1. Approaches for many-systems interoperability

The first does not scale to a project with about a dozen systems, for the third there is no obvious contender in the OPENDREAMKIT ecosystem. Fortunately, we already have a "standard" for expressing the meaning of mathematical concepts – **mathematical vernacular**: the language of mathematical communication, and in fact all the concepts supported in the OPENDREAMKIT VRE are documented in mathematical vernacular in journal articles, manuals, etc. The obvious problem is that mathematical vernacular is too (*i*) *ambiguous*: we need a human to understand structure, words, and symbols (*ii*) *redundant*: every paper introduces slightly different notions.

Therefore we explore an approach where we **flexiformalize**, i.e. partially formalize; see [Koh13] mathematical vernacular to obtain a flexiformal ontology of mathematics that can serve as an open communication vocabulary. We call the approach the **Math-in-the-Middle** (MitM) Strategy for integration and the ontology the **MitM ontology**.

Before we go into any detail on this ontology, and how it induces a uniform meaning space – see Sect. 4 for an example – we have to address another problem: the descriptions in the MitM ontology must simultaneously be system-near to make interfacing easy for systems, and serve as an interoperability standard – *i.e.* be general and stable. If we have an ontology system that allows modular/structured ontologies, we can solve this apparent dilemma by introducing **interface theories** [KRSC11], *i.e.* ontology modules (the light purple circles in Fig. 2) that

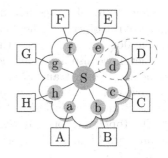

Fig. 2. Interface theories (Color figure online)

are at the same time system-specific in their description of mathematical concepts – near the actual representation of the system and part of the greater MitM ontology (depicted by the cloud in Fig. 2) as they are connected to the core MitM ontology (the blue circle) by views we call **interface views**. The MitM approach stipulates that interface theories and interface views are maintained and released together with the respective systems, whereas the core MitM ontology represents the mathematical scope of the VRE and is maintained with it. In fact in many ways, the core MitM ontology is the conceptual essence of the mathematical VRE.

3.2 Realizing and Utilizing a MitM Ontology

Our current candidate for representing the MitM ontology is the OMDoc/MMT format [Koh06, MMT]. OMDoc/MMT is an ontology format specialized for representing mathematical knowledge modularly in a theory graph: **theories** are collections of declarations of concepts, objects, and their properties that are connected by truth-preserving mappings called **theory morphisms**. The latter come in two forms: **inclusions** and **structures** that essentially

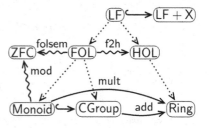

Fig. 3. A OMDoc/MMT theory graph

correspond to object-oriented inheritance (direct inheritance and inheritance modulo renaming and identification of symbols), and **views** that connect pre-existing theories – in these all axioms of the source theory have be to proven in the target theory. See [RK13] for a full account. Figure 3 shows an example of a theory graph. It has three layers:

(*i*) the (bottom) **domain level** which specifies mathematical domains as theories; here parts of elementary algebra. The hooked arrows are inclusions for inheritance, while the regular arrows are named structures that induce the additive and multiplicative structures of a ring.

(*ii*) the **logic level** represents the languages we use for talking about the properties of the objects at the domain level – again as theories: the meta-theories of the domain-level ones – the dotted arrows signify the meta-relation. At this level, we also have inclusions and views (the squiggly arrows) which correspond to logic translations (f2h) and interpretations into **foundational theories** like set theory (here ZFC). Incidentally models can be represented as views into foundations.

(*iii*) The top layer contains theories that act as metalogics, *e.g.* the Logical Framework LF and extensions which can be used to specify logics and their translations.

The theory graph structure is very well-suited to represent heterogeneous collections of mathematical knowledge, because views at the domain level can be used to connect differing but equivalent conceptualizations and views at the logic level can be used to bridge the different foundations of the various systems. The top level is only indirectly used in the MitM framework: it induces the joint meaning space via the meta-relation.

If we apply OMDoc/MMT to the MitM architecture, we arrive at the situation in Fig. 4, where we drill into the MitM information architecture from Fig. 2, but restrict at this stage to three systems from the OPENDREAMKIT project. In the middle we see the core MitM ontology (the blue cloud) as an OMDoc/MMT theory graph connected to the interface theories (the purple clouds) via MitM interface views. Conceptually, the systems in OPENDREAMKIT consist of three main components:

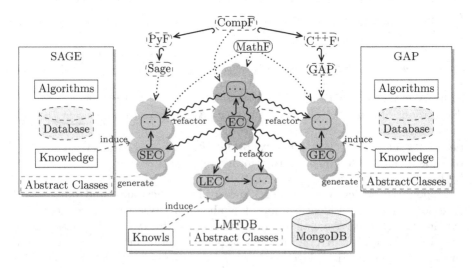

Fig. 4. The MitM paradigm in detail. PyF, C^{++}F and CompF are (basic) foundational theories for PYTHON, C^{++} and a generic computational model. SEC, LEC and GEC are theories for SAGE, LMFDB and GAP elliptic curves. (Color figure online)

(i) a *Knowledge Representation component* that provides data structures for the objects modeling mathematical concepts and their properties.
(ii) a *DataBase component* that provides mass storage for objects, and
(iii) a *library of algorithms* that operate on these.

To connect a system to an MitM-based VRE, the knowledge representation component is either refactored so that it can generate interface theories, or a schema-like description of the underlying data structures is created manually from which abstract data structures for the system can be generated automatically – in this version the interface theories act as an Interface Description Language.

In this situation there are two ways to arrive at a greater MitM ontology: the OPENDREAMKIT project aims to explore both: either (i) standardizing a core MitM by refactoring the various interface theories where they overlap, or (ii) flexiformalizing the available literature for a core MitM ontology. For (i), the MitM interface views emerge as refinements that add system-specific details to the general mathematical concepts[1]. For (ii), we have to give the interface views directly.

To see that this architecture indeed gives us a uniform meaning space, we observe that the core MitM ontology uses a mathematical foundation (presumably some form of set theory), whereas the interface theories also use system-specific foundations that describe aspects of the computational primitives of the respective systems. We have good formalizations of the mathematical foundations already; first steps towards a computational ones have been taken in [KMR13].

Our efforts also fit neatly alongside similar efforts underway across the sciences to standardize metadata formats (for instance through the Research Data Alliance's Typing Registry Working Group [Rda]), except for a typically much higher complexity in the typing since our objects of study are sometimes seen as types and sometimes as instances (think of groups for instance).

4   LMFDB Knowledge and Interoperability

The *L-functions and modular forms database* is a project involving dozens of mathematicians who assemble computational data about L-functions, modular forms, and related number theoretic objects. The main output of the project is a website, hosted at http://www.lmfdb.org, that presents this data so that it can serve as a reference for research efforts, and is accessible for postgraduate students. The mathematical concepts underlying the LMFDB are extremely complex and varied, so part of the effort has been focused on how to relay knowledge, such as mathematical definitions and their relationships, to data and software. For this purpose, the LMFDB has developed so-called *knowls*, which are

---

[1] We use the word "interface theory" with a slightly different intention when compared to the original use in [KRSC11]: There the core MitM ontology would be an interface between the more specific implementations in the systems, whereas here we use the "interface theories" as interfaces between systems and the core MitM ontology. Technically the same issues apply.

a technical solution to present LaTeX-encoded information interactively, heavily exploiting the concept of transclusion. The end result is a very modular and highly interlinked set of definitions in mathematical vernacular which can be easily anchored in vastly different contexts, such as an interface to a database, to browsable data, or as constituents of an encyclopedia [Lmfc].

The LMFDB code is primarily written in PYTHON, with some reliance on SAGE for the business logic. The backend uses the NoSQL document database system MONGODB [Lmfa]. Again, due to the complexity of the objects considered, many idiosyncratic encodings are used for the data. This makes the whole data management lifecycle particularly tricky, and dependent on different select groups of individuals for each component.

As the LMFDB spans the whole "vertical" workflow, from writing software, to producing new data, up to presenting this new knowledge, it is a perfect test case for a large scale case study of the MitM approach. Conversely, a semantic layer would be beneficial to its activities across data, knowledge and software, which it would help integrate more cohesively and systematically.

Among the components of the LMFDB, elliptic curves stand out in the best shape, and a source of best practices for other areas. We have generated MitM interface theories for LMFDB elliptic curves by (manually) refactoring and flexiformalizing the LaTeX source of knowls into sTeX (see Listing 1.1 for an excerpt), which can be converted into flexiformal OMDoc/MMT automatically. The MMT system can already type-check the definitions, avoiding circularity and ensuring some level of consistency in their scope and make it browsable through Math-Hub.info, a project developed in parallel to MMT to host such formalisations.

Listing 1.1. sTeX flexiformalization of an LMFDB knowl (original: Lmfd)

```
\begin{mhmodnl}{minimal−Weierstrass−model}{en}
    A \defi{minimal} \trefii{Weierstrass}{model} is one for which
    $\absolutevalue\wediscriminantOp$ is minimal among all Weierstrass models
    for the same curve. For elliptic curves over $\RationalNumbers$, minimal
    models exist, and there is a unique minimal model which satisfies the
    additional constraints $\minset{\livar{a}1,\livar{a}3}{\set{0,1}}$, and
    $\inset{\livar{a}2}{\set{−1,0,1}}$.
    This is defined as the reduced minimal Weierstrass model of the elliptic curve.
    \end{definition}
\end{mhmodnl}
```

The second step consisted of translating these informal definitions into progressively more exhaustive MMT formalisations of mathematical concepts (see Listing 1.2). The two representations are coordinated via the theory and symbol names – we can see the sTeX representation as a human-oriented documentation of the MMT.

Listing 1.2. MMT formalisation of elliptic curves and their Weierstrass models
theory minimal_Weierstrass_model : odk:?Math =

include ?elliptic_curve $\boxed{\text{D}}$

minimal : tm Ws_model → tm Ws_model $\boxed{\text{D}}$

is_minimal : tm Ws_model → prop \US = [A] (minimal A) $\doteq$ A $\boxed{\text{D}}$

minimality_idempotence : {A} ⊢ minimal (minimal A) $\doteq$ minimal A $\boxed{\text{D}}$

minimality_of_minimal_Ws_model :

{A} ⊢ is_minimal (minimal_Ws_model A) $\boxed{\text{D}}$

injective_minimal_Ws_model :

{A,B} ⊢ minimal_Ws_model A $\doteq$ minimal_Ws_model B → ⊢ A $\doteq$ B $\boxed{\text{D}}$

$\boxed{\text{M}}$

Finally, we have to integrate computational data into the interface theories. Based on recent ongoing efforts [Lmfb] to document the LMFDB "data schemata" we established OMDoc/MMT theories that link the database fields to their data types (string *vs.* float *vs.* integer tuple, for instance) and mathematical types (elliptic curves or polynomials) – the latter based on the vocabulary in the interface theories generated from the LMFDB knowls. This schema theory is complemented by a theory on functorial hence composable *MMT codecs*, which in turn acts as a specification for a collection of implementations in various programming languages (currently PYTHON, Scala, and C^{++} for SAGE, MMT, and GAP respectively) which are first instances of a computational foundation (see Sect. 3). For instance, one can compose two MMT codecs, say *polynomial-as-reversed-list* and *rational-as-tuple-of-int*, to signify that the data $[(2,3),(0,1),(4,1)]$ is meant to represent the polynomial $4x^2 + 2/3$. Of course, these codecs could be further decomposed (e.g. for signaling which variable name to use). The initial cost of developing these codecs is high, but the clarity gained in documentation is valuable, they are highly reusable, and they drastically expand the range of tooling that can be built around data management.

A Typical Application. Based on these MitM interface theories we can generate I/O interfaces that translate between the low-level LMFDB API, which delivers raw MONGODB data in JSON format into MMT expressions that are grounded in the interface theories. This ties the LMFDB database into the MitM architecture transparently. As a side effect, this opens up the LMFDB to programmatic queries via the MMT API, which can be queried and can then relay them to the LMFDB API directly and transparently.

5   Distributed Collaboration with GAP/Sage

Another aspect of interoperability in a mathematical VRE is the possibility of distributed multisystem computations, where *e.g.* a given system may decide to delegate certain subcomputations or reasoning tasks to other systems.

There are already a variety of peer-to-peer interfaces between systems in the OPENDREAMKIT project (see Fig. 1), which are based on the *handle paradigm*;

for example SAGE includes, among others, interfaces for GAP, SINGULAR, and PARI. In this paradigm, when a system A delegates a calculation to a system B, the result r of the calculation is not converted to a native A object; instead B just returns a *handle* h (or reference) to the object r. Later, A can run further calculations with r by passing it as argument to functions or methods implemented by B. Some advantages of this approach are that we can avoid the overhead of back and forth conversions between A and B, and that we can manipulate objects of B from A, even if they have no native representation in A.

The next desirable feature is for the handle h to behave in A as if it was a native A object; in other words, one wants to adapt the API satisfied by r in B to match the API for the same kind of objects in A. For example, the method call h.cardinality() on a SAGE handle h to a GAP object G should trigger in GAP the corresponding function call Size(G).

This can be implemented using the classical *adapter pattern*, mapping calls to SAGE's method to corresponding GAP methods. *Adapter classes* have already been implemented for certain types of objects, like SAGE's PermutationGroup or MatrixGroup. However, this implementation lacks modularity: for example, if h is a handle to a mere set S, SAGE cannot use the *adapter method* that maps h.cardinality() to Size(S), because this adapter method is only available in the above two adapter classes.

To get around this problem we have worked on a more semantic integration, where adapter methods are made aware of the type hierarchies of the respective systems, and defined at the highest available level of generality, as in Listing 1.3.

Listing 1.3. A semantic adapter method in SAGE

```
class Sets: # Everything generic about sets in Sage
    class GAP: # Adapter methods relevant to Sets in the Sage–Gap interface
        class ParentMethods: # Adapter methods for sets
            def cardinality(self): # The adapter for the cardinality method
                return self.gap().Size().sage()
        class ElementMethods: # Adapter methods for set elements
            ...
        class MorphismMethods: # Adapter methods for set morphisms
            ...
class Groups: # Everything generic about groups in Sage
    # This automatically includes features defined at a more general level
```

This peer-to-peer approach however does not scale up to a dozen systems. This is where the MitM paradigm comes to the rescue. With it, the task is reduced to building interface theories and interface views into the core MitM ontology in such a way that the adapter pattern can be made generic in terms of the MitM ontology structure, without relying on the concrete structure of the respective type systems. Then the adapter methods for each peer-to-peer interface can be automatically generated. In our example the adapter method for cardinality can be constructed automatically as soon as the MitM interface views link the cardinality function in the SAGE interface theory on Sets with the Size function in the corresponding interface theory for GAP.

We will now show first results of our experiments with interface theories and interface views, including several applications beyond the generation of interface theories that support distributed computation for SAGE and GAP.

5.1   Semantics in the Sage Category System

The SAGE library includes 40k functions and allows for manipulating thousands of different kinds of objects. In any large system it is critical to tame code bloat by

(i) identifying the core concepts describing common behavior among the objects;
(ii) implementing generic operations that apply on all objects having a given behavior, with appropriate specializations when performance calls for it;
(iii) designing or choosing a process for selecting the best implementation available when calling an operation objects.

Following mathematical tradition and the precedent of the AXIOM, FRICAS, or MUPAD systems, SAGE has developed a category-theory-inspired "category system", and found a way to implement it on top of the underlying PYTHON object system [Dev16,SC]. In short, a **category** specifies the available **operations** and the **axioms** they satisfy. This category system models taxonomic knowledge from mathematics explicitly and uses it to support genericity, control the method selection process, structure the code and documentation, enforce consistency, and provide generic tests.

To generate interface theories from the SAGE category system, we are experimenting with a system of annotations in the SAGE source files. Consider for instance the situtation in Fig. 5 where we have annotated the Sets() category in SAGE with

```
@semantic(mmt="sets")
class Sets:
    class ParentMethods:
        @semantic(mmt="card?card", gap="Size")
        @abstractmethod
        def cardinality(self):
            "Return the cardinality of ''self'''"
```

Fig. 5. An annotated category in SAGE

@semantic lines that state correspondences to other interface theories. From these the SAGE-to-MMT exporter can generate the respective interface theories and views.

In ongoing experiments, variants of the annotations are tested for annotating existing categories without touching their source files and providing the signature or the corresponding method names in other systems when this information has not yet been formalized elsewhere.

5.2   Exporting the GAP Knowledge: Type System Documentation

As in SAGE, the GAP type system encodes a wealth of mathematical knowledge, which can influence method selection. For example establishing that a group is nilpotent will allow for more efficient methods to be run for finding its centre. The main difference between SAGE and GAP lies in the method selection process. In SAGE the operations implemented for an object and the axioms they satisfy are specified by its class which, together with its super classes, groups syntactically all the methods applicable in this context. In GAP, this information is instead specified by the truth-values of a collection of independent **filters**, while the context of applicability is specified independently for each method. Breuer and Linton describe the GAP type system in [BL] and the GAP documentation [Gap] also contains extensive information on the types themselves.

GAP allows some introspection of this knowledge after the system is loaded: the values of those attributes and properties that are unknown on creation, can be computed on demand, and stored for later reuse.

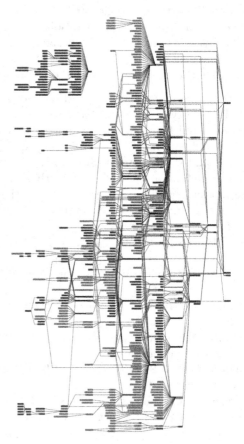

As a first step in generating interface theories for the MitM ontology, we have developed tools to access mathematical knowledge encoded in GAP, such as introspection inside a running GAP session, export to JSON to import to MMT, and export as a graph for visualisation and exploration. These will become generally available in the next GAP release. The JSON output of the GAP object system with default packages is currently around 11 MB, and represents a knowledge graph with 540 vertices, 759 edges and 8 connected components, (see Figs. 6 and 7). If all packages are loaded, this graph expands to 1616 vertices, 2178 edges and 17 connected components.

There is, however, another source of knowledge in the GAP universe: the documentation, which

Fig. 6. The GAP knowledge graph.

is provided in the GAPDoc format [LN12]. Besides the main manuals, GAPDoc is adopted by 97 out of the 130 packages currently redistributed with GAP. Conventionally GAPDoc is used to build text, PDF and HTML versions of the manual from a common source given in XML. The reference manual has almost 1400 pages and the packages add hundreds more.

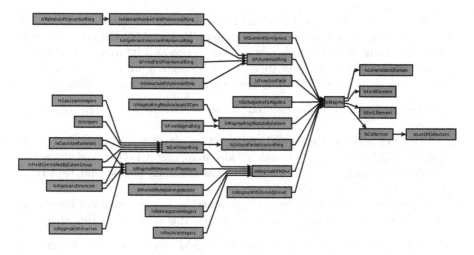

Fig. 7. The GAP knowledge graph (fragment).

The GAPDoc sources classify documentation by the type of the documented object (function, operation, attribute, property, etc.) and index them by system name. In this sense they are synchronized with the type system (which *e.g.* has the types of the functions) and can be combined into flexiformal OMDoc/MMT interface theories, just like the ones for LMFDB in Sect. 4. This conversion is currently under development and will lead to a significant increase of the scope of the MitM ontology.

As a side-effect of this work, we discovered quite a few inconsistencies in the GAP documentation which came from a semi-automated conversion of GAP manuals from the TEX-based manuals used in GAP 4.4.12 and earlier. We developed the consistency checker for the GAP documentation, which extracts type annotations from the documented GAP objects and compares them with their actual types. It immediately reported almost 400 inconsistencies out of 3674 manual entries, 75 % of which have been eliminated in the subsequent cleanup.

6   Conclusion

In this paper we have presented the OPENDREAMKIT project and the "Math-in-the-Middle" approach it explores for mitigating the system integration problems inherent in combining an ecosystem of open source software systems into a coherent mathematical virtual research environment. The MitM approach relies on a central, curated, flexiformal ontology of the mathematical domains to be covered by the VRE together with system-near interface theories and interface views to the core ontology that liaise with the respective systems. We have reported on two case studies that were used to evaluate the approach: an interface for the LMFDB, and a more semantic handle interface between GAP and SAGE.

Even though the development of the MitM is still at a formative stage, these case studies show the potential of the approach. We hope that the nontrivial cost of curating an ontology of mathematical knowledge and interface views to the interface theories will be offset by its utility as a resource, which we are currently exploring; the unification of the knowledge representation components

1. enables VRE-wide domain-centered (rather than system-centered) documentation;
2. can be leveraged for distributed computation via uniform protocols like the SCSCP [HR09] and MONET-style service matching [CDT04] (the absence of content dictionaries – MitM theories – was the main hurdle that kept these from gaining more traction);
3. will lead to the wider adoption of best practices in mathematical knowledge management in the systems involved; in fact, this is already happening.

Whether in the end the investment into the MitM will pay off also depends on the quality and usability of the tools for mathematical knowledge management. Therefore we invite the CICM community to interact with and contribute to the OPENDREAMKIT project, on this work package and the others. Possible contributions include

1. interfacing another system to the MitM architecture via interface theories
2. contributing to the MitM core ontology
3. MitM-refactoring existing integrations of mathematical software systems.

Acknowledgements. The authors gratefully acknowledge the other participants of the St Andrews workshop, in particular John Cremona, Luca de Feo, Steve Linton, and Viviane Pons, for discussions and experimentation which clarified the ideas behind the math-in-the-middle approach.

We acknowledge financial support from the OpenDreamKit Horizon 2020 European Research Infrastructures project (#676541), from the EPSRC Collaborative Computational Project CoDiMa (EP/M022641/1) and from the Swiss National Science Foundation grant PP00P2_138906.

References

[Aus+03] Ausbrooks, R.: Mathematical Markup Language (MathML) v. 2.0. In: World Wide Web Consortium Recommendation (2003)
[BL] Breuer, T., Linton, S.: The GAP 4 type system: organising algebraic algorithms. In: Proceedings of the 1998 International Symposium on Symbolic and Algebraic Computation, ISSAC 1998, pp. 38–45. ACM
[Bus+04] Buswell, S., et al.: The Open Math standard. Technical report Version 2.0. The Open Math Society (2004)
[CDT04] Caprotti, O., Dewar, M., Turi, D.: Mathematical Ser vice Matching Using Description Logic and OWL. Technical report, The MONET Consortium (2004)
[Dev16] The Sage Developers. SageMath the Sage Mathematics Software System (Version 7.0) (2016). http://www.sagemath.org

[EI]   EINFRA-9: e-Infrastructure for Virtual Research Environment. http://ec. europa.eu/research/participants/portal/desktop/en/opportunities/h2020/ topics/2144-einfra-9-2015.html

[Gap]   GAP-Groups, Algorithms, Programming, Version 4.8.2. The GAP Group (2016). http://www.gap-system.org

[HR09] Horn, P., Roozemond, D.: OpenMath in SCIEnce: SCSCP and POPCORN. In: Carette, J., Dixon, L., Coen, C.S., Watt, S.M. (eds.) MKM 2009, Held as Part of CICM 2009. LNCS (LNAI), vol. 5625, pp. 474–479. Springer, Heidelberg (2009)

[KMR13] Kohlhase, M., Mance, F., Rabe, F.: A universal machine for biform theory graphs. In: Carette, J., Aspinall, D., Lange, C., Sojka, P., Windsteiger, W. (eds.) CICM 2013. LNCS, vol. 7961, pp. 82–97. Springer, Heidelberg (2013). doi:10.1007/978-3-642-39320-4

[Koh06] Kohlhase, M.: OMDoc–An Open Markup Format for Mathematical Documents [version 1.2]. LNCS (LNAI), vol. 4180. Springer, Heidelberg (2006). http://omdoc.org/pubs/omdoc1.2.pdf

[Koh13] Kohlhase, M.: The flexiformalist manifesto. In: Voronkov, A., et al. (eds.) 14th International Workshop on Symbolic and Numeric Algorithms for Scientific Computing (SYNASC 2012), pp. 30–36. IEEE Press, Timisoara (2013)

[KRSC11] Rabe, F., Kohlhase, M., Sacerdoti Coen, C.: A foundational view on integration problems. In: Davenport, J.H., Farmer, W.M., Urban, J., Rabe, F. (eds.) MKM 2011 and Calculemus 2011. LNCS, vol. 6824, pp. 107–122. Springer, Heidelberg (2011)

[KW03] Kanayama, H., Watanabe, H.: Multilingual translation via annotated hub language. In: Proceedings of MT-Summit IX, pp. 202–207 (2003)

[Lmfa] LMFDB GitHub repository. https://github.com/LMFDB/lmfdb

[Lmfb] LMFDB inventory GitHub repository. https://github.com/LMFDB/ lmfdb-inventory

[Lmfc] LMFDB Knowledge Database. http://lmfdb.org/knowledge/

[Lmfd] LMFDB Knowledge Database entry for Minimal Weierstrass equation over the rationals. http://lmfdb.org/knowledge/show/ec.q.minimal_weierstrass_ equation

[LN12] Lübeck, F., Neunhöffer, M.: GAPDoc, A Meta Package for GAP Documentation, Version 1.5.1 (2012). http://www.math.rwth-aachen.de/~Frank. Luebeck/GAPDoc

[MMT]   Rabe, F.: The MMT Language and System. https://svn.kwarc.info/repos/ MMT/doc/html. Accessed 11 Oct 2011

[ODK]   OpenDreamKit Open Digital Research Environment Toolkit for the Advancement of Mathematics. http://opendreamkit.org

[Rda]   Research Data Alliance Type Registries Working Group. https:// rd-alliance.org/groups/data-type-registries-wg.html

[RK13] Rabe, F., Kohlhase, M.: A scalable module system. Inf. Comput. **230**, 1–54 (2013)

[SC]   Thiéry, N.M., et al.: Elements, parents, categories in Sage: a primer. http://combinat.sagemath.org/doc/reference/categories/sage/categories/ primer.html

[Wie92] Wiederhold, G.: Mediators in the architecture of future information systems. Computer **25**(3), 38–49 (1992)

Formal Dependability Modeling and Analysis: A Survey

Waqar Ahmad[1][(✉)], Osman Hasan[1], and Sofiène Tahar[2]

[1] School of Electrical Engineering and Computer Science,
National University of Sciences and Technology, Islamabad, Pakistan
{waqar.ahmad,osman.hasan}@seecs.nust.edu.pk
[2] Electrical and Computer Engineering Department,
Concordia University, Montreal, Canada
tahar@ece.concordia.ca

Abstract. Dependability is an umbrella concept that subsumes many key properties about a system, including reliability, maintainability, safety, availability, confidentiality, and integrity. Various dependability modeling techniques have been developed to effectively capture the failure characteristics of systems over time. Traditionally, dependability models are analyzed using paper-and-pencil proof methods and computer based simulation tools but their results cannot be trusted due to their inherent inaccuracy limitations. The recent developments in probabilistic analysis support using formal methods have enabled the possibility of accurate and rigorous dependability analysis. Thus, the usage of formal methods for dependability analysis is widely advocated for safety-critical domains, such as transportation, aerospace and health. Given the complementary strengths of mainstream formal methods, like theorem proving and model checking, and the variety of dependability models judging the most suitable formal technique for a given dependability model is not a straightforward task. In this paper, we present a comprehensive review of existing formal dependability analysis techniques along with their pros and cons for handling a particular dependability model.

Keywords: Reliability Block Diagrams · Fault Tree · Markov Chain · Petri Nets · Model Checking · Higher-order Logic · Theorem Proving

1 Introduction

The rapid advancement in technology in the past few decades has enabled us to develop many sophisticated systems that range from ubiquitous hand-held devices (like cell phones and tablets) to high-end computing equipment used in aircrafts, power systems, nuclear plants and healthcare devices. Ensuring the

---

The original version of this chapter was revised. The spelling of the author Waqar Ahmad has been corrected. The erratum to this chapter is available at DOI: 10.1007/978-3-319-42547-4_13

© Springer International Publishing Switzerland 2016
M. Kohlhase et al. (Eds.): CICM 2016, LNAI 9791, pp. 132–147, 2016.
DOI: 10.1007/978-3-319-42547-4_10

reliable functioning of these sophisticated systems is a major concern for design engineers. This concern is greatly amplified for safety-critical systems where a slight malfunction in the system may endanger human lives or lead to heavy financial set-backs. In order to avoid such scenarios beforehand, several dependability modeling techniques have been developed that can effectively model the failure characteristics of a system and thus analyze its failure behavior.

Dependability is primarily defined as the ability of a system to deliver service that can justifiably be trusted [1]. Dependability is an umbrella concept which is evolved from *reliability* and *availability* considerations [1]. Many authors describe dependability of a system as a set attributes, such as reliability, maintainability, safety, availability, confidentiality, and integrity [2]. Some of these attributes, i.e. reliability and availability, are quantitative whereas some are qualitative, for instance, safety [1].

Reliability is defined as the probability of a system or a sub-component functioning correctly under certain conditions over a specified interval of time [1]. Availability is a closely related concept to reliability and it can be defined as the probability that a component will be available when demanded [1]. To understand the difference between reliability and availability, it is important to realize that reliability refers to failure-free operation during an interval, while availability refers to failure-free operation at a given instant of time [1]. Availability can be viewed as a special case of reliability and is thus commonly considered as an attribute of reliability [3]. The availability of a system is typically measured as a function of reliability and *maintainability*, which is defined as the probability of performing a successful repair action of a system under a given time and stated conditions [1]. Additionally, if we keep the maintainability measure constant, the availability of the system is directly proportional to the reliability of the system [4]. This paper mainly focuses on reliability and availability attributes of dependability, since maintainability can be considered as a part of availability.

The first step in conducting the dependability analysis is the calculation of basic metrics of reliability and availability, such as mean-time to failure (MTTF) [1], mean-time between failure (MTBF) [1] and mean-time to repair (MTTR) [1], at the individual *component level* of the given system. The next step is the selection of an appropriate dependability modeling technique. Some of the widely used dependability modeling techniques include Reliability Block Diagrams (RBD) [5], Fault Trees (FT) [6] and Markov chains (MC) [7]. The selection among these modeling techniques depends upon numerous factors, which include the level of available details, size and complexity of the given system. These modeling techniques allow us to estimate the reliability and availability of the system at the *system level* and play a particularly useful role at the design stage of a system for scrutinizing the design alternatives without building the actual system. Once the modeling technique is selected, the third and the last step is the choice of the appropriate *system level* reliability and availability analysis technique. The dependability models, formed using these techniques, are analyzed using paper-and-pencil based analytical methods or simulation. However, these analysis methods cannot ascertain absolute correctness of the analysis mainly because of the human error and manual manipulations involved in the former and the sampling based deduction and the usage of pseudo random numbers and computer arithmetic in the later. Formal methods, on the other hand, use mathematical logic to precisely model the system's intended behavior and deploy mathematical reasoning to construct an irrefutable proof that the given system satisfies its requirements. This kind of mathematical modeling and analysis makes formal methods an accurate and rigorous analysis method compared to the traditional analytical and simulation based analysis. Thus, they are being strongly advocated for being used for the dependability analysis of safety-critical systems.

The purpose of this survey paper is to provide a generic overview of the formal methods that are being utilized for dependability analysis. These formal methods primarily include: (i) Petri Nets (ii) Model Checking and (iii) Higher-order Logic theorem proving as they have all been used for the dependability analysis using the three dependability modeling techniques: RBD, FT, and MC. The main focus of the paper is to study the utilization of formal methods in conjunction with the dependability modeling techniques for real-world applications and thus gain insights about the strengths and weaknesses of these formal methods and how to use them in the most effective manner. It is important to note that the paper is unique compared to existing surveys and tutorials on dependability analysis [3,8–10] due to its exclusive focus on dependability modeling techniques and their analysis with formal methods. For instnace, in [8] a unified framework for reliability with Markov reward models is described and then a survey of existing reliability analysis software tools is presented. Similarly, a survey of work related to dependability modeling and analysis of software and systems specified with UML is presented in [9]. In [3,10], tools and methods that have been used for enhancing the dependability of Wireless Sensor networks (WSN) and communication networks are also surveyed, respectively. Unlike above work, this paper discusses about the pros and cons of modeling techniques and formal methods for the dependability analysis of a broad range of systems.

The organization of the paper is as follows: Sect. 2 briefly describes commonly used dependability modeling techniques. Section 3 presents a detailed survey of formal methods that have been used for conducting accurate and rigorous dependability analysis of real-world systems. Section 4 provides the insights and the common pitfalls of the dependability modeling techniques and also a comparison of formal methods with traditional dependability analysis techniques. Finally, Sect. 5 concludes the paper.

2   Dependability Modeling Techniques

Dependability assessment techniques can be utilized in every design phase of the system or component including development, operation and maintenance. FT and RBD based models are usually used to provide reliability and availability estimates for both *early* and *later* stages of the design, where the system models are more refined and have more detailed specifications compared to the early stage system models [1]. While on the other hand, MC based models are mainly used in the *later* design phase to perform trade-off analysis among different design alternatives when the detailed specification of the design becomes available. In addition, when the system is deployed, these modeling techniques can be beneficial in order to estimate the frequency of maintenance and part replacement in the design, which allows us to determine the life cost of the system elements or components. In this section, we present a brief detail about some commonly used dependability modeling techniques to facilitate the understanding of the next sections.

2.1   Reliability Block Diagrams

Reliability Block Diagrams (RBD) [11] are graphical structures consisting of blocks and connector lines. The blocks usually represent the system components and the connection of these components is described by the connector lines. The system is functional, if at least one path of properly functional components from input to output exists otherwise it fails.

Table 1. RBDs with their mathematical expressions

RBDs	Mathematical Expressions
	$$R_{series}(t) = Pr(\bigcap_{i=1}^{N} A_i(t)) = \prod_{i=1}^{N} R_i(t)$$
	$$R_{parallel}(t) = Pr(\bigcup_{i=1}^{M} A_i) = 1 - \prod_{i=1}^{M}(1 - R_i(t))$$
	$$R_{parallel-series}(t) = Pr(\bigcup_{i=1}^{M} \bigcap_{j=1}^{N} A_{ij}(t))$$ $$= 1 - \prod_{i=1}^{M}(1 - \prod_{j=1}^{N}(R_{ij}(t)))$$
	$$R_{series-parallel}(t) = Pr(\bigcap_{i=1}^{N} \bigcup_{j=1}^{M} A_{ij}(t))$$ $$= \prod_{i=1}^{N}(1 - \prod_{j=1}^{M}(1 - R_{ij}(t)))$$
	$$R_{k|n}(t) = Pr(\bigcup_{i=k}^{n} \{exactly\ i\ components\ functioning\})$$ $$= \Sigma_{i=k}^{n}(\binom{n}{k}R^i(1-R)^{n-1})$$

An RBD construction can follow any one of three basic patterns of component connections: (i) series (ii) active redundancy or (iii) standby redundancy.

Table 2. Probability of failure of fault tree gates

FT Gates	Failure Probability Expressions
AND	$F(t) = Pr(\bigcap_{i=2}^{N} A_i(t)) = \prod_{i=2}^{N} F_i(t)$
OR	$F(t) = Pr(\bigcup_{i=2}^{N} A_i(t)) = 1 - \prod_{i=2}^{N}(1 - F_i(t))$
NOR	$F(t) = 1 - F_{OR}(t) = \prod_{i=2}^{N}(1 - F_i(t))$
NAND	$F(t) = Pr(\bigcap_{i=2}^{k} \overline{A}_i(t) \cap \bigcap_{j=k}^{N} A_i(t)) = \prod_{i=2}^{k}(1 - F_i(t)) * \prod_{j=k}^{N}(F_j(t))$
XOR	$F(t) = Pr(\bar{A}(t)B(t) \cup A(t)\bar{B}(t)) = F_A(t)(1 - F_B(t)) + F_B(t)(1 - F_A(t))$
NOT	$F(t) = Pr(\bar{A}(t)) = (1 - F_A(t))$

In the *series* connection, shown in Table 1, all components should be functional for the system to remain functional. The corresponding reliability expression is also shown in Table 1, where A_i represents the event corresponding to i^{th} component. In an *active* redundancy, all components in at least one of the redundant stages must be functioning in fully operational mode. The components in an active redundancy might be connected in a parallel structure or a combination of series and parallel structures as shown in Table 1. In a *standby* redundancy, all components are not required to be active. In other words, at least k out of n are required by the system to be functional, which can be seen in Table 1. There are three main requirements for building the RBD of a given system, i.e., the information about the (i) functional interaction of the system components; (ii) reliability of each component usually expressed in terms of failure distributions, such as exponential or Weibull, having appropriate failure rates; and (iii) mission times at which the reliability is desired. This information is then utilized by the design engineers to identify the appropriate RBD configuration (series, parallel or series-parallel) in order to determine the overall reliability of the given system. The detail about these commonly used RBD configurations and their corresponding mathematical expressions are presented in Table 1.

2.2   Fault Trees

Fault Tree (FT) [6] is a graphical technique for analyzing the conditions and the factors causing an undesired *top event*, i.e., a critical event, which can cause the whole system failure upon its occurrence. These causes of system failure are represented in the form of a tree rooted by the *top event*. The preceding nodes of the fault tree are represented by *gates*, which are used to link two or more *cause events* causing one fault in a prescribed manner. For example, an OR FT gate can be used when one fault suffices to enforce the fault. On the other hand, the AND FT gate is used when all the cause events are essential for enforcing the fault. Besides these gates, there are some other gates, such as exclusive OR FT gate, priority FT gate and inhibit FT gate, which can be used to model the occurrence of faults due to the corresponding cause events [6].

Once the fault tree model is constructed, both qualitative and quantitative analysis can be carried out. A qualitative analysis in this context allows the identification of all combinations of basic failure events, known as cut sets, which can cause the top event to occur. The *minimal* cut sets (MCS) are those cut sets that do not contain any subset of the basic cause events that are still a *cut set* and are obtained by applying Boolean algebraic operations on these cut sets. The smaller the number of basic cause events in these cut set, the more resilient to failures is the considered modeled system. The quantitative analysis is used to evaluate the probability of occurrence of the top event by considering these minimal cut sets, which significantly contribute to the system failures.

In Fault Tree analysis (FTA), each FT gate has an associated failure probability expression as shown in Table 2. These expressions can be utilized to evaluate the reliability of the system. The first step in the FTA is the construction of the FT of the given system. This is followed by the assignment of the failure distributions to basic *cause-events* and the identification of the Minimal Cut Set (MCS) failure events, which contribute in the occurrence of the top event. These MCS failure events are generally modeled in terms of the *exponential* or *Weibull* random variables and the Probabilistic Inclusion-Exclusion (PIE) principle [11] is then used to evaluate the probability of failure of the given system.

2.3 Markov Chain

A MC [12] is a stochastic process that consists of a set of states, i.e., $S = \{s_0, s_1, ..., s_n\}$, and arcs, which are used to point the transition from one state to another. The initial state s_{ini} and the probability p_{ij} represent the starting state and the transition probability from state s_i to state s_j, respectively. The process starts from an initial state and transitions from the current state to the next state occur on the basis of transition probabilities, which only depend upon the current state based on the Markov or the memoryless property. Markov chains are usually classified into two categories: Discrete Time Markov Chains (DTMC) and Continuous Time Markov Chains (CTMC). Markovian models are frequently utilized for reliability analysis in scenarios where failure or repair events can occur at any point in time [12].

Markov modeling has also been utilized for analyzing the *dynamic* behavior of the other reliability models, i.e., RBD and FT. The notion of dynamic behavior, for reliability analysis, represents the evolution of system topology/configuration with respect to time. In the case of Dynamic Reliability Block Diagrams (DRBD) [13], the system is modeled in terms of *states* of the components and the evolution of these components states is carried out by a sequence of *events* [13]. A typical DRBD contains the following states: (i) *Active*: the state of proper functioning of the component; (ii) *Failed*: the failure state of the component; and (iii) *Standby*: the state depicting the case when the component is not in functional or in active condition but it can be activated. In addition, there are other states such as *Hot*, *Warm* and *Cold*, representing the conditions when the system or component is disabled but energized, partially and completely disabled, respectively [13].

3 Formal Dependability Analysis Techniques

3.1 Petri Nets

A Petri Net (PN) [14] is a bipartite directed graph consisting of disjoint sets of places P and transitions T. The former, which is represented by circles, models the condition while the latter, signified by bars, represents the events or activities that may occur in the system. The directed arcs $(P \times T)$ and $(T \times P)$, represented by arrows, describe the input places P for the transitions T and output places P for the transitions T, respectively. Places may be empty or contain more than one token that is drawn by a block dot and term *marking* represents the tokens over the set of places. A transition is said to be enabled, in a given marking, if all its input places contain at least one token. An enabled transition can be *fired* and as a result a token will be removed from the input places of the transition and added to its output places.

Petri Nets and its variants are widely used as a reliability analysis tool for many real-world systems due to their ability to efficiently handle large problems of dynamic nature. For instance, PNs have been used for the reliability assessment of Web services [15] and a wind turbine hydraulic variable pitch system [16]. Many existing work have utilized the PNs for *availability* analysis, for instance, the availability of a mechanical system is hierarchically analyzed by dividing the complete system into three levels [17]. A system level PN model is constructed by composing the PNs of the subsystem levels, which are also composed from the PNs of the component level. Similarly, PNs have been used to analyze the availability of computational servers that are processing the jobs in a queue [18], a replicated file system to reduce the overhead in a distributed environment [19], a subsea blowout preventer (BOP), which is essentially required to provide safety for drilling workers, rigs and natural environment [20] and the C160 series equipment that can modify its own modules based on different process plan and forms a new configuration [21]. In addition, a considerable amount of work has been done by utilizing PN in conjunction with the dependability modeling techniques, described in Sect. 2, for dependability analysis as follows:

Reliability Block Diagrams. Many PN variants are extensively utilized to represent the RBDs to model the reliability of communication systems with dynamic nature. For instance, the live migration process in cloud computing networks makes the system dynamic and thus yields to a complex RBD model, which can be effectively handled using Petri Nets with the support of commercial tools, such as *SNOOPY* [22] and *CPN* [23]. Given the dynamic nature of visualization, due to the presence of hardware systems, software systems, live migration techniques, resource allocation algorithms and concurrent failures, virtualized networks are frequently modeled with RBDs, which are then transformed to Petri Nets for the reliability analysis [24]. The reliability of communication networks with *redundancy mechanisms* has also been efficiently analysed using RBD based Petri Nets [25].

PNs have also been used to ensure the security/safety aspects of networks in terms of reliability and availability by analyzing the safety/security aspects of network protocols, such as internet voting systems [26] and high-speed trains [27]. In addition to the communication network, PNs have been used to develop the RBDs to analyze the reliability of a logistic supply chain [28] and redundant electrical generator used to power-up the coast guard vessel [29]. Similarly, a Cojoint system model consisting of CPN and RBD has been effectively used to analyze the dependability and logistics of a fault-redundant space station [30].

Fault Trees. The PN approach has also been utilized, in conjunction with FTs, for the reliability analysis of embedded systems by translating the PN reachability into provability of linear logic sequents, which empowers the analysis by utilizing sequent calculus [31]. The *dynamic behavior* of networks components, such as timed behavioral nature, cannot be captured by simple FT models but PNs provide a very feasible alternative for this purpose. The system under consideration is modeled with a FT, which is then transformed into its corresponding PN based model for analysis. For example, the reliability of the broadband integrated service network (B-ISDN) has been assessed by modeling the dynamic re-routing mechanism of the traffic using the FT-based PN approach [32].

Markov Chains. A considerable amount of work has been done on analyzing reliability of systems using PNs with Markov chains. Some other prominent work in this direction include the reliability analysis of a preemptive M/D/1/2/2 client-server queuing system [33], the dynamic reconfiguration of FPGA [34], the data communication systems of the WLAN based train control system [35], cellular networks [36] and Wireless Sensor Networks (WSN) [37]. Moreover, some network protocols, like the courier [38] and Fibre Distributed Data Interface (FDDI) token ring protocol [39], have also been analyzed using the Petri Net approach. Similarly, the reliability of a file server system [40], financial system [41], distributed memories [42] and Low Earth Orbit (LEO) satellite has also been analyzed using PNs based on Markov chains [43]. Moreover, a Markov regenerative PN has been introduced in [44] to extend the capability of stochastic PN analysis and then its effectiveness is illustrated by utilizing this approach to approximate client-server systems.

3.2   Model Checking

Model Checking [45] allows to describe the behavior of a given system in the form of a state machine and verify its temporal properties in a rigorous manner. Probabilistic model checking extends traditional model checking principles for the analysis of MCs and allows the verification of probabilistic properties. Some notable probabilistic model checking include *PRISM* [46] and *ETMCC* [47].

Probabilistic model checking techniques have been considerably adopted to verify the reliability and availability properties of many systems, for instance, the

PRISM has been used to assess the reliability of e-health systems used in hospitals based on the Fast Health Interoperable Resources (FHIR) standard [48] and the Device Interoperability Middleware (DIM) used to bridge the gap between different healthcare vendors [49]. In addition, the *PRISM* model checker has been utilized for the reliability/safety analysis of airbone applications by augmenting it to the Matlab simulink [50], a RAID disk protocol used for reading the data from the disk sectors [51], multi-processor systems based on the Triple modular redundancy (TMR) model [52]. *PRISM* has also been utilized for quantitative reliability and availability analysis of a satellite system [53].

Fault Trees. The *COMPASS* tool [54] supports the formal FT analysis, specifically for aerospace systems. For verification purposes, *COMPASS* provides support of several model checking tools, like *NuSMV* [55] and *MRMC* [56]. This tool provide various templates containing placeholders that have to be filled in by the user. These templates are primarily composed of the most frequently used patterns that allow easy specifications of properties by non-experts by hiding the details of the underlying temporal logic. The tool generates several outputs, such as traces, FTs and Failure Mode and Effect Analysis (FMEA) tables, along with diagnostic and performance measures.

Markov Chains. Probabilistic model checking extends traditional model checking principles for the analysis of MCs and allows the verification of probabilistic properties. Probabilistic model checking techniques have been considerably adopted to verify the reliability properties of many systems, such as NAND multiplexing [57], an airbag system, an industrial process control system and the Herschel-Planck satellite system [58]. In [59], the reliability analysis of the Fast And Secure Protocol (FASP) is carried out by first defining the successful data transmission using STL and then the communication network is modeled in the form of a sender, receiver and a communication channel module in *PRISM*. Finally, the reliability property is then verified against the communication network using the *PRISM* model checker.

3.3   Higher-Order-Logic Theorem Proving

Interactive theorem provers, like *HOL4*, *Isabelle/HOL* and *Coq*, can be used to reason about probabilistic behaviors using the higher-order-logic formalizations of probability theory [60–62]. This feature has been widely used to conduct the dependability analysis of many systems. For instance, the probability theory in *HOL4* [61] has been used for the reliabililty analysis of combinational circuits [63] and reconfigurable memory arrays [64]. In these work, however, the reliability is evaluated based on probabilistic principles directly, i.e., no component to system-level assessment based on RBD or FT methods is done. Similarly, formally verified statistical properties of the continuous random variables have been used to reason about the fundamental reliability properties, including survival function and hazard rate [65]. These reliability properties are then used to analyzed the reliability of electronic system components [65].

Reliability Block Diagrams. The higher-order logic theorem prover *HOL4* has been recently used for the formalization of RBDs, including series [66], parallel [67], parallel-series [67] and series-parallel [68]. These formalizations have been used for the reliability analysis of a simple oil and gas pipeline with serial components [66], WSN protocols [67] and logistic supply chains [67].

Fault Trees. A higher-order-logic formalization of generic Fault Tree gates, i.e., AND, OR, NAND, NOR, XOR and NOT and the formal verification of their failure probability expressions have also been recently proposed in *HOL4* [69]. In addition, this work also presents a formalization of probabilistic inclusion-exclusion principle, which is then used to conduct the FT-based failure analysis of a solar array used in a Dong Fang Hong-3 (DFH-3) satellite [69].

Markov Chains. A foundational formalization of time-homogeneous DTMC with finite state space has been presented in HOL4 [70] and *Isabelle/HOL* [71]. These formalizations have been successfully used to formally analyze a binary communication channel [70], ZeroConf [71] and anonymizing crowds protocols [71]. None of these Markov chain formalizations has been used for reliability analysis so far.

4   Comparison and Discussion

4.1   Comparison of Dependability Modeling Techniques

The criteria for the selection of these modeling techniques, for a certain system, mainly depends upon the type of system and problem domain. A comparison among these modeling techniques is shown in Table 3. For instance, RBD is primarily used if we are interested in the successful working of the system while FT models the failure relationship due to the failure of individual components of the system. Also, both of these techniques utilize top-down analysis approach that starts at the system level and then proceeds downward to link system performance to failures at the component level. Due to this reason, these techniques work only for combinatorial types of problems, where a combination of components faults is used to determine the overall system failure. On the other hand, Markov chains are more flexible in terms of handling a wide variety of problems, as given in Table 3, including non-combinatorial problems, where systems are in different operational modes, such as active or failed. However, Markov chains fail to cater for large and complex systems due to the exponential growth in the number of states.

Based on the survey conducted in Sect. 3, we have found that FTs have been the mostly utilized dependability modeling technique by formal methods. On the other hand, the utilization of RBD and MC models for the dependability analysis is rapidly increasing specifically by PNs. The usage of RBD models with model checking for the formal dependability analysis is an area that is almost unexplored. We believe that this combination of modeling and analysis technique has a huge potential for ensuring accurate reliability analysis of a wide variety of safety-critical system.

Table 3. Comparison of dependability modeling techniques

Features	Reliability Block Diagram	Fault Tree	Markov Chain
Success domain	✓		✓
Failure domain		✓	✓
Top-down approach	✓	✓	✓
Identification and prevention of faults	✓	✓	✓
Combinatorial problems	✓	✓	✓
Non-combinatorial problems			✓
Large and complex systems	✓	✓	

4.2 Comparison of Dependability Analysis Techniques

A summary of various dependability analysis techniques is presented in Table 4. These techniques are evaluated according to their expressiveness, accuracy and the possibility of automating the analysis. Model checking and Petri Nets are not expressive enough to model and verify all sorts of reliability properties due to their state-based nature. The accuracy of the paper-and-pencil based proofs is questionable because they are prone to human errors. Simulation is inaccurate due to the involvement of pseudo-random number generators and computer arithmetics along with its inherent sampling-based nature. Theorem proving does not support all the reliability analysis foundations as of now. Finally, the paper-and-pencil based proof methods and interactive theorem proving based analysis involve human guidance and therefore are not categorized as automatic. However, there is some automatic verification support (e.g. [72]) available for theorem proving, which can ease the human interaction in proofs and thus we cannot consider interactive theorem proving as a completely manual approach. All three formal methods techniques promise to provide accurate results and thus can be very useful for analyzing the dependability aspects of safety and financial-critical systems.

We have used the question mark symbol in accuracy feature for paper-and-pencil to highlight its limitation of being prone to human error.

Table 4. Comparison of reliability analysis techniques

Feature	Paper-and-pencil proof	Simulation tools	Petri Nets	Theorem proving	Model checking
Expressiveness	✓	✓		✓	
Accuracy	✓ (?)		✓	✓	✓
Automation		✓	✓		✓

5 Conclusions

In this paper, we have discussed various dependability models constructed using the building blocks offered by the formalisms of reliability block diagrams, fault trees and Markov chains models. We have also presented a critical comparison, of the various dependability analysis techniques, i.e., analytical methods, simulation, and formal methods. Apart from providing the necessary background, we have also provided a detailed survey of the application of formal methods available in the open literature focused on studying dependability analysis of various real-world systems. The main contribution of this paper is that it is the first work presenting a comprehensive review of the various dependability modeling techniques in conjunction with formal methods along with a critical analysis describing their pros and cons in various contexts. Existing surveys on dependability analysis are either focused on software or communications networks and do not cover formal methods in depth.

Acknowledgments. This publication was made possible by NPRP grant # [5 - 813 - 1 - 134] from the Qatar National Research Fund (a member of Qatar Foundation). The statements made herein are solely the responsibility of the author[s].

References

1. Avizienis, A., Laprie, J.C., Randell, B.: Fundamental concepts of dependability. Technical report CS-TR-739, Newcastle University, UK (2001). http://pld.ttu.ee/IAF0530/16/avi1.pdf
2. Spitzer, C.R., Spitzer, C.: Digital Avionics Handbook. CRC Press, Boca Raton (2000)
3. Al-Kuwaiti, M., Kyriakopoulos, N., Hussein, S.: A comparative analysis of network dependability, fault-tolerance, reliability, security, and survivability. Commun. Surv. Tutorials 11(2), 106–124 (2009)
4. Weibull: (2015). http://www.weibull.com/hotwire/issue26/relbasics26.htm
5. Čepin, M.: Reliability block diagram. In: Čepin, M. (ed.) Assessment of Power System Reliability, pp. 119–123. Springer, Heidelberg (2011)
6. Vesely, W.E., Goldberg, F.F., Roberts, N.H., Haasl, D.F.: Fault tree handbook (NUREG-0492). Technical report, U.S. Nuclear Regulatory Commission (1981)
7. Gilks, W.R.: Markov Chain Monte Carlo. Wiley, New York (2005)
8. Trivedi, K.S., Malhotra, M.: Reliability and performability techniques and tools: a survey. In: Walke, B., Spaniol, O. (eds.) Messung, Modellierung und Bewertung von Rechen-und Kommunikationssystemen, pp. 27–48. Springer, New York (1993)
9. Bernardi, S., Merseguer, J., Petriu, D.C.: Dependability modeling and analysis of software systems specified with UML. ACM Comput. Surv. 45(1), 1–48 (2012)
10. Venkatesan, L., Shanmugavel, S., Subramaniam, C., et al.: A survey on modeling and enhancing reliability of wireless sensor network. Wirel. Sens. Netw. 5(03), 41–51 (2013)
11. Trivedi, K.S.: Probability & Statistics with Reliability, Queuing and Computer Science Applications. Wiley, Hoboken (2008)
12. Fugua, N.: The applicability of markov analysis methods to reliability, maintainability, and safety. Reliab. Anal. Cent. START Sheet 10(2), 1–8 (2003)

13. Distefano, S., Xing, L.: A new approach to modeling the system reliability: dynamic reliability block diagrams. In: Reliability and Maintainability Symposium, pp. 189–195. IEEE (2006)
14. Peterson, J.L.: Petri Net Theory and the Modeling of Systems. Prentice Hall, Upper Saddle River (1981)
15. Zhong, D., Qi, Z.: A petri net based approach for reliability prediction of web services. In: Meersman, R., Tari, Z., Herrero, P. (eds.) OTM 2006 Workshops. LNCS, vol. 4277, pp. 116–125. Springer, Heidelberg (2006)
16. Yang, X., Li, J., Liu, W., Guo, P.: Petri net model and reliability evaluation for wind turbine hydraulic variable pitch systems. Energies **4**(6), 978–997 (2011)
17. Kumar, G., Jain, V., Gandhi, O.: Reliability and availability analysis of mechanical systems using stochastic petri net modeling based on decomposition approach. Int. J. Reliab. Qual. Safety Eng. **19**(01), 1–39 (2012)
18. Jian, S., Shaoping, W., Yaoxing, S.: Petri-nets based availability model of fault-tolerant server system. In: Robotics, Automation and Mechatronics, pp. 444–449. IEEE (2008)
19. Dugan, J.B., Ciardo, G.: Stochastic petri net analysis of a replicated file system. Softw. Eng. **15**(4), 394–401 (1989)
20. Zengkai, L., Yonghong, L., Ju, L.: Availability and reliability analysis of subsea annular blowout preventer. In: International Conference on Energy, vol. 25, pp. 73–76. Science & Engineering Research Support Society (2013)
21. Beirong, Z., Xiaowen, X., Wei, X.: Availability modeling and analysis of equipment based on generalized stochastic petri nets. Res. J. Appl. Sci. Eng. Technol. **4**(21), 4362–4366 (2012)
22. Heiner, M., Herajy, M., Liu, F., Rohr, C., Schwarick, M.: Snoopy – a unifying petri net tool. In: Haddad, S., Pomello, L. (eds.) PETRI NETS 2012. LNCS, vol. 7347, pp. 398–407. Springer, Heidelberg (2012)
23. Beaudouin-Lafon, M., et al.: CPN/Tools: a tool for editing and simulating coloured petri nets ETAPS tool demonstration related to TACAS. In: Margaria, T., Yi, W. (eds.) TACAS 2001. LNCS, vol. 2031, pp. 574–577. Springer, Heidelberg (2001)
24. Wei, B., Lin, C., Kong, X.: Dependability Modeling and Analysis for the Virtual Data Center of Cloud Computing. In: High Performance Computing and Communications, pp. 784–789. IEEE (2011)
25. Guimarães, A., Maciel, P., Matos Jr., R., Camboim, K.: Dependability analysis in redundant communication networks using reliability importance. In: Information and Network Technology, vol. 4, pp. 12–17. IACSIT Press (2011)
26. Omidi, A., Moradi, S.: Modeling and quantitative evaluation of an internet voting system based on dependable web services. In: Computer and Communication Engineering, pp. 825–829. IEEE (2012)
27. Lijie, C., Tao, T., Xianqiong, Z., Schnieder, E.: Verification of the safety communication protocol in train control system using colored Petri net. Reliab. Eng. Syst. Saf. **100**, 8–18 (2012)
28. Li, Y.Z., Yi, H.Y.: Calculation method on reliability of logistics service supply chain based on stochastic petri nets. Int. J. u-and e-Serv. Sci. Technol. **7**(1), 103–112 (2014)
29. Robidoux, R., Xu, H., Xing, L., Zhou, M.: Automated modeling of dynamic reliability block diagrams using colored petri nets. Syst. Man Cybern. Part A Syst. Hum. **40**(2), 337–351 (2010)

30. Nebel, S., Bertsche, B.: Modeling and simulation methodology of the operational availability and logistics using extended colored stochastic petri netsan astronautics case study. In: Reliability and Maintainability Symposium, pp. 434–439. IEEE (2008)

31. Sadou, N., Demmou, H.: Reliability analysis of discrete event dynamic systems with petri nets. Reliab. Eng. Syst. Saf. **94**(11), 1848–1861 (2009)

32. Balakrishnan, M., Trivedi, K.S.: Stochastic petri nets for the reliability analysis of communication network applications with alternate-routing. Reliab. Eng. Syst. Saf. **52**(3), 243–259 (1996)

33. Radev, D., Rashkova, E., Denchev, V.: Analysis of markov reward models with stochastic petri nets. In: International Conference on Computer Systems and Technologies, pp. 1–6. ACM (2008)

34. Kohlík, M.: Dependability models based on petri nets and Markov Chains (2009)

35. Zhu, L., Yu, F.R., Ning, B., Tang, T.: Service availability analysis in communication-based train control systems using WLANs. In: Communications, pp. 1383–1387. IEEE (2012)

36. Jindal, V., Dharmaraja, S., Trivedi, K.S.: Markov modeling approach for survivability analysis of cellular networks. Int. J. Perform. Eng. **7**(5), 429 (2011)

37. Schoenen, R., Yanikomeroglu, H.: Erlang analysis of cellular networks using stochastic petri nets and user-in-the-loop extension for demand control. In: Global Communication Conference, pp. 298–303. IEEE (2013)

38. Youness, O., Elkilani, W., El-Wahed, W.A., Torkey, F.: A robust methodology for performance evaluation of communication networks protocols. In: Communication Networks and Services Research Conference, pp. 1–10. IEEE (2006)

39. Christodoulou, S., Zhou, M.: A petri net approach to modeling and performance analysis of fiber data distributed interface (FDDI) network. In: Emerging Technologies and Factory Automation, pp. 373–380. IEEE (1994)

40. Ibe, O.C., Choi, H., Trivedi, K.S.: Performance evaluation of client-server systems. Parallel Distrib. Syst. **4**(11), 1217–1229 (1993)

41. Tunik, A., Kharlashkin, I.: A formalistic method for the performance evaluation of communication networks of distributed computing systems. In: Industrial Electronics, vol. 2, pp. 874–878. IEEE (1992)

42. Sun, X., Lin, C., Liu, W., Xiao, Y.: Survivability evaluation of distributed service using stochastic petri net. In: Communications and Networking in China, pp. 1–5. IEEE (2009)

43. Zeng, W., Hong, Z.G.: SPN-based performance analysis of LEO satellite networks with multiple users. In: Machine Learning and Cybernetics, vol. 3, pp. 1425–1429. IEEE (2011)

44. Choi, H., Kulkarni, V.G., Trivedi, K.S.: Markov regenerative stochastic petri nets. Performance Eval. **20**(1), 337–357 (1994)

45. Baier, C., Katoen, J.P.: Principles of Model Checking. MIT Press, Cambridge (2008)

46. Lin, C.M., Yang, C.W., Teng, H.K., Chung, M.C., Lang, K.C., Teng, H.F.: Modeling CAN network using PRISM. In: Industrial Informatics, pp. 390–394. IEEE (2010)

47. Hermanns, H., Katoen, J.P., Meyer-Kayser, J., Siegle, M.: ETMCC: model checking performability properties of Markov chains. In: Dependable Systems and Networking, p. 1. IEEE (2003)

48. Pervez, U., Hasan, O., Latif, K., Tahar, S., Gawanmeh, A., Hamdi, M.S.: Formal reliability analysis of a typical FHIR standard based e-Health system using PRISM. In: e-Health Networking, Applications and Services, pp. 43–48. IEEE (2014)

49. Pervez, U., Mahmood, A., Hasan, O., Latif, K., Gawanmeh, A.: Formal reliability analysis of device interoperability middleware (DIM) based E-health system using PRISM. In: e-Health Networking, Applications and Services, pp. 1–6. IEEE (2015)
50. Gomes, A., Mota, A., Sampaio, A., Ferri, F., Buzzi, J.: Systematic model-based safety assessment via probabilistic model checking. In: Margaria, T., Steffen, B. (eds.) ISoLA 2010, Part I. LNCS, vol. 6415, pp. 625–639. Springer, Heidelberg (2010)
51. Gopinath, K., Elerath, J., Long, D.: Reliability modelling of disk subsystems with probabilistic model checking. Technical report, Technical Report UCSC-SSRC-09-05, University of California, Santa Cruz (2009). http://www.crss.ucsc.edu/media/papers/ssrctr-09-05.pdf
52. Ge, X., Paige, R.F., McDermid, J.A.: Analysing system failure behaviours with PRISM. In: Secure Software Integration and Reliability Improvement Companion, pp. 130–136. IEEE (2010)
53. Peng, Z., Lu, Y., Miller, A., Johnson, C., Zhao, T.: A probabilistic model checking approach to analysing reliability, availability, and maintainability of a single satellite system. In: Modelling Symposium, pp. 611–616. IEEE (2013)
54. Bozzano, M., Cimatti, A., Katoen, J.-P., Nguyen, V.Y., Noll, T., Roveri, M.: The COMPASS approach: correctness, modelling and performability of aerospace systems. In: Buth, B., Rabe, G., Seyfarth, T. (eds.) SAFECOMP 2009. LNCS, vol. 5775, pp. 173–186. Springer, Heidelberg (2009)
55. Cimatti, A., Clarke, E., Giunchiglia, E., Giunchiglia, F., Pistore, M., Roveri, M., Sebastiani, R., Tacchella, A.: NuSMV 2: an opensource tool for symbolic model checking. In: Brinksma, E., Larsen, K.G. (eds.) CAV 2002. LNCS, vol. 2404, pp. 359–364. Springer, Heidelberg (2002)
56. Katoen, J.P., Khattri, M., Zapreev, I.S.: A Markov reward model checker. In: Quantitative Evaluation of Systems, pp. 243–244. IEEE (2005)
57. Norman, G., Parker, D., Kwiatkowska, M., Shukla, S.: Evaluating the reliability of NAND multiplexing with PRISM. Comput. Aided Des. Integr. Circ. Syst. 24(10), 1629–1637 (2005)
58. Norman, G., Parker, D.: Quantitative verification: formal guarantees for timeliness. reliability and performance. Technical report (2014)
59. Conghua, Z., Meiling, C.: Analysis of fast and secure protocol based on continuous-time Markov Chain. Commun. China 10(8), 137–149 (2013)
60. Hurd, J.: Formal verification of probabilistic algorithms. Ph.D. thesis, University of Cambridge, UK (2002)
61. Mhamdi, T., Hasan, O., Tahar, S.: On the formalization of the lebesgue integration theory in HOL. In: Kaufmann, M., Paulson, L.C. (eds.) ITP 2010. LNCS, vol. 6172, pp. 387–402. Springer, Heidelberg (2010)
62. Hölzl, J., Heller, A.: Three chapters of measure theory in Isabelle/HOL. In: van Eekelen, M., Geuvers, H., Schmaltz, J., Wiedijk, F. (eds.) ITP 2011. LNCS, vol. 6898, pp. 135–151. Springer, Heidelberg (2011)
63. Hasan, O., Patel, J., Tahar, S.: Formal reliability analysis of combinational circuits using theorem proving. J. Appl. Log. 9(1), 41–60 (2011)
64. Hasan, O., Tahar, S., Abbasi, N.: Formal reliability analysis using theorem proving. Trans. Comput. 59(5), 579–592 (2010)
65. Abbasi, N., Hasan, O., Tahar, S.: Formal lifetime reliability analysis using continuous random variables. In: Dawar, A., de Queiroz, R. (eds.) WoLLIC 2010. LNCS, vol. 6188, pp. 84–97. Springer, Heidelberg (2010)

66. Ahmed, W., Hasan, O., Tahar, S., Hamdi, M.S.: Towards the formal reliability analysis of oil and gas pipelines. In: Watt, S.M., Davenport, J.H., Sexton, A.P., Sojka, P., Urban, J. (eds.) CICM 2014. LNCS, vol. 8543, pp. 30–44. Springer, Heidelberg (2014)

67. Ahmed, W., Hasan, O., Tahar, S.: Formal reliability analysis of wireless sensor network data transport protocols using HOL. In: Wireless and Mobile Computing, Networking and Communications, pp. 217–224. IEEE (2015)

68. Ahmed, W., Hasan, O., Tahar, S.: Towards formal reliability analysis of logistics service supply chains using theorem proving. In: Implementation of Logics, pp. 111–121 (2015)

69. Ahmed, W., Hasan, O.: Towards formal fault tree analysis using theorem proving. In: Kerber, M., Carette, J., Kaliszyk, C., Rabe, F., Sorge, V. (eds.) CICM 2015. LNCS, vol. 9150, pp. 39–54. Springer, Heidelberg (2015)

70. Liu, L., Hasan, O., Tahar, S.: Formal reasoning about finite-state discrete-time markov chains in HOL. J. Comput. Sci. Technol. **28**(2), 217–231 (2013)

71. Hölzl, J., Nipkow, T.: Interactive verification of Markov chains: two distributed protocol case studies. arXiv preprint (2012). arXiv:1212.3870

72. Slind, K., Norrish, M.: A brief overview of HOL4. In: Mohamed, O.A., Muñoz, C., Tahar, S. (eds.) TPHOLs 2008. LNCS, vol. 5170, pp. 28–32. Springer, Heidelberg (2008)

Systems and Data

Extending E Prover with Similarity Based Clause Selection Strategies

Jan Jakubův$^{(\boxtimes)}$ and Josef Urban

CIIRC, Czech Technical University, Prague, Czech Republic
jakubuv@gmail.com, josef.urban@gmail.com

Abstract. E prover is a state-of-the-art theorem prover for first-order logic with equality. E prover is built around a saturation loop, where new clauses are derived by inference rules from previously derived clauses. Selection of clauses for the inference provides the main source of non-determinism and an important choice-point of the loop where the right choice can dramatically influence the proof search. In this work we extend E Prover with several new clause selection strategies based on similarity of a clause with the conjecture. In particular, clauses which are more related to the conjecture are preferred. We implement different strategies that define the relationship with a conjecture in different ways. We provide an implementation of the proposed selection strategies and we evaluate their efficiency on an extensive benchmark set.

Keywords: Automated theorem proving · Large theory reasoning · Clause selection

1 Introduction

Many state-of-the-art automated theorem provers (ATPs) are based on the *given clause algorithm* introduced by *Otter* [5]. The input problem $T \cup \{\neg C\}$ is translated into a refutationally equivalent set of clauses. Then the search for a contradiction, represented by the empty clause, is performed maintaining two sets: the set P of *processed clauses* and the set U of *unprocessed* clauses. Initially, all the input clauses are unprocessed. The algorithm repeatedly selects a *given clause* g from U and generates all possible inferences using g and the processed clauses from P. Then, g is moved to P, and U is extended with the newly produced clauses. This process continues until a resource limit is reached, or the empty clause is inferred, or P becomes *saturated*, that is, nothing new can be inferred.

The search space of this loop grows quickly. Several methods can be used to make the proof search more efficient. The search space can be narrowed by adjusting (typically restricting) the inference rules, pruned by using *forward* and *backward subsumption*, reduced by pre-selecting relevant input clauses, or otherwise simplified. One of the main sources of non-determinism affecting efficiency

J. Jakubův and J. Urban—Supported by the ERC Consolidator grant nr. 649043
AI4REASON.

© Springer International Publishing Switzerland 2016
M. Kohlhase et al. (Eds.): CICM 2016, LNAI 9791, pp. 151–156, 2016.
DOI: 10.1007/978-3-319-42547-4_11

of the search is the selection of the given clause. Clever selection mechanism can improve the search dramatically: in principle, one only needs to do the inferences that participate in the final proof. So far, this is often only a tiny portion of all the inferences done by the ATPs during the proof search.

2   Clause Selection in E Prover

E [6] is a state-of-the-art theorem prover which we use as a basis for implementation. The selection of a given clause in E is implemented by a combination of priority and weight functions. A *priority function* assigns an integer to a clause and is used to pre-order clauses for weight evaluation. A *weight function* takes additional specific arguments and assigns to each clause a real number called *weight*. A *clause evaluation function* CEF is specified by a priority function, weight function, and its arguments. Each CEF selects the clause with the smallest pair (*priority, weight*) for inferences. E allows a user to select an *expert heuristic* on a command line in the format "$(n_1 * CEF_1, \dots, n_k * CEF_k)$", where integer n_i indicates how often the corresponding CEF_i should be used to select a given clause. E additionally supports an *autoschedule* mode where several expert heuristics are tried, each for a selected time period. The heuristics and time periods are automatically chosen based on input problem properties.

One of the well-performing weight functions in E, which we also use as a reference for evaluation of our weight functions, is the *conjecture symbol weight*. This weight function counts symbol occurrences with different weights based on their appearance in the conjecture as follows. Different weights δ_f, δ_c, δ_p, and δ_v are assigned to function, constant, and predicate symbols, and to variables. The weight of a symbol which appears in the conjecture is multiplied by γ_{conj}, typically $\gamma_{conj} < 1$ to prefer clauses with conjecture symbols. To compute a term weight, the given symbol weights are summed for all symbol occurrences. This evaluation is extended to equations and to clauses.

3   Similarity Based Clause Selection Strategies

Many of the best-performing weight functions in E are based on a similarity of a clause with the conjecture, for example, the *conjecture symbol weight* from the previous section. In this paper we try to answer the question whether or not it makes sense to also investigate a term structure. We propose, implement, and evaluate several weight functions which utilize conjecture similarity in different ways. Typically they extend the symbol-based similarity by similarity on terms. Using finer formula features improves the high-level premise selection task [2], which motivates this work on steering also the internal selection in E. We first describe the common arguments of our weight functions and then function-specific properties.

Common Arguments (v,r,e). We implement two ways of term variable normalization, selected by the argument v. Either (1) variables are α-normalized, naming them consistently by their appearance in the term from left to right (value "α"), or (2) all variables are unified to a single variable ("$\star$"). This provides differently coarse notions of similarity. Each of our weight functions relates a term to the global set RelatedTerms. This set RelatedTerms, controlled by the argument r, contains either (1) all conjecture terms ("ter"), (2) conjecture terms and their subterms ("sub"), (3) conjecture subterms and top-level generalizations ("top"), or to (4) conjecture subterms and all their generalizations ("gen"). Each of our weight functions implements a different function base-weight which assigns a weight to a term. We use three different ways of extending base-weight to compute a term weight, selected by the argument e. Either (1) base-weight value is used directly (value "1"), or (2) values of base-weight for all the subterms are summed ("Σ"), or (3) the maximal value of base-weight on all of the subterms is used ("$\vee$").

Conjecture Subterm Weight (Term). The first of our weight functions is similar to the standard *conjecture symbol weight*, counting instead of symbols the number of subterms a term shares with the conjecture. The weight function Term takes five specific arguments γ_{conj}, δ_f, δ_c, δ_p and δ_v and base-weight$_{Term}(t)$ equals weight δ_f for functional terms, δ_c for constants, δ_p for predicates, and δ_v for variables, possibly multiplied by γ_{conj} when $t \in$ RelatedTerms.

Conjecture Frequency Weight (Tfldf). *Term frequency – inverse document frequency*, is a numerical statistic intended to reflect how important a word is to a document in a corpus [3]. A *term frequency* is the number of occurrences of the term in a given document. A *document frequency* is the number of documents in a corpus which contain the term. The term frequency is typically multiplied by the logarithm of the inverse of document frequency to reduce frequency of terms which appear often. We define $\mathrm{tf}(t)$ as the number of occurrences of t in RelatedTerms. We consider a fixed set of clauses denoted Docs. We define $\mathrm{df}(t)$ as the count of clauses from Docs which contain t. Out weight function Tfldf takes one specific argument δ_{doc} to select documents, either (1) ax for the axioms or (2) pro for all the processed clauses, and base-weight$_{Tfldf}$ is as follows.

$$\text{base-weight}_{Tfldf}(t) = \frac{1}{1 + \mathrm{tfidf}(t)} \quad \text{where} \quad \mathrm{tfidf}(t) = \mathrm{tf}(t) * \log \frac{1 + |\mathsf{Docs}|}{1 + \mathrm{df}(t)}$$

Conjecture Term Prefix Weight (Pref). The above weight functions rely on an exact match of a term with a conjecture related term. The following weight function loosen this restriction and consider also partial matches. We consider terms as symbol sequences. Let max-pref(t) be the longest prefix t shares with a term from RelatedTerms. A *term prefix weight* (Pref) counts the length of max-pref(t) using weight arguments δ_{match} and δ_{miss}, formally, base-weight$_{Pref}(t) = \delta_{match} * |\text{max-pref}(t)| + \delta_{miss} * (|t| - |\text{max-pref}(t)|)$.

Conjecture Levenshtein Distance Weight (Lev). A straightforward extension of Pref is to employ the Levenshtein distance [4] which measures a distance of two strings as the minimum number of edit operations (character insertion, deletion, or change) required to change one word into the other. Our weight function Lev defines base-weight$_{Lev}(t)$ as the minimal distance from t to some $s \in$ RelatedTerms. It takes additional arguments δ_{ins}, δ_{del}, δ_{ch} to assign different costs for edit operations.

Conjecture Tree Distance Weight (Ted). The Levenshtein distance does not respect a tree structure of terms. To achieve that, we implement the *Tree edit distance* [8] which is similar to Levenshtein but uses tree editing operations (inserting a node into a tree, deleting a node while reconnecting its child nodes to the deleted position, and renaming a node label). Our weight function Ted takes the same arguments as Lev above and base-weight$_{\mathsf{Ted}}$ is defined similarly.

Conjecture Structural Distance Weight (Struc). With Ted, a tree produced by the edit operations does not need to represent a valid term as the operations can change number of child nodes. To avoid this we define a simple *structural distance* which measures a distance of two terms by a number of *generalization* and *instantiation* operations. Generalization transforms an arbitrary term to a variable while instantiation does the reverse. Our weight function Struc takes additional arguments δ_{miss}, γ_{inst}, and γ_{gen} as penalties for variable mismatch and operation costs. The distance of a variable x to a term t is the cost of instantiating x to t, computed as $\Delta_{\mathsf{Struc}}(x,t) = \gamma_{\mathsf{inst}} * |t|$. The distance of t to x is defined similarly but with γ_{gen}. A distance of non-variable terms t and s which share the top-level symbol is the sum of distances of the corresponding arguments. Otherwise, a generic formula $\Delta_{\mathsf{Struc}}(t,x_0) + \Delta_{\mathsf{Struc}}(x_0,s)$ is used. Function base-weight$_{\mathsf{Struc}}$ is as for Lev but using Δ_{Struc}.

4 Experimental Results and Evaluation

The best evaluation would be to measure how our weight functions enrich the autoschedule mode of E. This is, however, beyond the scope of this paper. Instead, we design experiments to help us estimate the quality of the new weights. For each new weight function we run all possible combinations of common arguments (*"v-r-e"*, see Sect. 3) and other manually selected arguments. First, we run the weight functions on the 2078 MPTP bushy problems [1] with a 5 s time limit. We compare the number of solved problems with the number of problems solved by the *conjecture symbol weight* (denoted ref) discussed in Sect. 2. Second, to estimate how complementary our weight functions are with existing functions, we pick a well-performing expert heuristic from the autoschedule mode of E, and we compute how many problems were solved which the expert heuristic was not able to solve in 10 s (denoted 2E+). The five best-performing combinations of arguments for each weight function are presented in Table 1. Column *speed* contains an average number of processed *(kilo-)clauses per second* to evaluate implementation efficiency. Our implementation is available for download[1].

From Table 1 we can see that the weights which rely on an exact match of a term with a related term or its part (Term, Tfldf, and Pref) perform best when values of base-weight are summed for all the subterms ($e = \Sigma$). On the other hand, weights which incorporate some notion of term similarity directly in base-weight do not profit so much from this. For weights Lev, Ted, and Struc we have tried to experiment with operation costs (column δ, for example, 151 means that δ_{del} is increased to 5 while other costs are 1). In general, the experiments show that different arguments have an impact on performance. Finally, the experiments also reveal a higher time complexity of the Lev and Ted weights (Levenshtein distance of two terms is in $O(n^2)$ while Ted is in $O(n^3)$). However, a higher time complexity does not have to be a drawback as Lev is still best performing.

---

[1] http://people.ciirc.cvut.cz/jakubja5/src/E-arg-2016-03.tar.gz.

Table 1. The five best-performing configurations for each weight function.

Term	solved	speed	%ref+
★-gen-Σ	749	5.6	5.3
α-gen-Σ	749	5.4	5.3
★-sub-Σ	718	5.7	1.0
★-ter-Σ	717	5.7	0.8
α-ter-Σ	717	5.5	0.8
ref	711	3.4	0.0

Term	2E+	speed	%ref+
α-gen-1	20	4.4	-0.7
★-sub-Σ	19	5.7	1.0
★-ter-Σ	19	5.7	0.8
α-ter-Σ	18	5.5	0.8
α-sub-Σ	18	5.5	0.6
ref	7	3.4	0.0

Tfldf	δ_{doc}	solved	speed	%ref+
α-gen-Σ	pro	738	3.1	3.8
α-gen-Σ	ax	736	3.7	3.5
★-gen-Σ	pro	735	3.3	3.4
★-gen-Σ	ax	733	3.6	3.1
★-ter-Σ	pro	716	3.6	0.7

Tfldf	δ_{doc}	2E+	speed	%ref+
★-sub-Σ	pro	17	3.5	0.3
★-gen-Σ	pro	16	3.3	3.4
★-ter-Σ	pro	16	3.6	0.7
α-sub-Σ	pro	16	3.3	0.1
★-sub-Σ	ax	16	3.9	0.0

Pref	solved	speed	%ref+
α-gen-Σ	788	4.0	10.8
α-top-Σ	772	4.2	8.6
★-gen-Σ	771	3.9	8.4
α-gen-1	768	3.9	8.0
★-sub-Σ	766	4.3	7.7

Pref	2E+	speed	%ref+
α-gen-Σ	21	4.0	10.8
★-gen-Σ	20	3.9	8.4
α-gen-1	18	3.9	8.0
★-sub-Σ	18	4.3	7.7
α-sub-Σ	18	4.2	7.5

Lev	δ	solved	speed	%ref+
★-gen-1	155	841	2.4	18.3
α-gen-1	155	836	2.4	17.6
α-gen-1	151	827	2.5	16.3
α-gen-1	111	824	2.5	15.9
★-gen-1	151	822	2.5	15.6

Lev	δ	2E+	speed	%ref+
★-gen-1	155	41	2.4	18.3
α-gen-1	155	39	2.4	17.6
α-gen-1	151	35	2.5	16.3
α-gen-1	111	35	2.5	15.9
★-gen-1	151	30	2.5	15.6

Ted	δ	solved	speed	%ref+
α-gen-1	511	797	1.2	12.1
α-gen-1	111	797	1.3	12.1
★-gen-Σ	155	789	1.0	11.0
α-gen-Σ	155	789	1.0	11.0
α-gen-1	155	789	1.2	11.0

Ted	δ	2E+	speed	%ref+
α-gen-1	111	33	1.3	12.1
α-gen-1	511	32	1.2	12.1
α-gen-1	155	28	1.2	11.0
★-gen-Σ	155	25	1.0	11.0
★-ter-1	511	23	2.4	6.2

Struc	δ	solved	speed	%ref+
★-ter-1	115	833	3.9	17.2
α-ter-1	115	832	2.0	17.0
★-sub-Σ	115	832	2.9	17.0
α-sub-Σ	115	831	1.4	16.9
★-sub-1	115	825	3.6	16.0

Struc	δ	2E+	speed	%ref+
★-sub-Σ	115	32	2.9	17.0
α-sub-Σ	115	32	1.4	16.9
α-top-Σ	115	31	1.5	16.0
★-ter-1	115	29	3.9	17.2
★-top-Σ	115	29	2.9	15.6

5 Conclusions and Future Work

We have implemented several new weight functions for E prover based on term similarity with a conjecture. The experiments suggest that our functions have a potential to improve the autoschedule mode of E as they are reasonably complementary with existing heuristics. In order to use our weight functions with the autoschedule mode of E, we would need to (1) find the best performing parameters of our weight functions, (2) find the best combinations of our weight functions with other weight functions, and (3) find the most complementary combinations and create a scheduling strategy. As a future research, we are planning to use parameter-searching methods such as BliStr [7] to achieve this task.

References

1. Alama, J., et al.: Premise selection for mathematics by corpus analysis and kernel methods. J. Autom. Reason. **52**(2), 191–213 (2014)
2. Kaliszyk, C., Urban, J., Vyskocil, J.: Efficient semantic features for automated reasoning over large theories. In: IJCAI, vol. 15 (2015)
3. Leskovec, J., Rajaraman, A., Ullman, J.D.: Mining of Massive Datasets, 2nd edn. Cambridge University Press, Cambridge (2014)
4. Levenshtein, V.I.: Binary codes capable of correcting deletions, insertions and reversals. Sov. Phys. Dokl. **10**, 707 (1966)
5. McCune, W.W.: Otter 3.0 Reference Manual and Guide, vol. 9700. Argonne National Laboratory, Argonne (1994)
6. Schulz, S.: E - a brainiac theorem prover. AI Commun. **15**(2), 111–126 (2002)
7. Urban, J.: BliStr: the blind strategymaker. In: Global Conference on Artificial Intelligence, GCAI 2015, vol. 36, pp. 312–319. EasyChair (2015)
8. Zhang, K., Shasha, D.: Simple fast algorithms for the editing distance between trees and related problems. SIAM J. Comput. **18**(6), 1245–1262 (1989)

Enhancement of Mizar Texts with Transitivity Property of Predicates

Artur Korniłowicz[✉]

Institute of Informatics, University of Białystok,
K. Ciołkowskiego 1M, 15-245 Białystok, Poland
arturk@mizar.org

Abstract. A typical proof step in mathematical reasoning consists of two parts – a formula to be proven and a list of references used to justify the formula. In addition, computer proof-assistants can use specialized procedures and algorithms to strengthen their computational power to verify the correctness of reasonings.

The Mizar system supports several mechanisms to increase automation of some reasoning steps. One of them is registration of chosen properties of predicates and functors when they are defined. We propose strengthening of the Mizar system by processing another common property used in mathematics – transitivity.

1 Introduction

The Mizar system [1–3] is a computer system invented for computer-assisted verification of mathematical papers. It consists of three main components: a language – the Mizar language, a bunch of computer programs including Verifier and a repository of formal texts – Mizar Mathematical Library (MML) – written in the language and automatically verified for their logical correctness. The Mizar language is a declarative formal language designed to write mathematical papers readable for humans and effectively processed by computers. The language is highly structured to ensure producing rigorous and semantically unambiguous texts. Apart from rules for writing traditional mathematical items (e.g. definitions, lemmas, theorems, proof steps, etc.) it also provides syntactic constructions to launch distinguished algorithms for processing particular mechanisms (e.g. term identifications, term reductions [4], flexary connectives [5]) increasing computational power of Verifier. The most interesting mechanism, from the point of view of this research, is the possibility of registering various properties of predicates and functors [6] at the stage of defining new notions. The current version of the Mizar system supports registration of `reflexivity`, `irreflexivity`, `symmetry`, `asymmetry` and `connectedness` for binary predicates; `involutiveness` and `projectivity` for unary operations; and `commutativity` and `idempotence` for binary operations. Table 1 presents how registrations of the properties are used in the MML and how they influence on proofs stored in the library. Consecutive columns show numbers of occurrences

© Springer International Publishing Switzerland 2016
M. Kohlhase et al. (Eds.): CICM 2016, LNAI 9791, pp. 157–162, 2016.
DOI: 10.1007/978-3-319-42547-4_12

Table 1. Properties of predicates and functors

Property	Occurrences	Articles	Errors	Articles with errors
Predicates				
`reflexivity`	138	91	356	44
`irreflexivity`	11	10	9	2
`symmetry`	122	82	498	47
`asymmetry`	6	6	6	4
`connectedness`	4	4	65	4
total	281	119	934	73
Functors				
`involutiveness`	38	32	163	18
`projectivity`	21	18	11	3
`commutativity`	155	86	1423	55
`idempotence`	20	13	155	9
total	234	115	1718	70

of each property, numbers of articles in which the properties were declared, numbers of errors occurring after removing registrations of the properties from texts, and numbers of articles with such errors.[1]

In this paper we propose strengthening of the MIZAR system by processing of another common property used in mathematics – `transitivity`. It is described in Sect. 2. In Sect. 3 we present some results of our implementation and describe its potential influence on the MML. In Sect. 4 we indicate several directions of further development of processing properties in MIZAR.

2   Transitivity

Transitivity is a very common property of predicates. It is a subject of research in various branches of mathematics. It is used to define, for example, orders, equivalences, etc. Many relations are tested to determine if they are transitive or not. Many mathematical theorems assert the transitivity of various relations.

We propose an enhancement of the MIZAR system supporting automatic processing of transitive predicates, where by automatic we mean that some computations during the verification process are executed based on knowledge gathered in the MML which is not explicitly referred to in processed proof steps.[2] To enable such an automation, when a new predicate is defined, if it is transitive, it should be declared as transitive (just like in the case of other properties

---

[1] Total numbers are not simply sums of columns, because errors occurring after removing different registrations could occur in the same articles.

[2] Other such automations are, for example, processing of adjectives [7] and definitional expansions [8].

supported by the MIZAR verifier [6]). Such a declaration has to be done within a definitional block with syntax

```
definition
  let x₁ be θ₁, x₂ be θ₂, ..., xₙ be θₙ, y₁,y₂ be θₙ₊₁;
  pred π(y₁,y₂) means :ident:
    Φ(x₁,x₂,...,xₙ,y₁,y₂);
  transitivity
  proof
    thus for a, b, c being θₙ₊₁
      st Φ(x₁,x₂,...,xₙ,a,b) and Φ(x₁,x₂,...,xₙ,b,c)
      holds Φ(x₁,x₂,...,xₙ,a,c);
  end;
end;
```

The correctness of the definition must be proven according to a special formula expressing the transitivity of the defined predicate. The formula is generated by the system. Having such a definition, whenever VERIFIER meets a conjunction of formulas $\pi(a,b)$ and $\pi(b,c)$ within an inference, the inference is enlarged by automatically generated formula $\pi(a,c)$ which may help to justify the proof step. For example, when one wants to prove the transitivity of <= for real numbers, that is the statement a<=b & b<=c implies a<=c, VERIFIER (as a classical disprover) assumes three premises: a<=b, b<=c and a>c. Then, by transitivity, it knows that a<=c which contradicts with a>c and finishes the proof.

3 Experiments

The implemented software was tested on MIZAR Version 8.1.02 working with the MML Version 5.36.1267.[3]

An important part of the package is a tool (TRANSDET) which detects theorems stored in the MML, that could be rewritten as registrations of the transitivity of some predicates (we will call such theorems *transitivity-like theorems*). In the current version of the library 127 such theorems were found in 90 articles. The Library Committee, who is responsible for the management, developing and revisions of the MML, will analyze all cases and decide which of them would be incorporated into the library. In the case of approval, a refactoring of the MML [9] will be required while maintaining licensing its content [10].

To present some examples detected in the MML[4] let us cite the transitivity of ordering of elements of a semilattice [11]

---

[3] Computations were carried out at the Computer Center of University of Białystok http://uco.uwb.edu.pl.

[4] The full list is accessible at http://alioth.uwb.edu.pl/~artur/transitivity/th2trans. txt.

```
theorem
for L being join-associative non empty \/-SemiLattStr,
    a, b, c being Element of L holds a [= b & b [= c implies a [= c;
```

and the transitivity of being isomorphic groups [12]

```
theorem
for G, H, I being Group holds
 G,H are_isomorphic & H,I are_isomorphic implies G,I are_isomorphic;
```

An important gain from rewriting detected transitivity-like theorems as declarations of the transitivity of used predicates is decreasing the number of explicit references to the theorems from all proofs collected in the MML. Table 2 presents top 10 most cited such theorems.[5] These numbers mean that 16855 out of all 629048 (2.7 %) references in the entire library can be removed while ensuring that all proofs remain valid.

Table 2. References to transitivity-like theorems

Article	References
XXREAL_0:2	12601
XBOOLE_1:1	3162
ORDERS_2:3	319
ORDINAL1:10	235
LATTICES:7	97
NAT_D:4	70
INT_2:9	44
WELLORD2:15	44
PBOOLE:13	43
BORSUK_6:79	31
...	...
total	16855

The software can be downloaded from http://alioth.uwb.edu.pl/~artur/transitivity.

4 Further Work

A possible direction to continue work is to implement processing of other commonly used in mathematics properties of relations, like, for example, antisymmetry, trichotomy, left- and right- Euclidean. Another topic is to introduce properties which are collections of other properties, like equivalence which is reflexive,

---

[5] The full list of non-zero numbers of references is accessible at http://alioth.uwb.edu.pl/~artur/transitivity/references.txt.

symmetric and transitive; or preorder which is reflexive and transitive; etc. Of course, one may declare a relation as reflexive, symmetric and transitive, but it would be probably worth to enrich the MIZAR language to make it closer and closer to traditional mathematical vernacular.

In the current stage of the MIZAR system, all properties of predicates can be registered for binary predicates only. So, for example, the theorem [13]

```
theorem :: REWRITE1:16
for R being Relation, a,b,c being object st R reduces a,b & R reduces b,c
 holds R reduces a,c;
```

is not transformable to a registration of transitivity, since the predicate `reduces` is ternary, not binary. But it is seen, that if we fix the value of one argument, the predicate can be understood as binary one, and we may think about its transitivity (or other properties of binary predicates). In general, properties dedicated for binary predicates, can be introduced for n-ary predicates, where $2 \leq n$, with $n - 2$ fixed arguments.

5 Conclusions

In the paper we presented an extension of the MIZAR system by introducing a new word to the MIZAR language (transitivity) and new rules for processing transitive predicates. We detected theorems describing the transitivity of various relations gathered in the MML. It can be concluded that our implementation will have strong impact on the shape of many proofs – many explicit references to the theorems can be removed. It may even result in reorganization of proof steps within entire proofs [14].

As the last observation, it can be said that this new feature of the MIZAR system was anticipated and expected by MIZAR users. Josef Urban, in one of his papers [15], annotated a theorem as follows[6]:

```
:: remove when transitivity implemented
theorem :: OSALG_1:2
for S being non empty non void OverloadedMSSign
 for o,o1,o2 being OperSymbol of S
  holds o ~= o1 & o1 ~= o2 implies o ~= o2;
```

References

1. Trybulec, A.: Mizar. In: Wiedijk, F. (ed.) The Seventeen Provers of the World. LNCS (LNAI), vol. 3600, pp. 20–23. Springer, Heidelberg (2006). doi:10.1007/11542384_4
2. Bancerek, G., et al.: Mizar: state-of-the-art and beyond. In: Kerber, M., Carette, J., Kaliszyk, C., Rabe, F., Sorge, V. (eds.) CICM 2015. LNCS, vol. 9150, pp. 261–279. Springer, Heidelberg (2015). doi:10.1007/978-3-319-20615-8_17

---

[6] http://mizar.uwb.edu.pl/version/current/html/osalg_1.html.

3. Grabowski, A., Korniłowicz, A., Naumowicz, A.: Four decades of Mizar. J. Autom. Reason. **55**(3), 191–198 (2015). doi:10.1007/s10817-015-9345-1
4. Korniłowicz, A.: On rewriting rules in Mizar. J. Autom. Reason. **50**(2), 203–210 (2013). doi:10.1007/s10817-012-9261-6
5. Korniłowicz, A.: Flexary connectives in Mizar. Comput. Lang. Syst. Struct. **44**, 238–250 (2015). doi:10.1016/j.cl.2015.07.002
6. Naumowicz, A., Byliński, C.: Improving MIZAR texts with *properties* and *requirements*. In: Asperti, A., Bancerek, G., Trybulec, A. (eds.) MKM 2004. LNCS, vol. 3119, pp. 290–301. Springer, Heidelberg (2004). doi:10.1007/978-3-540-27818-4_21
7. Naumowicz, A.: Enhanced processing of adjectives in Mizar. In: Grabowski, A., Naumowicz, A. (eds.) Computer Reconstruction of the Body of Mathematics. Studies in Logic, Grammar and Rhetoric, pp. 89–101. University of Białystok, Białystok (2009)
8. Korniłowicz, A.: Definitional expansions in Mizar. J. Autom. Reason. **55**(3), 257–268 (2015). doi:10.1007/s10817-015-9331-7
9. Grabowski, A., Schwarzweller, C.: Revisions as an essential tool to maintain mathematical repositories. In: Kauers, M., Kerber, M., Miner, R., Windsteiger, W. (eds.) MKM/CALCULEMUS 2007. LNCS (LNAI), vol. 4573, pp. 235–249. Springer, Heidelberg (2007). doi:10.1007/978-3-540-73086-6_20
10. Alama, J., Kohlhase, M., Mamane, L., Naumowicz, A., Rudnicki, P., Urban, J.: Licensing the Mizar mathematical library. In: Davenport, J.H., Farmer, W.M., Urban, J., Rabe, F. (eds.) MKM 2011 and Calculemus 2011. LNCS, vol. 6824, pp. 149–163. Springer, Heidelberg (2011). doi:10.1007/978-3-642-22673-1_11
11. Żukowski, S.: Introduction to lattice theory. Formalized Math. **1**(1), 215–222 (1990)
12. Trybulec, W.A., Trybulec, M.J.: Homomorphisms and isomorphisms of groups. Quotient group. Formalized Math. **2**(4), 573–578 (1991)
13. Bancerek, G.: Reduction relations. Formalized Math. **5**(4), 469–478 (1996)
14. Pąk, K.: Improving legibility of formal proofs based on the close reference principle is NP-hard. J. Autom. Reason. **55**(3), 295–306 (2015). doi:10.1007/s10817-015-9337-1
15. Urban, J.: Order sorted algebras. Formalized Math. **10**(3), 179–188 (2002)

Erratum to: Formal Dependability Modeling and Analysis: A Survey

Waqar Ahmad[1](✉), Osman Hasan[1], and Sofiène Tahar[2]

[1] School of Electrical Engineering and Computer Science,
National University of Sciences and Technology, Islamabad, Pakistan
{waqar.ahmad,osman.hasan}@seecs.nust.edu.pk
[2] Electrical and Computer Engineering Department,
Concordia University, Montreal, Canada
tahar@ece.concordia.ca

Erratum to:
Chapter "Formal Dependability Modeling and Analysis:
A Survey" in: M. Kohlhase et al. (Eds.):
Intelligent Computer Mathematics, LNAI,
DOI: 10.1007/978-3-319-42547-4_10

The original version of this chapter contained an error. The name of the author Waqar Ahmad was spelled incorrectly as Waqar Ahmed in the original publication. The original chapter was corrected.

The updated original online version for this chapter can be found at
DOI: 10.1007/978-3-319-42547-4_10

© Springer International Publishing Switzerland 2017
M. Kohlhase et al. (Eds.): CICM 2016, LNAI 9791, p. E1, 2016.
DOI: 10.1007/978-3-319-42547-4_13

Author Index

Printed in the United States
By Bookmasters